248.843   McCoy, Anna.
MCC
          Woman, act now.

    JAN   2009

                         32026002117429
$19.99

DATE			

FOREST PARK PUBLIC LIBRARY

BAKER & TAYLOR

Praise for *Woman, Act Now* and Coach Anna McCoy

Gives new meaning to the term "get busy." Highly motivational.

—*Richard Parsons*
Chairman of the Board, Time Warner, Inc.

Anna is uniquely talented to equip others to successfully execute their dreams. Her vast array of experiences indeed culminates in her work. She has earned the right to be read and she deserves to be heard!

—*Bishop T. D. Jakes*
Pastor and best-selling author

Woman, Act Now is a vital tool for all of us who desire to make a difference in our lifetime. Now is the time to take action and, Anna has provided the help that is needed to train us for the task ahead in a clear, personal, and highly motivational way.

—*Susan Kimes*
Founder, Chosen Women

When God gives you a vision, He puts in your path all the necessary parts for completion. I now realize why Coach Anna McCoy became a working exclamation point to Crusade Christian Faith Center. I believe that everyone who is exposed to the offerings of Anna McCoy will be infected with her contagious excitement and propelled to reach new dimensions of personal growth. A must-read for males and females alike.

—*Dr. Virgil D. Patterson Sr.*
Bishop, Crusade Christian Faith Center

Woman, Act Now is an exceptional book. Anna McCoy's unfaltering belief in our ability to create and recreate our lives and to live our dreams comes through on every page. She shares her vision, she shares her faith, and she shares herself. The chapters are packed with stories, exercises, and scriptural references. Anna is a champion of women leading fulfilling lives—and, most importantly, doing it now!

—*Paula Asinof*
Principal, Yellow Brick Path career consulting firm

Woman, Act Now is masterfully woven with a personal touch and should be required reading for every visionary. It is not limited to women only, for it applies to all of us.

—*Al Hollingsworth*
CEO, Aldelano Corporation
Founder, BOSS the Movement

Anna McCoy is *Woman, Act Now* personified. She has done a wonderful job of turning her enthusiasm for life, women, and living one's dreams into not only a readable, but also a very motivational, guide to move each of us several steps closer to living the lives we dream of. Anna's wisdom, faith, and sense of humor show that this need not be a chore but a journey of love and happiness. Read it, do the exercises, and watch your life change! I look forward to using this book with my coaching clients to help enrich their lives.

—*Lynn Banis*
Owner, Discovery Point Coaching

This book is a manual for getting life done. It will encourage, challenge, and equip you to close the execution gap successfully and move your ideas to material reality.

—*P. B. Wilson*
Best-selling author

Anna's passion and genuine desire to see people from all walks of life transform themselves from survival to significance, live life with confidence, and fulfill their God-given dreams and goals are evident in everything she does. Anna does not tolerate excuses but graciously inspires people to reach higher and go further. She is a loving, humorous, and anointed woman of God of whom I say, "I'll have what she's having!"

—*Irene Penner*
CFO, J&D Penner Paving Stone and Concrete

This is a how-to manual of rare excellence, penned by one of the brightest most innovative business minds of our time. It's a must-read for those who desire to establish themselves in tomorrow's global marketplace.

—*Jill Wagner*
Author

Woman, Act Now maps a blueprint for success with a host of practical and powerful insights for anyone seeking a long-lasting life of achievements. This book defines focus and purpose.

—*Adriane Gaines*
General Manager, AM 1600 WWRL radio station

Anna McCoy's words go straight to the heart and inspire; they go straight to the head and invoke vision. *Woman, Act Now* is the next best thing to taking Anna home with you to coach you to your greatness. Anna challenges me to make real what I dream while she lives her dream.

—*Peggy Dean*
Founder, Peak Performance Corporation

Anna McCoy is a dynamic woman who uses her energy and passion to encourage others to achieve their purposes. In personally executing the principles I have learned from Woman Act Now, which are conveyed in this book, my firm's revenues have doubled, my staff has grown, and my clientele has vastly increased. These principles have changed my business and my life. Take an action now—your dreams are waiting!

—*Dianne Jones McVay*
The Jones McVay Firm, PLLC

Woman, Act Now

Woman, Act Now

Learn, Launch, and Live Your Dream

Coach Anna McCoy

WHITAKER
HOUSE

Editorial services provided by David Yeazell.

WOMAN, ACT NOW
Learn, Launch, and Live Your Dream
Hardcover Edition

Anna McCoy
Woman Act Now, Inc.
2000 E. Lamar Boulevard
Suite 600
Arlington, TX 76006
www.womanactnow.com

ISBN: 978-1-60374-068-5
Printed in the United States of America
© 2009 by Anna McCoy

Whitaker House
1030 Hunt Valley Circle
New Kensington, PA 15068
www.whitakerhouse.com

Library of Congress Cataloging-in-Publication Data

McCoy, Anna, 1965–
  Woman, act now / by Anna McCoy.
      p. cm.
  Summary: "Applies business principles and scriptural teachings to the development of self-image and reputation in order to empower women to identify their strengths, minimize their weaknesses, pursue excellence in all aspects of life, and ultimately fulfill their personal and professional dreams"—Provided by publisher.
  ISBN 978-1-60374-068-5 (hardcover : alk. paper) 1. Christian women—Religious life. 2. Self-perception in women. 3. Self-perception—Religious aspects—Christianity. 4. Self-actualization (Psychology) in women. 5. Self-actualization (Psychology)—Religious aspects—Christianity. I. Title.
  BV4527.M37 2009
  248.8'43—dc22

                                                          2008042941

1 2 3 4 5 6 7 8 9 10 11 12 **W** 17 16 15 14 13 12 11 10 09

Acknowledgments

&

I am so appreciative of my husband, Richmond, whose unfailing commitment to my destiny continues to push me forward. I am grateful for my dad and mom, Raymond and Mary, who have so diligently invested their love into my life and helped me to understand the importance of loving deeply. My sisters, Sonya and Michelle, offer inspiration and constant encouragement—thank you both for your support and prayers.

I am indebted to the following people for seeing my vision and helping me to pursue all my dreams:

The members of Jabez International Fellowship Tele-Bible Study who pray for my success, listen to my stories, and love me still.

My sidekick and executive assistant, Shonna, who keeps me focused and holds me accountable every day to following the principles I teach.

David Yeazell, for working with me on this project from start to finish and encouraging me to grow in confidence as each word was written.

Judith Ellis, who pushed me as hard as I push others—thank you for being the "midwife" who helped me birth my dreams.

The members of Woman Act Now, who believed I had something to offer them and who entrusted their hearts and vision to my instruction and leadership. I am so proud of you for pursuing your dreams, and I eagerly await their manifestation.

The readers of this book—thank you for making the investment, both in my efforts and, on a greater scale, in your own success.

My spiritual parents, Al and Hattie Hollingsworth—your imprint can be seen throughout the pages of this book.

My SWAT sisters—thank you for preparing me to lead!

Bishop Virgil and Jerri Patterson, whose investment in my destiny resonates in everything I do.

My pastors, Bishop T. D. and Serita Jakes—your wisdom and leadership continue to equip me for my future.

To my publisher, Bob Whitaker Jr., and the entire team at Whitaker House—thank you for believing in me and giving me this opportunity to walk in my purpose and leave my legacy of words and principles for the benefit of others.

—*Coach Anna McCoy*

Contents

❦

Part IV: *Execute*

Part V: *Make the Connection*

Foreword

⟨∂⟩

A nna is my partner, my coach, my best friend, and the love of my life. She is committed to serving me, loving me, and encouraging me to be the best I can be, and I am honored to share all that she is with the world. Anna, my friend, I am so very grateful to be your husband. You make me proud!

Anna is a unique individual who possesses a rare combination of the ability to visualize and create concepts, ideas, and plans and the talent, skill, and stick-to-itiveness to execute with total excellence. She is able to take the intangible and manifest it into actuality through various methods, namely, key conversations that turn into relationships, which then turn into opportunities. Anna knows that being in the right place at the right time is just a matter of making the most of every moment. She has the true heart of a teacher and mentor. She loves all people, and they know it instantly. Anna is committed to instilling and imparting all that she has learned and experienced in her life, be it on Wall Street, creating our multibillion-dollar real estate company; serving as an executive in corporate America; or ministering in churches. She is an extraordinary woman, no matter the context in which she is known: as wife, daughter, mother, sister, aunt, mentor, coach, or friend.

Anna has an exceptional sense of humor, which she uses to communicate business principles that can be difficult to understand and assists individuals in getting serious about their lives and taking action. She is a tremendous athlete and fierce competitor, especially with herself. Our two dogs love and obey her.

Anna has a powerful writing style and a way of crafting words so as to break down complex mental and emotional issues so that they cease to be roadblocks for others. I have had the pleasure of watching her communicate concepts to people in a way that, afterward, it was apparent they just got it! She is committed to teaching women to live principles-centered lives so that they can take action to move forward in their personal, professional, and relational lives while maximizing their God-given gifts and talents.

This is not a book that you can read in one sitting; it is a manual for your success that must be digested one bite at a time. Implement the principles that Anna puts forth, for they are real and powerful; their efficacy is proven in Anna's own life, which she orders by executing these very principles. Take advantage of the benefits offered by the great organization Woman Act Now; you are poised to lead, and when you become a member, you join a group of women who will support you and hold you accountable to pursuing and achieving your dream. Woman, act now!

—Dr. Richmond McCoy
Husband, friend, and mentor

Introduction

A Dream or a Wish?

In the 1940 Disney animated classic, *Pinocchio*, Jiminy Cricket sings the famous song by Leigh Harline, "When You Wish upon a Star." Lyricist Ned Washington's familiar refrain became one of the best-loved mantras for dreamers of many generations, including mine.

As I read those simple yet profound lyrics, they confirmed to me that any one of us can wish upon a star, regardless of who we are. But the words in the second stanza, "If your heart is in your dream…" showed me that wishing and dreaming are two different things. I concluded that wishing is an act of the mind, while dreaming is an act of the heart. For our ideas to move from the wishing stage to the dreaming stage, our hearts must be behind them—it is the powerful collision of these two concepts that makes dreams come true. Dreaming converts our wishes into concrete opportunities of purpose.

In Part I of this book, "Dream," you will learn about the power of the imagination, as well as how you can create conditions and an environment in which your imagination will soar. You will be encouraged to dream vividly and envision your future. You will learn how to achieve clarity of thought, align your values with your actions, and write out your specific vision. And, finally, you will learn how to avoid what I call "Dream Busters"—those attitudes, actions, and relationships that can cause you to derail en route to achieving the fulfillment of your dreams.

Many individuals have shared with me how they wish they could do something new and exciting, such as running a marathon, starting a business, finding a mate, or securing a better job. Unfortunately, in most cases, their wishes do not come true. Why? Because a wish is powerless to produce change; a dream, on the other hand, has the power to bring an unseen reality into manifestation.

Dreaming and wishing are two entirely different things. *Merriam-Webster's 11th Collegiate Dictionary* defines the verb *wish* as "to have a desire for (as something unattainable)." Wishing is seeing something that already exists and hoping to obtain it—without necessarily having to do the work entailed. So, as a result, you sit back in your comfortable recliner and wish: "I wish I had a better car. I wish I had a better job. I wish I could travel to someplace exotic, such as Paris, Rome, or Shanghai. I wish, I wish, I wish!"

Your wish will remain unattainable if you don't take the steps necessary to convert it to action. It is always "out there" somewhere, just beyond reach; you desire it, but you continue to stare out the window, hoping that things will change or wishing that your life were different. Often, you wish because of something you lack—you develop the desire for things that others possess when you realize that you don't possess them.

Of course, you can get some things by wishing—you can get complacent, lazy, unfulfilled, and old before your time—just spend a day sitting in your recliner staring out the window and see what happens! Dreaming, on the other hand, is having an inward perception of fulfilling an outward reality. *Merriam-Webster's* defines *dream* as "a visionary creation of the imagination...a strongly desired goal or purpose...something that fully satisfies a wish." A dream is something you believe you might have the necessary abilities, skills, intellect, or relationships to execute. It is out of a place of being—of accepting and understanding who you are and what you can contribute to the world—that you begin to dream.

Dreams come in all sizes. You might begin to dream big dreams. Your dreams might start out small, or they might fall somewhere in the middle. But whatever their size, your dreams envision what is inside your heart and provide you with a road map to bring your thoughts into existence. Dreaming is seeing what you have inside—your potential—instead of looking around and wishing for what others have. Remember, your *dream* fully satisfies your *wish*, and *action* is the bridge that brings these two concepts together.

To see any positive transformation happen in your life, you have to move from having a wish to dreaming a dream.

I am not writing this book for those who are content to wish. If you are content with your wishing, put the book down and resume gazing complacently out the window. I am writing for a dreamer. I want to address the woman who will reach into the heavens through her imagination and bring those things that are unseen into the earthly realm, who can dream despite all odds and obstacles, who can believe in her own significance and value her contributions to society. I am writing to the woman who refuses to die with unful-filled dreams and untapped talents. I am writing to the woman who knows that it's time to let her dream live again, or perhaps live for the first time. I am writing to the woman who has a dream but is stuck in the "valley of execution," yet believes that she can resur-rect her dream with the proper guidance and direction.

This book is the beginning of a movement and a revolution for women who are tired of talking about what they want to be or what they could have done. By reading this book, you will learn how to dream again, believing in yourself more and more. You will discover your strengths, limit your threats, build your personal brand, and execute your ideas as you connect with other fantastic women of destiny and purpose.

I must preface that the basis of my belief in the value of dreams is my faith in the Bible, the infallible Word of God. It is my goal to live a life in which I demonstrate the character of Jesus, recogniz-ing that without my faith in God as my source of hope, I would not see effectively the plans that He has for me—plans to give me a hope and a future. (See Jeremiah 29:11.) It is this hope that I desire to share with readers, trusting that it will cause you to go deeper, see more of who you are, and pursue the future that God will show you as you dream, believe, and execute your ideas.

The time to act is now, and by "now," I mean even as you read this book! Almost every chapter includes an exercise that invites introspection, critical thinking, and personal application on your part. Some exercises even require physical participation. You will recognize these opportunities to act, for each is designated by the Woman Act Now logo. Woman, act now!

Part I

 *Dream*

I   *Welcome to Dreamland*

There is a favorite place in my life that I call Dreamland. It is a land in the imagination—a mental, emotional, and spiritual environment teeming with opportunity. It is a place you, also, can venture to, and most times, you will bring back something that is life changing. I want you to be a dreamer who reaches into Dreamland—a place that is within you, yet beyond you—a place of great potential.

If you've never paid Dreamland a visit, you may not see the entirety of what you can be or do during your first visit. But you have to start somewhere, so join the refrain of all the dreamers who have gone there before you: "I am going to this place called Dreamland. I've got to get there to see the greater picture and the bigger things, the potential within me that has not been released. I refuse to waste away in the recliner of unfulfilled wishes—I must get to Dreamland today!"

When you get to Dreamland, you will see business opportunities, relationships, financial prosperity, inventions, and ideas that may not currently exist in your world. They may exist in someone's world in Asia, in South America, in Africa, or elsewhere, but they have yet to be manifested in your home, neighborhood, or city. In Dreamland, you will see things that have the potential to literally change your life, your family, and your generation.

You must make the conscious choice to enter Dreamland, and you must then force yourself to do just that. It can be difficult to go to Dreamland, especially if you are content to stay in your current circumstances, believing they are your only possibilities. As dreamers, we have forgotten how to imagine because we have trusted others—the broadcast media, movies, radio talk shows, newspapers, friends, and coworkers—to imagine for us. We are awestruck because of what we see and hear from others, but we have little faith in what we can see for ourselves.

There is more to see if you will take the journey yourself and understand that big dreams are abundant and available for you. However, *you* must make the journey; no one can make it for you and bring back a dream or an idea with your name on it. The only door between your unfulfilled wishes and the potential of your dreams is you. The door to your life is within you, opening from the inside out. Wishing pushes open the door from the outside in and offers pipe dreams, get-rich-quick schemes, and false hopes. Dreaming, on the other hand, courageously invites destiny into your life from within.

What will you do? Will you open the door to the possibilities of who you are and who you will be? Which will you be—a wisher who joins the multitudes of people around the world who wish for things based on what they see, and hope to possess those things with little effort; or a dreamer who reaches into a place that is within yourself, yet beyond yourself, and brings something into the material reality of this world?

> *"The realization of the self is only possible if one is productive, if one can give birth to one's own potentialities."*
> —Johann Wolfgang von Goethe

෨

Dream Vividly

When I encourage my coaching clients to visit Dreamland, I help them to identify and remove all of the constraints and barriers, real or imaginary, that they or others have put on their lives.

This process is necessary for them to be able to take that long-overdue trip—and, once they've reached their destination, to dream vividly. Dreaming vividly involves all of the five "senses" and allows us to see what something looks, feels, and smells like; the people who should be involved in the project; and the location where it will take place—long before any of it becomes a reality.

Removing constraints and barriers to dreaming vividly allows you to dream without limits. The process of constructing a building serves as an excellent analogy to illustrate the concept of dreaming vividly. When you build any kind of structure—be it a high-rise, home, hospital, or church—to the bystander, it looks like the building just rises up out of the ground. Picture any recent construction projects in your own town. A vacant lot is a barren, rutted piece of land one day—the next day, it's a solid structure with a purpose that provides products, services, and jobs to your community.

I used to live in West Los Angeles, California, where I worked in sales. I would canvass the Crenshaw District, home to the West Angeles Church of God in Christ. During the time I lived in L.A., the church started a building project to construct a new sanctuary. I remember driving past the building site frequently during the initial construction phase. At the time, the neighborhood consisted predominantly of older storefront buildings, and it had a 1960s feel to it. Even though I heard talk about the construction plans and saw the large billboard that announced "The Future Home of West Angeles Church of God in Christ," it seemed unlikely to me that they'd find a place to construct such a building in that community.

Every time I passed that site, I wondered where in the world they were going to put that building. Directly across the tracks, off Jefferson and Crenshaw, there was a big industrial warehouse and parking lot. For months, I assumed they would tear down that structure and build their sanctuary on the site, for adjacent to it stood the towering billboard that announced its imminent construction.

In my mind, based on what already existed in that place, I could not picture a church building that would seat thousands. I had no perception of what could be; I only heard the words that were used to raise money and solicit people to support the vision of a new church facility. My only perception of something like it was the enormous size of Crenshaw Christian Faith Center's dome that stood in the heart of Los Angeles, and I thought something that big certainly couldn't fit in the West Los Angeles neighborhood.

After a year or so, a construction fence was erected—big sheets of plywood were put up, surrounding the building site. We knew something was going on behind the plywood construction fence, but we had no idea what the end result would be. We knew that they had finally broken ground to begin building that facility, but the vision was hidden.

At that point, I left Los Angeles for a time. When I returned a few years later, there, right in the middle of the 'hood of West Los Angeles, was a huge, beautiful cathedral that had risen out of the ground. It was amazing! On April 28, 2001, West Angeles Cathedral held its first service in the new sanctuary. I had the opportunity to tour the facility shortly after it opened. In 2005, I was a guest speaker featured on Bishop T. D. Jakes's God's Leading Ladies Tour. I stood in the pulpit of that great church and spoke to thousands of women about financial responsibility.

Dream Beyond Eye Level

Obviously, I did not have a dream to see a large church in West Los Angeles. Nor was I dreaming vividly (remember, I would have torn down the warehouse and put the church on the wrong side of the railroad tracks). But I believe the pastor, Bishop Charles Blake, was a dreamer and had dreamers around him to see the project beyond the limitations that their former neighborhood posed.

Dreamers have to see through what already exists, pursuing an aerial view and seeing the dream from all possible angles. I saw only what was at eye level. I would suppose that Bishop Blake and his team saw beyond the former condition of their neighborhood, a community in desperate need of redevelopment. They probably envisioned the potential in that place and built their new church across the street from the old church, while many people, if given identical circumstances, would have left the area to locate a large tract of empty land on the edge of town. Not so for this ministry. Bishop Blake undoubtedly had a dream to restore his community, to bring back to life an area both deserving and needy. He sought to empower the people through development, enabling them to dream again and to see the many possibilities mid the desolation.

Bishop Blake's church rose up out of the concrete, and before you knew it, people were entering the building dressed in their Sunday best. The dream and vision they had worked on for twenty years had come to fruition. Those plywood boards finally came down, exposing to the world the beautiful sanctuary called West Angeles Cathedral.

Not only did the vision of the physical building come to pass, but what the church's leadership really wanted to see—people flocking to that building—was also realized. In their vivid dreams, the building served a greater purpose for its members: it was to be a house of God in a community where thousands of people—families, senior citizens, and neighborhood youth—could gather to hear the gospel of Jesus Christ. Bishop Blake's dream was bigger than what I saw and what already existed. It was, indeed, undoubtedly bigger than other people's words or opinions allowed for. As a result, the community of West Los Angeles, California, is living the dream of one man. A single dream has the power to effect a profound impact on your life, as well as on the lives of many others, when seen above eye level.

Dream Dimensionally

To construct a building, you have to employ the services and expertise of an architect. You discuss with the architect what you want to build, the size that the building should be, and the dimensions of the property on which it will stand. The architect takes your input and creates a detailed artistic rendering of the future. Often, when he brings you the rendering, he will first sketch it in the form of a blueprint—a one-dimensional diagram on a sheet of paper that gives you an idea of what the rendering will look like. This step saves time, for it allows you to change your mind before the rendering is completed.

If you approve the one-dimensional drawing of your vision, the project will progress to the next level: the architect creates a multidimensional model to give you an even better understanding of what your completed project will look like. In fact, while this book was being written, West Angeles had renderings posted on their Web site of the various phases the building went through before it was built. One such rendering depicted the inside of the sanctuary. It featured rows of seats, as well as the pulpit, behind which a man was standing. He was meant to represent Bishop Blake. The architect had to convince Bishop Blake and his team that they were seeing the same thing that he saw on the inside, in his mind's eye. The renderings included not only the building, but also automobiles, trees, landscape, and even people walking in and out of that building.

You must become the architect of your own dream. No longer let your dreams die because of the limitations that you or others place on your life. Sit down and draw a vivid picture of what your dream looks like, then add the multidimensional elements—trees, cars, landscape, and people walking in and out of your vision. This will define the purpose of your dream in detail.

Your dream is important! Within your dream may be the ability to generate wealth, cure disease, or advance the welfare of the poor. Within your dream is your family's future, your child's college education, your retirement plan. Within your dream is an answer to someone's need. But to get there, you have to envision what your future will look like.

It does not matter how small or large you think your dream is; there is a process through which you must walk to make it a reality. That is what *Woman, Act Now* is all about: teaching and empowering women to be the architects and executioners of their dreams. As you begin to write and sketch out your dream in your mind and heart, we are going to pull it out together and put it on paper so that you can begin to walk out your dream. But for now, learning to dream vividly means giving yourself permission to see in color, to smell, to touch, to taste, and to feel the essence of what you can be or do—you want all of the five senses to become active in your imagination. You want them to be so real to you that you would never think of giving up. We want to get your possibilities to your potential, the place where everything in you moves steadily forward until your dream becomes reality.

Dream vividly! Learn how to walk out your ideas in Dreamland. Most of us stop at an idea, but great ideas are carefully and thoughtfully walked out in the imagination. Go back again and again until you see the finished product. If you can master this process of trusting your imagination by walking out your ideas in your mind, your actions will be like déjà vu when you begin to execute them physically; you will have been there before, and achieving your dream will be easier and attainable.

The Characteristics of a Dreamer

1. A dreamer is courageous; she dares to dream impossibilities beyond her current circumstances.

2. A dreamer honors her imagination as a place of great potential where treasures are discovered.

3. A dreamer invites destiny into her life from within.

4. A dreamer employs all five senses, engaging in the experience in order to equip herself with the clearest vision possible while in Dreamland.

5. A dreamer dreams without limits.

6. A dreamer sees beyond what physically exists.

7. A dreamer constructs, deconstructs, and reconstructs when necessary.

8. A dreamer seeks others who can see what she sees and confirm her reality.

9. A dreamer focuses on the aerial view.

10. A dreamer goes back to Dreamland over and over with an expectation of getting more details each time.

11. A dreamer walks out her thoughts in her mind, processes them in her imagination, and executes them in the physical.

12. A dreamer becomes the architect of her ideas, moving them from one dimension to the next until they are manifest in the physical dimension.

Are You a Dreamer?

1. Think of a time when you were convinced that your current situation was your only possibility. How did you handle this situation?

2. What was the last treasure you discovered simply by using your imagination?

3. Where do you go to dream?

4. Why is it important to let your dreams live?

5. Identify any barriers or limits that you or others have placed on you that you feel are keeping you from dreaming.

6. Identify three individuals who can see what you see and confirm your reality.

7. Write down the last thing you imagined but never acted on, then identify what prevented you from acting on it.

8. How have you developed your mind to dream?

9. How often do you take time to dream?

2

The I-FACTOR Zone:
It's All about Imagination

To visit the place called Dreamland and become a person who fulfills a dream, you have to tap into your imagination. I help individuals achieve a place of heightened imagination by what I call the "I-FACTOR Zone": the place where you and your imagination meet. "I" is a personal pronoun referring to whoever is speaking or writing. *Merriam-Webster's 11th College Dictionary* defines *personal* as "of, relating to, or affecting a particular person; relating to, or affecting, an individual." In other words, "I" refers to me. *Merriam-Webster's* defines "imagination" as "the act or power of forming a mental image of something not present to the senses or never before wholly perceived in reality...a creative ability." The Zone is the meeting place of "me" and my imagination to bring my heart's desire into reality.

Using your imagination is something you can do as an ongoing exercise. Many people start by finding a quiet place where they can escape the distractions of life; there, they may meditate or pray to create the conditions for the imagination to run wild. It is in this quiet place that the I-FACTOR takes you to Dreamland. The I-FACTOR is an acronym to help you remember how to dream. The "I" is all about the imagination. In part, it stands for the imagination in you, the factor that *is* you! The word *factor* is defined in *Merriam-Webster's* as "one that actively contributes to the production of a result." The I-FACTOR Zone is the combination of you and your imagination shutting the world out so that you can explore the opportunities of your imagination within you.

The mind is extraordinary. When you see images and opportunities in your imagination, the mind does not distinguish whether those images and opportunities are real—true, factual—or not. In its definition of *imagination*, *Merriam-Webster's* says the mental images formed by the imagination are "not present to the senses or never before wholly perceived in reality." So, if I begin to flood my mind with the images of what I want to do and accomplish in life, my mind does not know if I am conscious or unconscious; I could be dreaming, or those images and associated actions might actually be a present reality.

The mind is a beautiful gift. It can operate in both the past and the future, as well as the present. It interacts with the past via memory, but it can also interact with the future in a function of imagination. The I-FACTOR helps you to build upon your past experiences in order to maximize the opportunities of your future.

It is important to recall the times of success in your life. For example, you may remember the joy of passing your first driver's test, dreaded parallel parking component and all. Remember how frightened you were, hoping that you would do everything right and impress the man or woman next to you holding the clipboard and pen? Out of the corner of your eye, you could see them writing; you heard the pen scratch with every check mark, and, perhaps, like I did, you first thought, *Whoops, did I do something wrong?* Perhaps you said to yourself, *I have my hands positioned on the steering wheel at ten and two o'clock.* You may even recall the voice that called out those commands, "Left here, right here," while all you could think about was hand over hand, keeping them both on the steering wheel at all times as you turned each corner. Finally, you heard the dreaded command: "Pull over here and parallel park."

The experience I just described certainly doesn't sound like much of a success, but it was. What I depicted sounds as painful as it was when I experienced it. However, as I walked away with my driver's license, I realized that I had done more than just pass a test. Earning my driver's license gave me the freedom to drive myself to work, to go out with my friends, or to run household errands—something my parents found extremely convenient. Obtaining my license boosted my self-confidence, strengthened my self-esteem, and provided me with self-assurance. It was a rite of passage into maturity, convincing me that I was no longer a girl but rather a young woman accepting responsibility for my actions at the age of sixteen.

I can recount numerous experiences from my past that continue to give me confidence to trust the dreams and ideas of my future. Your memory is a useful tool if you use it as a positive reference rather than allowing negative experiences to consume your thoughts. It is necessary to have wins in your life so that when you are confronted with impossibilities, you can remember the determination and perseverance you demonstrated earlier in life to win again.

Dr. Mike Murdock is a prolific writer, and most of his work aims to provide readers with principles for living called "Wisdom Keys." One such principle is, "You will always move in the direction of your strongest and most dominant thought." He writes in his book *Dream Seeds* that great achievers usually have learned to replay the memories of their past triumphs and replay the pictures of their desired successes. Your imagination helps you to picture your future success. As I work with my team to set daily goals and objectives, I am constantly taking us to the Zone. When we plan, we walk it out, we replay, and we preplan our strategy, changing things that don't work and keeping those that do; when the day arrives, we experience what we saw in Dreamland.

The more individuals I coach on achieving their dreams, the more I discover that most people don't know how to visualize their success. When I ask a client to describe in detail what she sees in her dreams, she will often shrink back behind such phrases as "I don't know" and "I can't think of anything." She may also get quiet, saying nothing. As I examined my own method of entering Dreamland in my own imagination, I realized that I need a certain sense of quietude, of stillness. When I enter Dreamland, I am sitting quietly and meditating on my ideas.

Sometimes, I even enter Dreamland amid noise as a way of escaping the outer racket. The constant, regardless of silence or noise, is that I have control when I enter Dreamland. No matter my surroundings, my imagination always brings me an image of what I desire. In order for me to be able to share these principles with others, I first observed my own frame of reference, attitude, and presuppositions when I went to Dreamland. I soon discovered that I had cleared my mind and released the barriers of impossibilities, creating a mental picture and environment where my imagination could run wild.

In contrast, when I asked my clients to see what they wanted, they immediately began to tell me about the things that would keep them from achieving their goals; they began to speak about barriers they perceived to be impenetrable. One day, as I sat pondering how to help people imagine, I realized that life is filled with many things that stifle our imaginations, with the result that we do not achieve or press ourselves beyond our current circumstances. We get trapped in our recliners of wishful thinking, looking out the window of life and hoping for a change to come instead of imagining the possibilities of what could be and then acting upon them. Why do we do this? Because we are so involved in the minutiae of our daily lives; we are pressed down and overwhelmed by reality. That is why you have to exercise your imagination and bring the power of your mind back under your control. Dream now!

If your body was to become flabby and out of shape, you would probably take walks, go to the gym, or do something to exercise your muscles and get your body back into shape. If your mind is becoming flabby—a process that's accelerated by sitting in the recliner of wishful thinking—it's time to take a break, cast off complacency, and go to a place where things will look the way you want them to look. I guarantee you, if you really focus on and live in the I-FACTOR—the place in your imagination where you try to achieve what you want in your life—you will see results.

Jim Carrey is an accomplished actor, comedian, writer, impressionist, singer, songwriter, laborer, painter, and sculptor. When he was struggling early in his Hollywood career, the actor once wrote himself a check for ten million dollars and postdated it for Thanksgiving Day 1995.

Carrey was completely accurate in his visualization. Days before his father's death, he was offered a ten million-dollar contract to costar in the film *Dumb and Dumber*. Oprah asked Carrey about this check during a show on which he was her guest. Carrey replied, "I wrote the check to myself for Acting Services Rendered. I folded it up, put it in my wallet, and carried it around with me for a couple of years. I would take it out and look at it over and over until it became tattered and torn. It was disintegrating and before it was completely destroyed I had been told about the ten million-dollar contract to do the film." This is a lesson in visualizing your success. Big dreamers achieve big things.

Imagine writing a check to yourself with a future date and really believing that you have potential, passion, and persistence to pursue your career or idea. Many news articles tell of Carrey's trips to the Hollywood Hills, where he would visualize his success until he felt the euphoria of his vision as if it were real. Make a decision to walk out your thoughts; desire to feel the experience and reward of achieving your goal. Don't give up on your dream. Write that check. I did. I wrote a check and dated it for July 2010. It represents a check from my publisher in the amount of two million dollars for royalties on books sold. I expect to be a best-selling author; I expect to appear on *Good Morning America*, the *Today Show*, *Oprah*, and other media outlets, sharing my passion and dream of helping women achieve their best.

The Carnival Ride

One of my fondest childhood memories is visiting the carnival. Some of the bigger carnivals had a ride called the Gravitron, now called Starship 2000, which consisted of a large cylinder shaped like a big spaceship. All the riders entered the cylinder and positioned themselves with their backs against the inner wall of the cylinder.

After you were positioned with your back against the wall, the operator emphasized the importance of keeping the backs of your hands and the heels of your feet pressed against the wall behind you. Once you were in place and had heard the instructions, the cylinder started to spin—and what happened next blew your mind. You realized that the floor had given way, and it appeared that you were standing in midair.

We all know we need to stand on something to stay upright. What we do not understand is that the centrifugal force generated by the ride's rapid spinning pushes the riders against the padded walls, which also begin to slide up on rollers to remove the riders' feet from the floor. When they tell you to look down, you realize that the floor is four feet below you, or perhaps you are four feet above it. I remember being amazed by that ride. As a young girl, I knew nothing of physics, and it was mind-boggling to see the floor drop beneath my feet, leaving me suspended and seeming to defy gravity.

Some of you need to have the floor drop out from under you so that you can imagine what you can do. Everything that you thought was holding you up is not necessarily true or effective. Rather, it is the power of our imaginations—our power to dream—that actually holds us up. Dream now! It's time to reimagine!

In your imagination, I want you to position yourself in a silo similar to but smaller than the Gravitron, consisting of seven impenetrable steel panels. Everything in your past or present that you feel has kept you from your dream—money, people, bad relationships, limited connections, or a lack of talent—exists outside the silo. Visualize seven panels, each one representing a principle to help your imagination create the conditions and environment necessary for success. This is the Zone.

The Zone strengthens you. The Zone empowers you. The Zone prepares you. The Zone challenges you to think beyond your circumstances. The Zone teaches you how to respect what is inside of you as you achieve repeated success by seeing what you have dreamed materialize. The Zone will present to you the best of who you are and what you have to offer the world, in spite of what presently exists. Woman, you must go there, find your treasure, and bring it back to the world.

Getting in the Zone is like being a basketball player who has repeatedly practiced his free-throw shot and has committed the movement to muscle memory. During the game, in the moment it counts, he shoots the ball at the final buzzer; before it even hits the basket, he is celebrating because he knows that he is in the Zone. The I-FACTOR Zone is where you align your thoughts, elevate your thinking, and practice seeing your future. When the physical moment arrives, make the shot and celebrate.

Each letter of the acronym "I-F-A-C-T-O-R" represents an element of the Zone. These seven elements specify the conditions that will catapult you into the Zone of your imagination. We have just covered the first element.

I: *It's All about the Imagination*
F: *Failure Is Limited*
A: *Achievement Is Inevitable*
C: *Consider Endless Possibilities*
T: *Touch the Impossible*
O: *Optimism Is King*
R: *Reality Doesn't Matter*

F: *Failure Is Limited*

Life requires overcoming obstacles, confronting problems, and persisting until you succeed. Success is the result of experiencing the benefits of removed obstacles, solved problems, and achieved goals. *Failure* is limited in the I-FACTOR Zone. Failure is not a personality trait; it is behavior, outcomes, or results. Outside of the I-FACTOR Zone, failure comes when we do not execute our goals or when we make mistakes. We are not failures, however; failure is not an identity.

Understand what I am saying: failure relates directly to your actions. The benefit of seeing the limitations of failure in your imagination is that you do not have to focus on outcomes that are not successful; instead, you are to picture the behavior and actions that bring success. Remember, the mind is an incredible machine, and you create your own conditions to dream. When you set limits and bounds on failure in your imagination, failure cannot succeed.

I want to challenge your thinking and change the way that you view failure. From now on, refer to failure as "feedback." Failure is the Law of Feedback in motion. The Law of Feedback gives you an answer to your actions. If your actions do not bring about the intended results, consider the "failed" results as positive feedback. What do I mean by positive feedback, you ask?

Most successful people feel that failure provides information that is actually helpful, as it enables them to get where they want to go if they didn't get there on the first try. As Benjamin Franklin once said, "I didn't fail the test, I just found one hundred ways to do it wrong." Oprah Winfrey says, "Do the one thing you think you cannot do. Fail at it. Try again. Do better the second time. The only people who never tumble are those who never mount the high wire. This is your moment. Own it." When you fail, get up and do it again, but differently.

Successful people view failures as stepping-stones to achieving what they want. I once interviewed Mike Roberts, CEO of the Roberts Companies and author of the book *Action Has No Season*, on my radio broadcast, *The Real McCoy Show*. During the interview, we talked passionately about the idea of failure and its impact on individuals—how it keeps them from achieving their best. I asked Mike to speak to the audience about his mind-set concerning failure and the paradigm shift people can undergo to achieve success. He responded,

What would your life be like if you could eliminate the fear of failure? A simple concept, but let's break down the two words—fear and failure. Fear does not really exist; it is a mental construct resulting from an experience. But fear itself does not exist as lighting, rain, or sleet—our mental experience of its effect does. When you were born, you didn't know what [fear] meant and you didn't know what it felt like. As easy as it has been placed in your experiences—in your memory—you can eliminate it.

Failure is an interesting word born out of the expectation of others...often placed to control us. But failure doesn't exist either, because the most you can argue in a given experience is that the outcome is not quite the same as you predicted. So, let's think for a moment; should we be living our lives with nothing but memories or should we be living with imagination? I think we should always look forward and live each moment to its fullest extent.

Unsuccessful people view failures as personal and permanent. Failure, however, is neither; it is feedback, simply an outcome or result. When you see failure as limited in your imagination, your fears of rejection, insignificance, and criticism are removed, allowing you to explore your opportunities unencumbered. In the Zone, the discouraging voices, past mishaps, mistakes, and insecurities are kept at bay. In your imagination, you have everything you need in order to be, to do, and to achieve what you want. Live in the moment; live in the imagination, not in your memories. You unlock your incredible potential when you rely on what can be instead of on what was. Live in your *now*!

A: *Achievement Is Inevitable*

The opposite of failure is achievement. In your imagination, achievement is inevitable. That means there is nothing that can hold you back. Whether you like it or not, and whether you do enough or not, you win. You are going to achieve the thing that you are dreaming about. In order to achieve success in the Zone, you have to put forth effort. Your greatest effort is needed to find a place to quiet your spirit, focus your thoughts, and dream. Sit in a comfortable chair with your feet slightly apart, and let your entire body begin to relax. During this time, visualize what you want, stay there until you see it, refuse to be distracted by your racing thoughts, arrest and quiet them, and refocus on what you want. Capture your stream of consciousness, walk out every detail of your scenario, and experience the achievement of your goals in the Zone.

C: *Consider Endless Possibilities*

In this place of imagination, you are not limited to a single path; you can consider endless possibilities. You can think through many different scenarios and have as much or as little as you like. You have to practice seeing the possibilities in the zone; lacking focus in your imagination can be the death of your dream. Avoid being satisfied with one route to winning; find several before you stop imagining. The more paths you see, the more opportunities you will have to overcome obstacles when you try to walk out your dreams and turn them into material realities. You have to develop a mental stick-to-itiveness in the Zone.

T: *Touch the Impossible*

I want you to touch the impossible—everything that you thought you could not have, be, or do—and I want you to touch the possibility in your imagination. I want you to be that doctor or lawyer. I want you to invent that product or start that business. All of the things that you thought were impossible now have a place where they can be achieved. Dreaming requires you to do work, but no one else is going to be able to see what you see. Others can agree or affirm what you see after you paint the picture, but no one shares your filter of reality.

I want you to think about a time when you started something and wanted to quit before you completed the project. Maybe you bit off more than you could chew, or you simply underestimated the amount of effort, time, and energy the task would require. You wanted desperately to quit, but something on the inside—or someone on the outside—refused to let you quit, either by encouragement or threat. Think deeply about what pushes you forward in spite of the strong urge to quit and remember this each time you are tempted to give up on your possibilities.

I was a freshman at Spelman College when my dad put the fear of God in me. Prior to my driving to Atlanta from my hometown of Goodrich, Texas (sixty miles northeast of Houston), my dad pulled out the operator's manual for my car and began a ten-point check. He showed me how to locate the dipstick, how to check the transmission oil, how to connect the battery cables, and a lot more. He stressed the importance of changing the oil every five thousand miles, rotating the tires, and keeping my car clean. I knew in that moment that he was preparing me to deal with any potential problems with my vehicle, and that he thought it was very important for me to know everything I could about it. My dad can fix anything, and I thank God that I inherited the trait and the attitude of a Do It Yourselfer (DIY). This DIY attitude has saved me a lot of money that I would normally have paid to someone else—but it's also cost me a lot of money to learn how to do things myself!

My father's lowdown on the importance of vehicular maintenance, combined with my DIY attitude, led me to believe that I could rotate the tires on my 1984 Mercury Topaz. You must understand that I was a responsible young woman, and my dad had stressed how important it was to rotate the tires every ten thousand miles or so to balance out the wear. I was a starving student and didn't have the money to pay for a professional tire rotation, so I decided to do it myself. I wish that the Internet had been available to me back then, for I would have done a Google search on rotating tires. I am certain that this would have saved me a lot of time and back pain! I had only one jack. It is recommended that you have jack stands on which you can rest the car, as you should jack up the front and use a jack stand as a brace. I didn't do it that way.

When I got the front wheel off, it dawned on me that I was in trouble. I was ready to quit, but I heard the voice of my dad telling me how important it was to rotate those tires. I wanted to prove that I was committed and responsible, so I sat on the side of the car contemplating how I could rotate those tires before running out of patience and giving up completely.

I figured it out, but I don't recommend that you try to do it. I took the spare tire from the trunk, took off the front tire, replaced it with the spare, and lowered the car. Next, I jacked the back of the car, took off the tire, and replaced it with a front tire until I had replaced each one. I had not only endured a couple of hours in the Georgia heat, but I had also pushed past my desire to quit. I was going to do it. I was going to taste the victory of rotating my own tires, keeping my commitment to my dad, and being a responsible driver. I found a way to rotate the tires in spite of my lack of money.

When I find myself wanting to quit, I think about moments like the tire rotation episode. Experiences like that are milestones—memories that help us touch and experience prior victories so that we can encourage ourselves to go forward in our present challenges. I realize that moments like those create backbone, character, and courage to persevere in life. They are the moments of quiet desperation when we had to solve our problems alone, and we chose to continue in spite of overwhelming obstacles. The result is that a bit of greatness is implanted deeply in our beings, giving us staying power for our futures.

O: *Optimism Is King*

Your imagination is a kingdom, and like every kingdom, it has a king. The king of your imagination is optimism. Optimism reigns supreme in the Zone of your imagination—it is the authority. Why? Because you will be tempted to think all kinds of thoughts that will be contrary to your abilities, your beliefs, and your passions. When negative thoughts invade your mind, employ the weapon of optimism to remind yourself that anything is possible. "Having a positive mental attitude is asking how something can be done rather than saying it can't be done," says Bo Bennett, who founded Igroops.com and authored *Year to Success*. I have grown to appreciate Bo's talent, passion, and desire as he consistently motivates thousands through his many successful Web sites.

Bo's insightful remark means that even when the negative thoughts of fear, doubt, and disbelief start to come against you, optimism rises up and tells you, "Not so!" As the ruler of the kingdom, optimism establishes the law. You may say this is unrealistic, but remember—we are talking about creating an environment where you can dream again. Visualize the details of your success. Most of us do not do this; instead, we look at the big picture and ignore everything in between the idea and the result.

Helen Keller, a role model for millions, said, "Optimism is the faith that leads to achievement. Nothing can be done without hope and confidence."

R: *Reality Doesn't Matter*

Reality doesn't matter in the imagination. Your world can be spinning around you and everything may be falling apart, but when you set this seventh panel in place, you realize that you are enclosed in a safe place where reality doesn't matter.

I encourage you to sit back and relax, because it's time to dream. It's time to get into the place of the I-FACTOR Zone. It is a disciplined habit, not something you can do by happenstance. The I-FACTOR principles empower you to develop so that you can begin to execute upon the earth those things that you see in eternity through your imagination. By the time you physically walk out your vision, it is already something from the past—simply a rerun of the thoughts and ideas you saw in your imagination.

3

Values, Clarity, and Vision

After you have been through the experience of the I-FACTOR and you start thinking about your dreams and visions, opportunities you want to pursue, and the areas of life in which you particularly want to excel, ask yourself whether the endless possibilities of your dreams and imagination align with your values.

Values

Values are intrinsic elements that underlie who you are. They are defined by what you value—what you hold dear or consider supremely important. Some people value their families; others value money, time, or hard work. What do you value? Do you value who you have become? Your values are determined by what matters most to you and what you deem valuable in your life.

Where do values come from? Values are personal, social, cultural, economic, and spiritual. We adopt values from various sources, including family, political systems, culture, personal experiences, and corporate environments. Values undergird who we are; they guide our behavior and actions.

Corporations define their values in mission statements, which they use to gauge their success. For example, Microsoft values making technology easy to use for its customers. I have always been interested in computers and technology. In the 1980s, I enrolled in a course in word processing, which operated on a DOS platform and involved memorizing multiple keystrokes to cut, paste, copy, and delete. Microsoft made word processing so much easier when it employed Graphical User Interface (GUI). If you review Microsoft's latest operating system, you will find it full of graphics and icons that facilitate a more user-friendly experience. The value of simplifying technology and making it accessible to every home has driven Microsoft and its founders to significant achievements in the personal computer software industry.

Despite the economic upheaval in the fall of 2008, when the company was taken over by Wells Fargo, Wachovia is one of my favorite financial institutions. I have had a positive experience at every Wachovia branch I have visited. It is the bank's intent that the employees know the customers by name, and the employees are always helpful. They even know my dogs, Ricky and Tommy—the bank tellers routinely send me doggie bones in the drive-through. This is the vision and value statement by which Wachovia operates, as stated on their Web site, www.wachovia.com:

> Wachovia's vision is to be the best, most trusted and admired financial services company. Our Operating Committee—after receiving ideas and feed back from employees—adopted the following statement of the company's values in the spring of 2002:
>
> 1. Integrity
>
> *Trust and honesty are essential to us. We do what we say we will do. We communicate with candor. We admit our mistakes. We are people who can be trusted.*
>
> 2. Respect and Value the Individual
>
> *We embrace diversity, seeking new ideas and listening and learning from each other. We appreciate the unique capabilities and contributions of each person. We foster personal growth. We are at our best when fully engaged with our families, friends and communities.*
>
> 3. Teamwork
>
> *We achieve far more as a team than as individuals. We do not*

tolerate those who put their own self-serving interest above those of our customers, colleagues and shareholders.

4. Service

We are passionately committed to service. Through our dedication to service, we create value for customers, communities and shareholders.

5. Personal Excellence and Accountability

We are committed to the highest level of personal performance. Each of us takes our roles and responsibilities seriously.

6. Winning

As a team, we play to win. We are optimistic, confident and driven by a sense of urgency and a desire to excel. We are focused on the long-term success of Wachovia.

Wachovia's employees have demonstrated many of these values in their interactions with customers. The quality of the values we embrace, combined with the degree to which we're committed to them, determines the level of accomplishment we experience. Wachovia provides me with the experience of having a personal banker rather than being another bank on the block.

Aligning Actions with Values

Have you identified the values that are essential to you? This is very important. When you identify your values, you begin to align your actions with them. If you have dreams, ideas, or thoughts that you believe God has poured into your heart, your actions will align with your values, character, nature, and personality. I have three important values that govern my life.

My first value is representing God in the best possible way as an advocate for the gospel of Jesus Christ.

To fulfill this value, I study the Bible in order to learn how to live an effective and righteous life. I also spread the gospel by preaching, teaching, and ministering its message of hope and salvation to others. But even more effective than preaching is the way I live the gospel on a daily basis, through the demonstration of my character, integrity, and leadership. In every area of life, I strive to reflect the character, nature, and personality of Jesus Christ—I try to be kind, loving, generous, long-suffering, and meek (in most cases). Serving God and being faithful to the principles taught in the Bible are easier to do when they are strong spiritual values.

Identifying your values creates a framework for your behavior. Since I am an advocate of Christ, I have purposed in my heart to expect and experience the highest good in people and in life. I have learned to appreciate people for who they are. I have grown to respect the decisions that others make about their lives, especially in areas where I find myself in need of direction. I honor others' efforts and what they choose to do with their lives, and I never measure them as being inadequate because of what they do.

Each of us has a daily role to play in the world, and the key is to play it well, no matter where you may find yourself. I have committed to live a life of making choices that align with the principles taught in the Bible. Therefore, I am rarely confused about matters of integrity and compassion, even when I have missed the mark by a few degrees.

My second value is being the best wife that I can be for my husband, Richmond McCoy.

To be the best wife that I can be, I think about my day-to-day life and the practical aspects of loving my husband, being a support, a friend, and an encouragement to him. When he requests my help with a need or project, I am not perplexed, because I want to be sure he knows that he is a priority in my life. Why? Because being my best for him is a core value of my life.

Trust me, it is not always easy to align my actions with this value, as my husband and I do have our differences. However, what stabilizes my ultimate decision is my desire for a successful and satisfying relationship with him. During difficult moments, I ask myself how much I value my relationship with my husband versus how much I value making a choice that might induce long-term pain and suffering in the relationship. Having a value of being the best wife and friend to him has liberated my life. It has eliminated my need to "keep score" in our relationship. It has helped me to take responsibility for my actions and master my emotions. The more my actions regarding my marriage align with this value, the more joy my husband and I experience.

My third value is contributing to the excellence of other people.

This value embodies the essence of who I really am—I love seeing others excel in their lives. Everything to which I commit myself, heart and soul, has to do with educating, empowering, and enriching the lives of others—for example, the entrepreneurs I've trained with passion for the past fifteen years. I am convinced that I was born to be a positive influence in the lives of many. So far, I have been fulfilling that purpose through ten years of multiple television appearances and speaking engagements.

But I have more yet to do. This is my personal mission statement: "I am an advocate for the righteousness of a living God, proclaiming the gospel to all I meet so that they may achieve their God-given purposes." To fulfill this mission, I position myself in places where I can most effectively contribute to the excellence of other people.

Many of my dreams and visions have materialized out of this value in my life. My value of empowering others attracts opportunities to speak to and encourage others. Since I empower people with information, I am passionate about the need to communicate with others, and I seek out avenues that allow me to do this. My message is one of hope—I encourage individuals that they can achieve their dreams and visions; that they are important, special, and uniquely designed.

My daily routine involves sharing the knowledge and resources I possess and helping individuals to be better at being who they are, for people are extremely valuable to me. I am an avid researcher and prolific reader, habits I am sure were deposited in me to use for the benefit of others. I constantly search out information that I can store and pass along. I know that if I find myself in pursuit of information on a particular subject matter, someone will need that specific information in the future, and I will be the connector in his or her life. The reason I do all of the above is because my value system is based on contributing to the excellence of other people.

I have purposed in life not to be a divider of people, nor to subtract from the people with whom I interact. I am a superb multiplier and one who adds to the well-being of everyone who enters my presence. We all should spend our lives in the presence of people who add and multiply rather than divide and subtract. My value of wanting to contribute to the lives of others keeps this question in my mind: "Are the people I meet better for having known me?" The answer to that question is, in most cases, I hope, a resounding, "Yes!" I consider people valuable, regardless of who they are.

I encourage you to resolve your values; then, spend your time and energy developing what's really important in your life. Being diligent in defining what is valuable to you will mature you. Aligning your values with your actions causes you to move forward in life. When you discover and define your values, and when you align your actions with those values, it begins to focus your life, eliminating insignificant things and maturing your purpose. Values are the foundation of your life, and defining them will empower you to do what matters most, leading you to greater personal and professional development.

Clarity

In this book, we have discussed dreaming, defining values, and doing what matters most to you. By following that process, I have found greater clarity about what I want to do, and I have accomplished more in my life as a result of this clarity. I believe that in all of the ways in which I have pursued my dreams, clarity has been the element most crucial to my success.

Clarity is a property of something clear or transparent. Clarity can refer to one's ability to clearly visualize an object or concept in thought or understanding. Clarity of purpose eliminates distractions that could keep you from achieving your goals and provides clear direction instead.

Purpose is a destination, but clarity is the compass that will point you there. Clarity shows you the specific destination you need to pursue, whereas a lack of clarity—unclear goals, ideas, and dreams—will only send you in a general direction. For example, if you were given the directions, "Go north," you could follow those directions and end up just about anywhere. Clarity, on the other hand, gives you an exact destination to move toward. Instead of just going north, clarity tells you, "Go north to 'The Farthest North Truck Stop in the World' in Coldfoot, Alaska, which is located sixty miles from the Arctic Circle." Now you know where you are going, and with that knowledge, you can prepare exactly what you need to take along. If you are going to Coldfoot, Alaska, you'd better be prepared for winters ranging from ten degrees to twenty degrees below zero, Fahrenheit. Would you want to make a trip to Coldfoot without knowing these details?

Don't go off in a general direction and just end up wherever you end up in life. Instead, be intentional about your life's journey. Success is intentional; rarely is it accidental. I certainly wouldn't want to accidentally wind up in Coldfoot, Alaska, without a plan.

How do you achieve clarity? Clarity comes through thinking about your goals, writing them down, and developing a detailed vision. The day I wrote this chapter, I had a coaching call with a client who was finding it difficult to meet her objectives, and she told me she wanted to get back on track. After she listed off the things she wanted to achieve, I shared with her that I was writing on the topic of clarity and how I desperately wanted to articulate my thoughts on how goal-setting and clarity work in tandem. My client and I have spent many hours discussing her weekly goals, and I consistently ask her, "How will you do it? What steps will you take?"

Setting unclear goals will waste your time. Having clarity means also having vision, methods, and systems that help you take the steps to achieving your goals. At the end of my conversation with the client, she experienced an "Aha!" moment—she truly understood that setting goals is pointless without first creating the details in your imagination.

Clear Goals Are Essential

If you don't take time to define your life's path, others will do it for you, and you will find yourself at a destination where you never intended to be. Setting clear goals and objectives is incredibly important, for your personal and professional spheres alike. I have read many books about setting goals, writing one's mission statement, and developing strategies. All of the books about these topics share a common thread of agreement: if you want to get somewhere in life, you need a map that clearly marks your route.

Most people who have attended business school or taken courses in strategic planning are familiar with the concept of S.M.A.R.T. goals. These goals define for us what a goal should look like, but they don't say anything about the attitude you should have while pursuing your goals, much less the benefits of reaching them. Execution is the result of action, which is seen in your attitude and is manifested once you have met your goal. Building on this acronym, I have developed the idea of "SMARTER" goals:

S—Goals Must Be Specific. Clear, specific goals are essential to your personal and professional success. The more specific the goal, the more clarity you will have in reaching your destination. Once you have defined specific goals, you need to remind yourself about them constantly. Write them on Post-it notes to stick on your mirrors, enter them into your cell phone, or write them down and keep them in a place where you can refer to them often.

Action: Write out goals.

M—Targets Should Be Measurable. If you set a goal to increase your sales for the year, setting a target of making twenty prospecting calls per week is a measurable goal.

Action: Set measurable targets.

A—Goals Should Have Accountability. Find a partner, coach, mentor, spouse, or friend with whom you can share your goals. Give him or her the permission to hold you accountable for meeting them.

Action: Find support for accountability.

R—Goals Must Be Realistic. Setting unrealistic goals only leads to failure and disappointment. Setting realistic, attainable goals, however, will empower you and keep you moving forward.

Action: Set realistic goals.

T—Targets Should Be Time-based. Goals that are not time-based are goals that you are not committed to completing. Make sure that your time allowance includes a starting date and an actual time frame in which you will complete the assignment. If your goal is to make twenty prospecting calls per week, how will you schedule your time? Will you schedule the execution of making calls daily or choose a specific day and time that will be adequate for making those calls?

Action: Set a start date and a time frame.

E—Goals Should Be Met with Enthusiasm. Goals are the road map that aligns your values with your actions. Choose to be enthusiastic and passionate about achieving your goals.

Action: Choose enthusiasm and passion.

R—Goals Should Be Rewarding. We set life goals for various reasons, but each goal has an intrinsic or extrinsic reward associated with it. Ask yourself why you are doing what you do. Is the reward greater than the effort? Make sure that you can identify the reward of reaching a goal so that you can remember the reward during those times when you are tempted to abandon a project.

Action: Identify the reward of reaching your goal.

Setting goals is more than writing out your top-ten list of resolutions for the New Year or outlining the latest project you want to do. Setting goals requires action. Most people who fail to achieve the goals they set fail primarily because they don't remember a specific goal or because they don't think through the details to make the goal effective. Set smarter goals that will give you smarter results.

Vision

Another great term that conveys a similar meaning to that of dreaming, and that helps to bring clarity to the purpose to which you have been called, is *vision*. *Merriam-Webster's* defines *vision* as "a thought, concept, or object formed by the imagination...a manifestation to the senses of something immaterial...."

Vision is important. The Bible says, *"Where there is no vision, the people perish"* (Proverbs 29:18 KJV). Without vision, your focus becomes impaired; you don't know where you are going, and you risk getting stuck doing something that is not life-giving. Having vision gives you a broad view—a road map of where you are going—and it will ensure that you arrive successfully at your destination.

A vision is the large picture of what you want to do, and clarity of focus helps you to break it down into more manageable pieces that you can accomplish one at a time. If you lack vision, or if your clarity of focus is impaired, you will start down the road of life and soon wonder where you are going. Unfortunately, without clear vision, you may achieve results that are unexpected or unintended because you didn't dream them in the first place.

Dreaming leads to vision. Dreaming is saying that you will no longer settle for the reality of your life, because you want to explore something better. Vision is essentially foresight; it is the imagination active in dreaming. When you invite vision into your life, you will live forward. Vision is seen before the actualization of the dream occurs. Foresight is the single most important key to vision, which is developed in the imagination. Vision prepares the way to reality; it prepares the way to success.

Write the Vision

In order for you to grab ahold of your vision, it will be necessary for you to write it down. A popular proverb says, "The shortest pencil is longer than the longest memory." When you get into the place of dreaming and forcing yourself to think about what lies ahead, it will be too difficult for you to remember everything.

If you were to spend two hours sitting in a room—talking with other people, engaged in various activities—you would probably forget much of what took place during those two hours. Even though you were physically present in the room, if I asked you to close your eyes and recount what you saw, it would reveal how short your memory is.

If I asked you to take notes during your time in the room, writing down everything that you saw—from the wall hangings to the ceiling lights to the number and color of the chairs—you would still miss some details about the items in the room. If I asked you to walk out of the room and we reviewed what you and others saw in the room, it would become apparent that different people noticed and remembered different details. Some would have missed the doorstop behind the door, others the power outlets around the wall. Each individual in that room would have seen a limited number of things, and each would be amazed by how differently things are observed—even in the same room, looking at the same surroundings.

If your memory of physically perceived things—sights, sounds, smells—is unreliable, it is just as unreliable when it comes to your consciousness of your future. It is important for you to be able to capture your dream and vision and, when you do, to write them down immediately. Otherwise, the thoughts you have in your imagination will escape you in the physical. And visiting Dreamland just once will not be enough; you will have to revisit this place of vision many times to see clearly what it is you are supposed to do.

Similar things will happen to you when you go back and envision things in that place of dreaming, pressing yourself to think about what you need to do, as well as the opportunities that await you. That is when you start to develop clarity about your purpose, your plan, and how to get it done.

4

Dream Busters

A Dream Buster is something that kills your dream—it takes the wind out of your sails before you even have the chance to start dreaming. Most of us have experienced one or more Dream Busters at some point in our lives. They usually come from ingrained behavior patterns, wrong attitudes, or toxic relationships that affect our ability to think and act beyond our perceived limitations. Below are a few of the significant Dream Busters that, if not addressed, can derail your vision.

1. No More Pie

One Dream Buster is what I call the "No More Pie" syndrome. Like me, you've probably found yourself in a situation where you had one pie to serve for dessert, but after doing a head count of your guests, you cut only eight pieces when you actually needed ten. To remedy the situation, you take a step back, then start to cut some of those slices in half. In the "No More Pie" syndrome, the pie represents your time:

Slice one—husband, significant other, or partner

Slice two—children

Slice three—work, career

Slice four—moonlight business

Slice five—extended family obligations

Slice six—physical fitness

Slice seven—major project that you must complete

Slice eight—volunteer opportunities

Slice nine—book that you want to write

Slice ten—phone calls that you need to make

You need ten slices but have only eight. So, which two slices will be divided to yield four? Will you spend less time with your husband and children, give up that trip to the gym, or cancel your volunteer commitment? I would venture to say whoever is holding the knife will usually be the one who will give up an entire slice of pie to try to accommodate the whole.

Aren't you tired of licking the filling off of the knife and scraping the pan in the name of fairness, love, and attention? When will your passion be great enough to fight for your dream? It doesn't matter what you do—there will always be someone who wants more of you. There will always be someone who complains that you are not doing enough, giving enough, or being enough. All of these emotions, pressures, and competing needs of others will throw you completely off course from the path to achieving your goals. When this happens, they act as Dream Busters in your life.

When you continually put your life on the back burner so that others can have their pieces of pie, can you trust your creativity, your ideas, or your passions? It is difficult to lift off, lunge, or leap forward if you are always trying to please those around you. Guess what? Time continues to pass, and because you gave up your plans and goals in an attempt to meet the needs of others or to appease them, you are left holding the empty pie tin that once held your hopes and dreams.

To avoid the Dream Buster of "No More Pie" syndrome, you must learn to find the balance between doing what matters most in your life and meeting the demands and needs of others. Sometimes, what matters most may be making more slices of pie; other times, it may mean saying, "There is no more pie; it's all gone." Often, there is just not enough pie for everyone in your life, and you must be willing to say so. You must be willing to stand up to those sad, disappointed faces who will eventually leave your presence and move forward in their lives, trying to get a piece of your next pie—or the pie of anyone else who crosses their paths.

2. *Procrastination*

We all understand the meaning of the term *procrastination*, and, if we're honest, we will admit that we are all procrastinators, in some way or another. Some put off the occasional project for a few days until it is more convenient to finish it; others have a chronic habit of procrastination that keeps them from achieving their dreams.

I routinely coach individuals to help them achieve their dreams. I have discovered that procrastination is one of the primary reasons that clients cannot fulfill their dreams. During my coaching sessions, I help my clients set up timelines marked with concrete action steps in order to assist them in reaching the goals they want to achieve. I find it interesting that many of them come to our weekly sessions and have not accomplished the basic goals that we set to help them realize their dreams.

Even though we break down their big dreams into bite-sized action steps, many people put off even the small steps and then wonder why they are never able to realize the bigger goals in their lives. The culprit is the Dream Buster of procrastination! A procrastinator is one who chronically puts things off. If you procrastinate, you know what you need to do, but you do not do it. You know when a task needs to be completed, and you even know how to execute it, but you just do not get it done. If you habitually delay or postpone the tasks of life, procrastination becomes a lifestyle for you.

When I assess my clients at the outset of our coaching relationship, many tell me that they are procrastinators but still work extremely well under pressure. I ask them, "Have you ever considered that when you don't give yourself sufficient time, you are not putting your best foot forward or creating your best product because you underestimate the time required to complete a particular task?" Procrastinating hinders your ability to achieve your dream and vision. When you continue to fall short in your attempts at execution, you establish a pattern of disappointment in your life, and procrastination is a direct enemy of execution.

Just because you procrastinate does not necessarily mean that you don't accomplish anything. I am a procrastinator, but I am able to plan my procrastination in such a way that it does not hinder my progress. Perhaps you feel the same way. I do get tasks accomplished, and I have an extremely optimistic attitude that allows me to say, "Even if I do not do it today, I'll have time to do it tomorrow."

Whenever I procrastinate, however, I find that I do not allow myself enough time to be excellent in what I do. No matter the task, if you allow yourself adequate time to complete it, you allow yourself an opportunity to readjust, reinvent, redesign, and reimagine all of the components that will make your project more successful. But when you are under the wire and feeling the pressure of time limitations, the only results you can deliver are based on the time you allow.

I enjoy watching the cable network show *Project Runway*. This particular show gives aspiring designers the opportunity to showcase their creative talents. One of the main pressures placed on the competing designers is a time constraint—they have to be accurate about estimating how long each task will take and must divide their time wisely. Failing to prioritize, talking too much, being lax in energy and effort, and postponing the production of the more difficult designs until the last minute are some of the many reasons a designer might be eliminated from the show. It is crucial to give yourself enough time to work out the details of your desired results. Make the details direct and succinct, eliminating unnecessary factors. Streamline the process.

3. Reinforcing the Lifestyle

Habitual procrastination will keep you from achieving your dream and vision. Unfortunately, many people develop the habit of procrastinating because it is often reinforced with rewards. For instance, imagine being assigned a project at work to produce a proposal in two weeks' time. As a procrastinator, you waited to put the proposal together until the night before it was due. You worked late into the night, gulping down large volumes of caffeinated beverages to keep you awake. Minutes before leaving for work, you printed off the final pages of the proposal to present to your boss.

Amazingly, your last-minute execution didn't seem to affect the outcome of the project—everybody in the office was overwhelmed by the great job you did on the proposal. This is an example of a reward system based on delay—it's as if your colleagues are rewarding you for your last-minute action. Your proposal probably had a few misspelled words and could definitely have been a tighter document, had you dedicated a bit more time and attention to it. But because you were rewarded for your efforts in spite of your laziness, you will likely follow the same pattern of procrastination the next time you undertake a project with a deadline.

Sure, you got the proposal done in time, and you got a great review. Even though it may have taken the same amount of effort had you started it several weeks before the due date, you would have had more time to rehash the contents, review your wording, and edit it multiple times—and you still may have received the same accolades. But there are other things to consider, such as the long-term effects of stress on your health and the sustainability of excellence when work is consistently done in this way—with or without immediate rewards.

When I was a student at Spelman College back in the mid-1980s, one of the courses I took was English. I entered that class presuming that I was not particularly skilled in English. Because of my lack of confidence, I decided that I didn't want to put forth much effort in the class. I figured I'd do what was necessary to get a passing grade. Well, I just barely passed—that's what happens when you wait until the very last minute to complete your assignments. English is not the class for which you should wait until the last minute to do your assignments; it's all about words—and a lot of them!

In all college-level courses, the professor gives you a syllabus at the beginning of the semester. The syllabus indicates when your term papers and other class projects are due—usually during the third or fourth month of the semester. Even with the professor's due dates clearly listed on my syllabus, I waited until the night before my term paper was due to begin. That proved an unwise decision, as the term paper was supposed to be ten to fifteen pages long.

I really had no experience with writing term papers prior to college. And in those days, we did not have the convenience of the Internet to access information as we do today. Both my roommate and I waited until the last minute to write our papers. The assignment was to write a review of one of three great literary classics: John Steinbeck's *The Grapes of Wrath*, Charles Dickens' *A Tale of Two Cities*, or *Great Expectations* by the same author. I don't even remember which book I chose, but that's probably because I hadn't read the book. Needless to say, I was not prepared!

I began to panic. The book was too long—hundreds of pages in length—and there was no possible way I could read that book, especially since I started after five o'clock the night before the paper was due. I resolved to use CliffsNotes. I don't have to tell you what happened next: after a sleepless all-nighter, I did produce a ten- to fifteen-page report, which I submitted to the professor the next day.

The next class, the professor wore a look of disdain as he handed back my paper—with a big, red F on the cover. I looked at it and said, "What?" and immediately changed the F to an E, even as he watched. My thought was that the professor could have given me at least an "E" for effort!

The professor recognized, however, that I had not put any effort into writing that paper. The result: I withdrew from the class, and it was reflected in my grade point average, as well as in my success (or lack thereof) in my other classes. It was like a downward spiral. Thereafter, I procrastinated in every class and produced the worst grades of my life, achieving a GPA of 1.8—not a great example from someone who had been the salutatorian of her high school class. Not only was my GPA nothing to write home about, but I was also scared to go home during summer break.

The resource of time is an asset, and until we value it, respect it, and use it wisely, we will continue to procrastinate; our performance will remain mediocre, and we will fail to achieve our goals to the best of our abilities. Looking back, I am sure that my paper was filled with mistakes and grammatical errors, as well as the obvious content flaws, all clearly showing that I had not given much time to reading the book or to editing my work.

Most of us procrastinators have developed the habit from years of experience—in our workplaces, in our relationships, or in raising our children. We wait until the last minute, convinced that we can perform well under pressure. The deception is that we really believe we are in control; we think that we can handle our business within the tightest of time constraints. When it comes to executing our dreams, this attitude can bust them wide open and derail our efforts.

4. Loss of Confidence and Self-esteem

A characteristic of procrastinators is a loss of confidence. One of my coaching clients has been particularly influenced by this fact. When she cannot achieve the things she sets out to do, her self-esteem takes a big dive. Procrastination, again, is the real culprit. It is not that she is too busy with a full plate of activities crying for her attention, nor is it a case of lacking talent, creativity, or skills to accomplish the tasks before her. Rather, she has a difficult time saying "no," identifying her priorities, and delegating responsibilities to others. She is a doer; she gets a lot done but wants to be more effective with her time, talents, and resources. When she's not effective in these matters, she struggles with low self-esteem.

These words of wisdom, gleaned at a Stephen Covey Focus course, are a great example of the confusing process of identifying priorities:

Because we don't know what is really important to us, every-
thing seems important. Because everything seems important,
we have to do everything. Other people, unfortunately, see us
as doing everything, so they expect us to do everything. Doing
everything keeps us so busy; we don't have time to think
about what is really important to us.

—Anonymous

Do you think that there are too many things on your plate? Is there enough time in a day or enough people in your life to help you clean your plate? If you're a procrastinator, you probably use the excuse that you are overloaded without enough time or help to explain why you can't get anything done. The result is that when others heap additional work on your plate, this work becomes a reason or excuse as to why you were late for a meeting or why you did not finish that report on time. "I simply had too much to do," you say. This type of statement becomes more than an attempt to justify why you aren't achieving your goals. It becomes a Dream Buster—one that keeps you from your purpose in life.

5. Manipulation

Some procrastinators use the fact that they don't get things done to manipulate other people into doing things their way. For instance, let's say you are scheduled to attend a meeting at work, and although you know that your colleagues are awaiting your arrival, you have something else you'd rather do. In your mind, you make the excuse that this other thing is more important than the meeting, and you delay your arrival accordingly. You are essentially manipulating the behavior and response of the people who are waiting for you; you know that your delay is causing anxiety and stress in the group.

Procrastinators may recognize that they develop this habit in an attempt to cope with the pressures of day-to-day living. You may be a good planner who diligently schedules her activities, but you use procrastination to actually deal with those pressures and delay your timeliness based on how you cope.

Basically, procrastinators cope with day-to-day pressures by waiting until the last minute to get things done. Many procrastinators embrace delays as a way to stay in control, so that other people cannot bother them or expect more from them than they want to give. They use their busyness as an excuse to delay or put off responsibilities that they know they ought to do. What better way to remain "in control" and cover the fact that sometimes you are just flat-out stubborn in refusing to work with your team or partner?

Another manipulative technique that procrastinators use is seeing themselves as frustrated victims. Victims do not assume responsibility for their actions or their lack of success, blaming them instead on other people, the "victimizers." This type of procrastinator is flabbergasted by his own procrastination, as if it is an outside force and no fault of his own. Procrastinators with the victim mentality attempt to manipulate the sympathy of others instead of doing their part to change the attitudes and behaviors that created their problem in the first place.

Once you grow sufficiently tired of your issues with self-esteem and manipulation and are prepared to cast off your procrastination, you can turn the habit around by doing things in your "now" moment. The benefits of overcoming procrastination are many. Think about how you would feel if you succeeded in achieving many of the goals that you set in your daily schedule. You would experience the satisfying feelings of success, reward, pleasure, and peace of mind. You would also feel strong and capable—a boost to your self-esteem from simply getting things done. On the contrary, when you procrastinate, you lack focus and feel helpless, inadequate, and weak. You may even feel useless; your life might seem out of your control. At the end of the day, consider the benefits of overcoming procrastination. Peace of mind, self-respect, a sense of accomplishment and competence, and achieving your goals are great victories—ones with significant personal and professional rewards.

6. Self-doubt

If you practice self-doubt, it means that you don't believe in yourself—you don't think that you have the capacity, talent, skills, or relationships necessary for achieving your goals. Perhaps you are living under a cloud of past failures—business ventures that fell through, relationships that ended bitterly—and you do not feel that you have what it takes to succeed. Maybe you don't feel smart; maybe you think you're a poor salesperson; maybe you don't think that you understand finances or any of the other areas of expertise that help people succeed in business. The worst thing you can do, when it comes to your dream, is doubt yourself and your abilities. Self-doubt is a significant Dream Buster.

Self-doubt stems from a false notion that you should have it all together, that you should have all the answers to any circumstance or problem you face. Quite frankly, it just doesn't work that way—for anyone. You will never have all the answers. But with the input of others, you can arrive at the answers you seek. Life consists of a series of shared moments, issues, questions, and the like. We are not islands, isolated from one another. Other people can have a positive impact on our lives, contributing in meaningful ways to our personal triumphs and professional successes. In a business environment, teamwork usually improves a product or service. What one cannot do, another person can. We contribute to the success of one another, as well as to the success of the whole—be it a business, a family, a community, or a country.

One of my pets is a dog named Tommy. A few months ago, Tommy was hit by a car. We were certainly concerned about him, especially his leg, which appeared to be broken. By the end of the ordeal, I had gained a great appreciation for the veterinarian who treated Tommy and the medical facility where his surgery took place. When we met with the veterinarian and she told us what was wrong with Tommy, we were overwhelmed with feelings of appreciation for her expertise.

Imagine the number of years of experience and training that she brought to bear on our dog's broken leg. Think about the passion and love for animals that drew her into the field of veterinary medicine, where she learned to better understand animal medicine and help animals in need. I didn't need to be an expert in veterinary science because, in the time of crisis, we had a trained veterinarian to take care of our dog.

I offer this example because when we reach out to achieve our dreams and visions, whether in business, the arts, ministry, or education, we never enter a new field with all the answers. There are always other people who can contribute to the accomplishment of our goals. So, how do you overcome the Dream Buster of self-doubt in your life? The following are a few things I suggest that you do:

First: Take an inventory of your skills.

What are you trained, skilled, and gifted to do? Where do you lack knowledge or a needed skill set? You need to identify the skills you have that will help you to achieve your dream.

It is wonderful that online and distance learning programs are available in our society. It took me fifteen years to be able to complete my undergraduate degree in business—primarily because I needed to take one additional course to complete the degree, but the course was not offered at any local school. The course was a California state requirement, but because I no longer lived in California, I could not enroll to take it. Having relocated, I couldn't take the course until it became available by distance learning.

Assess your skill sets, do an inventory, and if you see a lack in your training, find a mentor, or take a class to fulfill that lack. If you doubt your abilities in a certain area, study and train to become competent in that area so that you can strengthen your self-esteem.

Self-doubt does not need to determine your success in life; it need not doom you to failure. Taking an inventory of your relationships and skills allows you to build a network of encouragement around you and to sharpen your skills in the areas where they're lacking.

Second: Take an inventory of your relationships.

Review every relationship in your life (family members, friends, colleagues) and identify the people who are planting fruitful seeds in you—the people who confirm your reality and encourage you to achieve your dreams. Eliminate the "subtracters and dividers" (the people who diminish or take away from your chances at success) and embrace the "adders and multipliers" (the people who enhance or contribute to your chances at success).

If you find your current circle of relationships deficient in helping you achieve your dream, begin to invite others into your life who are more skilled or experienced, and begin to ask them questions. We live in a society in which we take can in information, yet we're often embarrassed to ask questions. Because we have so much information at our fingertips, it reinforces the myth that we should be able to figure out everything without any help from other people.

To counteract hesitation when it comes to asking questions, surround yourself with people who have expertise in an area of interest similar to yours. If you want to start an organization for women, open a flower arranging business, or climb a mountain, you need to connect with people who are already doing these things so that you can learn from their experiences.

7. *Toxic Relationships*

Dr. Lillian Glass, author of *Toxic People*, describes a toxic person as "anyone who manages to drag you down, make you feel angry, worn out, deflated, belittled or confused." It may be difficult for some people to admit that they are in a toxic relationship, for the "toxic" individual may be an intelligent, self-sufficient person in other aspects of life. Most people in toxic relationships, however, have the sense that something is just not right. When people fail to acknowledge toxic relationships or fail to deal with them in a healthy manner, these relationships can completely destroy their ability to dream.

Friends

College is a time when you develop many relationships that will remain with you for a lifetime. Even people who achieve great notoriety or prominence remain faithful to the friendships they formed before they hit the spotlight. It is wonderful when you can maintain relationships with close friends from earlier years.

I remember one young woman with whom I had a brief friendship in college. The friendship was full of drama and pressure. I quickly realized that she was not the type of person with whom I wanted to maintain a relationship. I remember telling her that even though she probably thought ours was a close, lasting relationship, I thought differently: to me, ours was a high maintenance relationship, and I really wanted to have low maintenance relationships. Two people in a low maintenance relationship are comfortable in one another's presence. There's a sense of knowing that even if they may not talk or visit very often, they can pick up right where they left off when they finally do talk on the phone or meet for lunch. They also know that they can call on one another in times of need. They always respect each other's differences, and they simply get along. Neither one has a greater degree of dependence on the other, nor does either one place the responsibility on the other to carry the relationship. They have mutual understanding, equal commitment, and shared responsibility.

During college, I was not familiar with the term "toxic relationship," but I believe that it accurately describes what I experienced. My relationship with the girl I mentioned involved meeting emotional needs and social pressures to the point where I could not maintain our friendship and still be a normal, active student. It was weighty, abusive, and distracting. I purposed in my heart to surround myself with people who added value to my life instead of those who pulled me down.

Thus, I ended my relationship with her because its nature of high maintenance was taking a toll on my emotional, mental, and social health. Many of us are in relationships with other women:

sisters, cousins, friends, and coworkers. Inevitably, we will enter into relationships that require much more than we are able to give. I have heard many women say that it seems like they are always the givers in their relationships.

I am not the kind of friend most people would call with a problem at two o'clock in the morning. That type of phone call stopped many years ago when I recognized the toxic nature of my relationship with my college friend. Now, when I enter into relationships with people, I let them know what is acceptable and unacceptable.

Toxic relationships can keep us from achieving our dreams because they simply take up too much of our time. We said earlier that procrastination means putting off doing something; relationships can cause us to procrastinate. Every time you answer your phone at two o'clock in the morning, you are taking away from your sleep, sense of well-being, and energy level. When you sacrifice your time and energy for others, you will have to momentarily procrastinate pursuing your dreams; they will slip into the background.

You certainly want to invest time and energy into those family members and friends who are important to you, but you want to divest yourself of toxic relationships that drain you to the point that you have little time and energy to devote to your own goals and dreams.

A toxic individual can be a friend, a parent, a spouse—any person who is simply sucking the life out of you. Imagine the sound when you slurp the final drops of soda through a straw. That noise is a good representation of what it is like when a person is sucking the life out of you—forceful and determined, this person will slurp up every drop of energy in your glass.

You need to find the kind of people who add positive things to your life—people around whom you feel comfortable exhaling, freely releasing air and breathing in without the fear that they'll suck the air out of you before you can take another breath. Every woman needs to have friends, but when it comes to achieving your dream and vision, you have to consider how much time you really have for relationships in any given day.

When you allow your long-term best friend to share for hours about the minute details of her latest crisis, is it really helping either of you? Does she really need your help, or is she just dumping her emotional woes on you? Is it time to reach out and help her, or time to distance yourself for a season? The answer depends on what you are doing in your life. Relationships are seasonal, and we must be aware when the seasons change. If you are in the dead of winter, let it go—don't force the advent of spring and risk perpetuating a harmful relationship for yet another year.

I often find that people who maintain toxic relationships do not have time set aside for their own lives—they put their personal goals and pursuits on hold. This often means that they will give up their time for anybody because they do not know what to do with it themselves. You should begin to think about how you can shift those relationships around to make room in your life for ones that are more positive, nurturing, and empowering.

One way to do this is by linking with opportunities provided by organizations such as Woman Act Now, which has chapters all over the country, and your local chapter can help to nurture and encourage you, tell you how great you are, hold you accountable, and instruct you in the methods that will help you bring positive changes to your life. Visit www.womanactnow.com.

Mom and Dad

Another type of toxic relationship that can need attention is the parent/child relationship. This is a sensitive matter, because our parents' homes are where we developed our earliest habits, positive and negative alike. If your relationship with your parents is toxic, it will take away from who you are without adding any value in return. Many people have toxic relationships with their parents, but they fail to recognize the toxicity because it was the norm—it's the way in which they were raised.

The term "dysfunctional family" has gained popularity and use in recent years. If we are honest, we'll admit that we all come from families with a degree of dysfunctionality; we all live dysfunctional lives, to a certain extent. But if you are a woman, married or single, living on your own (away from your parents' house), you have to determine whether the boundaries between you and your family are healthy. Is the relationship one of positive concern and nurture, or one of unwanted interference? If your parents are meddlesome to an unhealthy degree, you will need to raise your standards and clarify your boundaries.

Dealing with parents who are controlling, manipulative, overbearing, and interfering is a daunting challenge, and there is no simple advice about how to change a dysfunctional relationship that has gone on your entire life. One piece of advice, though, is that you must live for you. Take responsibility for your own actions, not for the actions of others who cause you to feel guilty and fill you with seeds of self-doubt. Unfortunately, we can spend our entire lives trying to fix relationships based on what looks right to others. Guard your heart and your mind when processing what you hear so that any negative words will not automatically erode your confidence.

Coworkers

Another type of relationship you need to pay attention to is your professional relationships with people in the workplace: your managers and coworkers. Colleagues in the workplace don't communicate with the same restraint that they did years ago. When you watch movies filmed during the 1940s and 1950s, you find that the actors depict people who used the English language properly and communicated with one another in a more civil, formal style than most people do today.

In the twenty-first century, workplace communication has grown loose and informal—offices are characterized by casual wear, casual talk, and casual behavior—and, as a result, the communication is often unclear or ineffective. Most people are in high maintenance relationships at work. Often, the norm is conflict, jealousy, arguments, sulking, and hassles with the people you work with. Even though some relationships at work just do not gel, there must be some way that you can navigate those relationships and still be successful in your workplace.

The key is to detoxify your work environment. If you are in business, look at the partners and determine whether relationships with them are high maintenance. What is being demanded of you in your relationships in the workplace? If you are in a partnership, are you both still aligned in vision and purpose? It is usually fairly simple to notice when you are misaligned or if there is a lack of communication. In personal or professional relationships, when you find it painful to talk, discuss, or make decisions, these may be signs of toxicity. This does not necessarily mean that you have to sever those relationships, but it does mean that you have to change your expectancy level if you are going to stay in the relationships.

To keep your dream from being derailed by a relationship Dream Buster, look for any toxic, high maintenance relationships in your life. Should you identify any, replace them with low maintenance relationships that will be mutually beneficial.

8. Lack of Self-credibility

Credibility is an important characteristic in business, and it's equally important in your personal life. Personal credibility can either propel you forward or preclude the fulfillment of your dreams; your dreams are hindered or fulfilled based on how you keep your word to yourself.

A lack of credibility to self falls in the same category as low self-esteem and self-doubt. You have probably said to someone whose confidence you were trying to inspire, "My word is my bond." But how often do you apply this same reassuring statement to yourself? How often do you keep the bond that you make to yourself? Examine your track record in following through with the goals that are important to you versus following through with things you promised to do for others.

What are the things you enjoy doing or really need to do? Have you had lunch with that longtime friend, scheduled that annual doctor's appointment, taken a vacation, hired a fitness trainer and nutritionist, or learned how to ballroom dance? You're probably saying to yourself, *I'll get around to it someday*. But "someday" may never come—too many people experience this reality. Do you really value yourself? Does your purpose, the reason you're alive, matter to you? It matters if it shows up in your actions and you begin to take your life seriously; it matters when you begin to do something extraordinary with the time you've been given.

There's an inner voice that whispers, bidding you to act, to produce great results. Listen—it guides you. Make a plan and act on it by keeping your word to you! Keep the commitments you make to yourself by actually acting upon them; doing this will bring you joy, peace, strength, and love. You will be encouraged to achieve the big and small things alike that matter most to you. This inner voice that whispers also screams, "Woman, act now!"

Disappointment ensues when you have promised yourself yet another thing but have given it up because you see it as insignificant. The inner voice screams louder still until you hear it, making you aware of the true significance of this seemingly trivial thing. You experience the pain of wrath through frustration, broken dreams, and restlessness. You may want to start a business, but you don't connect with that guiding voice. You don't act on it. Or, you do act—apart from it. Inaction and defiant action can both result in a negative outcome. You become more discouraged, for you know the truth: you won't follow through, because, to you, your word is not your bond. You lack credibility with yourself. And when this happens, dreams are deferred, self-confidence is shaken, and peace is lost.

If you say that you are going to do something but fail to follow through with it, your lack of credibility to self becomes a Dream Buster. That's when the inner voice turns into many voices. Fueled by self-doubt, these voices constantly remind you of your past failures and shortcomings. They remind you that you have never been able to do this or that before. You may have said that you were going to accomplish many things, but you never did what you said. You tried different options, but you still didn't reach your goals.

The voices that bombard your thoughts could be both internal and external—from your own subconscious, as well as from people around you.

The lack of credibility to self is a strong, brutal Dream Buster. It is often the internal voice of doubt and lack of commitment that initiates the external voices attacking your dream. If heeded, these voices are powerful. They begin to tell you that you are too young or too old, that you're not smart enough, or that you have no experience.

With all of these different voices, it is important to look honestly at yourself, first. If you do this, others will not judge you. Or, at least, their judgments will be lessened to the point that they eventually have no significance at all. You have already acknowledged your problem of credibility with yourself.

If you acknowledge that you have issues with keeping your own word to yourself, you need to overcome this behavior and become that person who honors herself by keeping her word. It is not always the large decisions, but rather the series of small decisions, that bring about great change in your life. Begin small and execute achievable agreements.

Some of your agreements will sound like the eternal line, "I'm going to start a new diet tomorrow." Many of us know all too well how rarely that vow is fulfilled. Similar agreements are, "Tomorrow, I'll begin an exercise program," "I plan to pray more," "I will meditate more often and find the place of wholeness in myself." But how many of us actually do any of those things when "tomorrow" arrives and becomes "today"?

But *Woman, Act Now* anyway! What we do today directly affects our tomorrows. Remove doubt and act! Self-evaluation, along with corresponding actions away from the presence of others, will reassure you in times of doubt and make a positive impact on your personal and professional life.

Lack of credibility with yourself, on the other hand, convinces you to distrust yourself, your decisions, and your actions. It is not somebody on the outside—a friend, boss, or coworker—who is pushing you down; rather, it is you. You do not trust yourself because of your track record. You can begin to overcome the issue of a lack of self-credibility by setting small, achievable goals and defining specific results. By setting achievable goals, you will develop the corresponding habit of keeping your word to yourself.

To help you develop the habit of keeping your word to yourself, we will consider the four primary aspects of life: mind, body, soul, and spirit. These aspects are laid out in Scripture, perhaps most notably in 1 Thessalonians 5:23: *"Now may the God of peace Himself sanctify you completely; and may your whole spirit, soul, and body be preserved blameless at the coming of our Lord Jesus Christ."* Begin to keep your commitments by acting upon your word to yourself— *Woman, Act Now!* Decide what you need in order to function effectively in every area of your life. Decide how to act on those needs and be proactive in situations that will give you the opportunity to take action.

A lack of credibility to self begins when you don't act upon the commitments you have made to yourself—remember this Dream Buster?—and the result is that any belief in your abilities starts to erode. When you have dreams that never come into being, it can destroy the dream inside of you because you lack personal credibility in your mind.

The lack of credibility to self can also be enacted when you make other people and their dreams and goals more important than your own. If you consistently find that you are working late into the midnight hour, exhausting your energy completely and still not managing to accomplish any personal tasks or objectives that you set for that day, you need to question your motives. Why is the work of others more important than your own?

Compare the amount of time you spend on personal projects with the amount of time you help others to complete projects of their own. If you discover that you're spending significantly more time helping others with their projects, this indicates that you consider them more important than your own. You must begin to put your tasks and goals first. By putting those of others first, you value them more, and their purposes for being here matter more to you than your own purpose. They have gone home for the night; they are enjoying favorite pastimes and taking care of their families; they are sleeping soundly...but what about you?

If you find yourself in a situation where you cannot give any attention to yourself, begin to systematically release yourself from responsibilities to others until you have properly given yourself the time needed to accomplish your goals. You must come first. If at the end of your life you are asked what you did to accomplish your purpose, how will you respond? God has a plan for each of us—an individual purpose, as well as a collective purpose, to spread the gospel. The Great Commission charges us to *"go into all the world and preach the gospel to every creature"* (Mark 16:15). And in 1 Peter 4:5, we read, *"They will give an account to Him who is ready to judge the living and the dead."*

Part of God's plan for us is that we serve others, meeting their needs by giving of our own energy, talents, and time. Jesus taught this to His disciples in the gospel of Matthew:

When the Son of Man comes in his glory, and all the angels with him, he will sit on his throne in heavenly glory. All the nations will be gathered before him, and he will separate the people one from another as a shepherd separates the sheep from the goats. He will put the sheep on his right and the goats on his left. Then the King will say to those on his right, "Come, you who are blessed by my Father; take your inheritance, the kingdom prepared for you since the creation of the world. For I was hungry and you gave me something to eat, I was thirsty and you gave me something to drink, I was a stranger and you invited me in, I needed clothes and you clothed me, I was sick and you looked after me, I was in prison and you came to visit me." Then the righteous will answer him, "Lord, when did we see you hungry and feed you, or thirsty and give you something to drink? When did we see you a stranger and invite you in, or needing clothes and clothe you? When did we see you sick or in prison and go to visit you?" The King will reply, "I tell you the truth, whatever you did for one of the least of these brothers

*of mine, you did for me." Then he will say to those on his left,
"Depart from me, you who are cursed, into the eternal fire prepared for the devil and his angels. For I was hungry and you
gave me nothing to eat, I was thirsty and you gave me nothing to drink, I was a stranger and you did not invite me in, I
needed clothes and you did not clothe me, I was sick and in
prison and you did not look after me." They also will answer,
"Lord, when did we see you hungry or thirsty or a stranger or
needing clothes or sick or in prison, and did not help you?" He
will reply, "I tell you the truth, whatever you did not do for one
of the least of these, you did not do for me."*

(Matthew 25:31–45 NIV)

If we are not fulfilling our purpose in the grand scheme of
things, we are not being effective at meeting the needs of others.
Being misaligned never brings value to the whole in the long run,
even if it appears beneficial at first glance. The emotional, spiritual,
physical, and mental aspects of life are parts of a balanced whole.
Giving of yourself at the expense of yourself, though, constitutes
a Dream Buster. Finding a balance in your life by employing small
tools of action will cause the aspects of your life to realign, and
balance will also help to destroy any Dream Busters that might be
threatening your equilibrium.

9. Ill-suited Employment

It is amazing how many of us are ill-suited for the jobs we do.
As I travel around the country teaching on Kingdompreneurship—
God's way of doing business—I am aware that many of us are not
in proper alignment because of our employment. For many of you,
your job has no connection to the dream or vision you have for
your life. It may not provide adequate avenues or opportunities for
fulfilling your life goals.

Conversely, you may be in a situation in which you have been
trained to do what you are called to do; if that's the case, great!
However, if you made a commitment to your employer to work

eight hours a day, but you work ten or more hours a day without overtime pay, where is your commitment to yourself? Those additional two hours a day add up, demanding of you a fifty-hour work-week instead of the forty-hour one you had agreed upon. By doing this, you are implicitly saying that your employer matters more to you than you matter to yourself. If you have pushed your dream to the background and your employer's demands to the foreground, think about how those additional hours could be used to advance your purpose and then reconsider your commitment. You might consider talking to your boss or manager about his or her expectations, stating your own and reaching a compromise.

Some of the reasons we put our dreams in the background include fear, embarrassment, thinking our dreams are too small or too large, or feeling unfit to accomplish them. Whatever your reason, *Woman, Act Now*! Your dream matters, and you need to move it to the foreground of the stage of your life. The way to overcome any lack of self-credibility or self-doubt is to take small yet significant steps toward accomplishing your dream. Bust the Dream Busters! Begin to take your life back by reclaiming your time and putting your dreams in the forefront.

When you take your life back, you mark your life. Set aside some time to do what you desire, and break it off in small chunks. Otherwise, the freedom may be a bit overwhelming, causing you to forget why you freed yourself to begin with. Begin to work on your dream for fifteen minutes a day; by the end of the week, you will have worked one hour and forty-five minutes. You will feel much better when you set aside this time rather than doing nothing at all about your dream.

"Hope deferred makes the heart sick, but when the desire is fulfilled, it is a tree of life" (Proverbs 13:12 AMP). Restore credibility to yourself by helping your deferred dream become a reality!

5 Dream Catchers

Once you've removed the Dream Busters from your life, replace them with Dream Catchers. According to tradition, a Dream Catcher is "a circular framed net with a hole in the center that is used by some American Indian peoples to help block bad dreams and catch good ones" (*Merriam-Webster's Dictionary*). The legend of the Dream Catcher comes from the Wounded Knee School in Manderson, South Dakota.

Long ago when the world was young, an old Lakot spiritual leader was on a high mountain and had a vision. In his vision, Iktomi, the great trickster and teacher of wisdom, appeared in the form of a spider. Iktomi spoke to him in a sacred language that only the spiritual leaders of the Lakota could understand. As he spoke, Iktomi the spider took the elder's willow hoop which had feathers, horse hair, beads and offerings on it and began to spin a web.

He spoke to the elder about the cycles of life...and how we begin our lives as infants and we move on to childhood, and then to adulthood. Finally, we go to old age where we must be taken care of as infants, completing the cycle. "But," Iktomi said as he continued to spin his web, "in each time of life there are many forces—some good and some bad. If you listen to the good forces, they will steer you in the right direction. But if you listen to the bad forces, they will hurt you and steer you in the wrong direction." He continued, "There are many forces and different directions that can help or interfere with the harmony of nature, and also with the Great Spirit and all of his wonderful teachings."

All the while the spider spoke, he continued to weave his web starting from the outside and working towards the center. When Iktomi finished speaking, he gave the Lakota elder the web and said... "See, the web is a perfect circle but there is a hole in the center of the circle. Use the web to help yourself and your people to reach your goals and make good use of your people's ideas, dreams and visions. If you believe in the Great Spirit, the web will catch your good ideas—and the bad ones will go through the hole."

The Lakota elder passed on his vision to his people and now the Sioux Indians use the dream catcher as the web of their life. It is hung above their beds or in their home to sift their dreams and visions. The good in their dreams is captured in the web of life and carried with them...but the evil in their dreams escapes through the hole in the center of the web and is no longer a part of them. They believe that the dream catcher holds the destiny of their future.

(From *Sunrise* magazine, October/November 1996. Copyright © 1996 by Theosophical University Press.)

When I was thinking about what it means to be a dream catcher, I was unfamiliar with the Indian tribal traditions that are the origins of these objects. My husband and I talked about how in our relationship, he is a diamond maker; I am a dream catcher. He is a brilliant man full of ideas and vision who encourages, motivates, and empowers—and is tough, at times, when he needs to be.

After our first few years of marriage, I began to understand my husband's methods. He is always looking for one of the many diamonds in me. He sees me as a diamond mine, full of precious jewels that need to be uncovered and polished. He "mines" my diamonds by his encouraging words, tender affections, and constant support. When he discovers a new diamond, he fully understands what he must do to refine the diamond in me.

I, on the other hand, am a dream catcher; as such, I catch dreams, visions, and ideas. I have demonstrated this ability throughout most of my life, always contributing to the creation, viability, and formation of ideas—my own and others' alike. I have purposed to catch the dreams of my husband and execute them in our daily life as a couple. A dream catcher is one who can identify a dream, vision, or idea and hold it in the reservoir of her heart until the proper season in which to execute it.

To become a dream catcher, you must purpose in your heart to have room for big dreams. You must continually empty your mind to ensure that your heart is never too full to contain a dream. Dream catchers long to dream and to manifest the dreams within them. They take inventories of the reservoirs of their hearts, looking for dreams that have grown old in order to reenergize, refocus, and recommit to these dreams until they are birthed.

Dream catchers often start as ordinary people whose lives are mundane or routine until, one day, something out of the ordinary happens. It could be a tragedy or a triumph—a terminal illness, the birth of a child, an inspiring program—but something significant or extraordinary enables the Dream Giver to release a dream. When that happens, you have to catch the dream. If your life is full of clutter, do you have room to receive a dream?

CNN produced a moving and inspirational program, *CNN Heroes: An All-Star Tribute*, that honored everyday people in a live Hollywood-style, red carpet event that was broadcast around the world. The program was fit for Hollywood's finest, but instead it honored the world's finest—people who had demonstrated acts of heroism during moments of crisis or birthed dreams of kindness, care, and restoration out of personal painful experiences. Here are some of the stories of dream catchers—ordinary people doing extraordinary things for others.

1. "It's a privilege to be in Kenya," Steve Peifer told the *CNN Heroes* audience. "We came to Kenya after one of our children died. Scripture says he who seeks to lose his own life will find it. When my son died, I felt like I lost my

own life. Kenya gave it back to me. I'll always be blessed that we ended up in Kenya. There's such a need in Kenya. There's such an opportunity right now."

2. Queen Brown's youngest son was killed on the streets of Miami, Florida, a victim of gun violence. Determined to turn her devastating loss into a positive message, Brown has become a crusader against violence. She hosts a radio talk show—funded from her own pocket—during which listeners can share their experiences with urban violence.

3. "I want to thank my late mother-in-law...who just passed this last Saturday. She lived to be very proud of me. Despite unstable health, Elaine was with me in Africa when I opened this clinic. She continued to support me until the last minute of her life. She would have loved to be here today, but I'm sure she is watching over, just as she used to say of my family members who didn't make it," Peter Kithene said. "To those living in dire need in Africa and other parts of the world, I say the world is watching over. Hang in there, do not give up, love and support one another."

4. When twelve-year-old leukemia patient Pat Pedraja learned minorities like him make up less than one-third of the U.S. bone marrow registry and often die without donors, he began traveling the country to encourage minorities to register. As a result of his efforts, more than 5,000 donors signed up in three months.

5. When she was only four weeks old, Ana Dodson was adopted from Peru by an American couple living in the state of Colorado. After Ana's first visit to her native country in 2003, she started a nonprofit organization called Peruvian Hearts. To date, it has raised nearly $40,000 for orphans living the life that could have been hers.

These are just a few stories of dream catchers who have made a positive impact on their world because of dreams deposited within them, whether through triumph or tragedy, that have helped thousands of people. No matter how insignificant you may think you are, you can birth a big dream in your family, your community, or the world. I dare you to dream, and dream big. Like the stories above, your dream is usually closer to you than you think: you see it every day, but it may never come into focus until it becomes personal to you, you catch it, and you bring it into reality.

Part II

Believe

6

Knowing Yourself

"Ninety percent of the world's woe comes from people not knowing themselves, their abilities, their frailties, and even their virtues. Most of us go almost all the way through life as complete strangers to ourselves."

—Sydney J. Harris

"It takes courage to grow up and turn out to be who you really are."

—e. e. cummings

"We know what we are, but know not what we may be."

—William Shakespeare, *Hamlet*

Who are you? What makes you tick? What makes you happy? What fills you with joy? What makes you angry? What motivates you? This chapter is going to help you discover the real you. I want you to remove the façades, become transparent, and dig deep. I want you to face and deal with any pain in your life, choosing to move forward into your purpose.

Knowing who you are is essential for living the life you desire. I want to help you to believe in yourself. I want you to believe in your abilities and talents, but I also want you to assess yourself honestly. Identity and significance are fundamental to our well-being. We all want to know who we are, as well as to be certain that our lives have meaning. But if you are like me, you have asked the question: Who am I, really? The problem is that many of us do not truly know ourselves. And if we do know ourselves, we might also wonder about our identities and how others see us.

> *Man's search for meaning is the primary motivation in his life*
> *and not a "secondary rationalization" of instinctual drives.*
> *This meaning is unique and specific in that it must and can be*
> *fulfilled by him alone: only then does it achieve a significance*
> *which will satisfy his own will to meaning.*
>
> —Victor Frankl

છ૭

Identity: What is it? I often tell people, "If you don't define who you are, others will define you." It's true, isn't it? We need to have a strong sense of self; otherwise, we are likely to fall victim to the manipulation of others, prone to feel powerless (and subsequently to lack the ability to make choices for ourselves). Deep introspection—reflecting thoroughly on our thoughts, ideas, past experiences, and behaviors—helps us to discover and define who we really are.

Do you have a clear perspective on who you are? I want you to find a mirror, look at yourself, and introduce yourself to you. When introducing yourself to you, I want you to speak of yourself only in the third person; avoid using I, me, I am—instead use your name (often), she, and her. For example, the self-introduction of a woman named Susan might sound something like this:

> *I'd like to introduce my friend, Susan, to you. She is one of the*
> *most loving, caring, kind, and considerate women I know. She*
> *goes out of her way to help others. She can talk to anyone; she*
> *never meets anyone whom she considers a stranger for long.*
> *Susan is a young executive with three incredible children. She's*
> *been married to her husband for twelve years. She is interested*
> *in doing things that matter. When you talk to Susan, she is*

always upbeat, thankful, grateful, and magnificently blessed. She sees the wonder and the beauty that life has to offer.

Now, find a mirror and introduce yourself as you would a friend. I want you to introduce the best parts of who you are to yourself. If you have a webcam or video camera, record yourself so you can remember the wonder and the beauty of who you are.

After you complete the initial introduction of yourself, your next exercise is to introduce yourself again, this time highlighting all of the things that aren't so great about yourself. Nobody's perfect; as Paul wrote in Romans 3:23, *"All have sinned and fall short of the glory of God."* Like the first introduction, record this one, if you can. Here is an example, again using "Susan":

Susan is not always happy; she is unfulfilled, she overcommits to projects and activities, and most of the time, she just wants to jump off the merry-go-round of her life that is spinning out of control. Susan doesn't know how to say no. She is too helpful and polite to others who take advantage of her generosity; she neglects the important affairs that matter to her. Susan knows that she is a gifted singer, but she refuses to train and cultivate her gift because she has too much else to do. She likes to receive attention, recognition, and praise; without these self-esteem boosters, she feels unimportant and her ego takes a blow.

The purpose of this exercise is to help you get out of yourself, observe who you are from a more objective standpoint, and get to know yourself. I have used this exercise in many meetings and coaching sessions, and the immediate response is usually, "Oh, I don't know what to say." Women commonly react with embarrassed smiles or nervous laughter; others say that the exercise is difficult or makes them uncomfortable because they don't like talking about themselves. My question to such responses is always, "Are you sure the issue is that you don't like talking about yourself?" Truth be told, most people love to talk about themselves. If you fear this exercise, could the real issue be that you are afraid to reveal the "real" you?

German poet Johann Wolfgang von Goethe suggested that getting to know ourselves is a frightening proposition. "'Know thyself'? If I knew myself, I'd run away," he said. But have no fear—knowing yourself, in fact, gives you the opposite feeling. It gives you the courage to be who you were placed on the earth to be. Have courage! Another famous poet, e. e. cummings, put it this way: "It takes courage to grow up and turn out to be who you really are."

When we meet new people or get together with friends, we talk freely about ourselves without even realizing it. Think about when we meet other women and start up a conversation. Inevitably we want to relate, we want to be similar, and we want to find something in common; we are on a journey to discover commonality, things we share. We want to build rapport with others. We want to feel significant to others, to know that we register on their radar screens. People desire to be alike, although we want to be unique in the midst of our alikeness. No one wants to be completely different, because we don't want to feel or look like freaks. The beauty of humanity is that we are all alike and share a commonality when we consider such things as general characteristics, physiology, and neurology.

I recently watched a talk show where the guest was a transsexual individual who had changed his identity from male to female. The focus of the program was the effects on the family unit when a parent undergoes a gender change and is essentially lost; he or she disappears and is replaced by a clone of the opposite sex. My attention was captured by a seven-year-old boy, swinging on a monkey bar as he was being interviewed. The young boy was asked the question, "What don't you like about your new mommy?" He responded, "It's okay, because I know it's my dad, but he's my momma now, but I want my dad back so I can be like my friends. I don't want to be different; I want it to be the same. My friends make fun of me."

I was amazed at this child's response, because although we encourage uniqueness and teach our children to accept others who are different from them, even small children want to be the same. Being the same as others helps us to avoid ridicule, confrontation, and disharmony. If you have found it difficult to do the third-person exercise, then perhaps you have been hiding in the likeness of humanity rather than truly finding your unique self.

How can you be certain that the "you" you find is really you? I am certain that honesty is the best policy. You already read about the importance of aligning your values with your actions, gaining clarity, and defining a specific vision. I want to take you another step forward and get to know who you are. Let's be honest with ourselves. If you go deeper, if you think about what matters to you, then you will get to know yourself.

The problem with Susan in our identity example is that she really does not know who she is. Susan is a nice person, but she's generous and giving to a fault. It's like she gives even when she doesn't want to. But after so many years of sacrificing herself so completely, she does not know who she really is or what she really wants to do. She also fears that others will perceive her as different if she changes. So, she continues to give.

At church, Susan continues to sit on many auxiliaries. She serves as chairperson of the finance committee at church. At work, she readily accepts unwanted assignments, frequently volunteers to travel, and regularly keeps long hours. She does not know how to say no. On Saturdays, she's the super mom, shuttling her daughter's soccer team to and from games, helping with her children's school projects, doing the laundry, and planning the family weekend entertainment.

On Sundays, her pastor speaks often from the pulpit about her faithfulness. This attention pleases Susan. Susan is awarded honors at work for her hard work and efficiency. Soccer moms love her! Her children love the fact that she picks up after them, and her husband delights in sitting nightly in front of the TV while she prepares dinner and serves it to him in his comfortable recliner. Susan is loved by all. But does Susan love herself?

It is safe to assume that Susan could not possibly love herself as she should, and that she could not be happy with such expenditures: too many withdrawals and too few deposits. The love factor is huge in determining how you feel about yourself. Do you love yourself? What do you think Susan could do to improve her self-image?

Is Susan even aware that she may not be getting what she needs as she's giving so much of herself to so many causes and to so many people? As women, we often find ourselves in situations that compromise who we really are. As women, we often give to a fault. Does your giving ever interfere with how you feel about yourself? As we move forward, I need you to commit to digging deeply, searching your heart, and allowing your stream of consciousness to flow honestly without inhibition. Are you ready to enter the I-FACTOR Zone to see the real you?

One of my dear friends passed away during the time of writing this book. At his funeral, I had the honor of reading his obituary to the audience. This man was bright, creative, youthful, loving, charismatic, and strikingly handsome. I felt I knew him well, to some degree, although not completely intimately—he was rather private and spent most of his time with his family. The obituary was filled with words about him that were colorful, respectful, loving, and humorous; they told the story of his life, what mattered most to him, and how much he mattered to his family.

No words in my friend's obituary spoke of his weaknesses, his disappointments, or his regrets. There were no comments about his attitudes or beliefs. These things didn't matter anymore; they had no relevance, at least not on this day of his memorial. (His family may have their own intimate memories, but they were not publicly announced or displayed.) My friend was a young man, just shy of forty-two when he died—a part of my own generation.

Now, when a friend of yours dies unexpectedly, at or near your age, you feel an immediate impact. But in that moment of grief, I found myself thinking about writing my own eulogy rather than leaving it up to my family or friends to write. It would be an easier task for me to do now than it would be to leave it to others to write during the difficult and emotionally draining time they will experience just after I am gone.

Imagine for a moment that you find yourself on the receiving end of a phone call from a friend or family member about someone's death. It's funny how you can sense the sound of bad news even when you are miles away from a person. You've just received news of a death, and you are grief-stricken; you begin to work yourself through the stages of grief. When called upon to talk about your friend's life, you begin to think about your own life. You say to yourself that the condition of your friend could be your own condition today, tomorrow, or next year.

It was during my friend's "home-going service," as funerals are commonly called in black charismatic circles—amidst the exuberance of rejoicing over our friend's life and believing that he had gone home to be with the Lord—that we gained a real sense of joy and peace. The apostle Paul described dying in faith as being *"far better"* than remaining in this earthly life, for in dying, believers go to be with the Lord in heaven. (See Philippians 1:21–26.) But that day, we remained on earth at my friend's home-going service, rejoicing and praising God for the opportunity to have shared our loved one's life.

If you have ever experienced a home-going service at a black charismatic church, you know that there is nothing else like it. At these services, you forget that you are at a funeral service. They seem more like regular Sunday morning services, and you find yourself rejoicing rather than grieving, wondering what in the world is wrong with anyone who expresses grief. But be forewarned: rejoicing is contagious, even during times of grief, because God takes the sadness we feel about unfortunate situations and reverses it; He turns times of mourning into times of rejoicing. The psalmist, King David, wrote in Psalm 30:11–12,

You have turned for me my mourning into dancing; You have put off my sackcloth and clothed me with gladness, to the end that my glory may sing praise to You and not be silent. O LORD my God, I will give thanks to You forever.

Who are you? You are your own answer. No one knows you like you know yourself. Can you write well of yourself? The eulogy, which is usually delivered by a preacher, rabbi, or priest, is defined as a speech or writing in praise of a person or thing, especially a set oration in honor of a deceased person. I have attended funeral services at which the person delivering the eulogy had no familiarity with the deceased person; it was evident when you listened to the words that were spoken—bland platitudes that said nothing about the deceased individual's character, identity, or personality. An obituary is a notice of a person's death, usually printed in a newspaper, and it often includes a biographical sketch of the person's life, as well as a list of the names of surviving relatives. Your life will be reduced to a mere sketch in the minds of all those who come to honor you—three lines of black and white in your local newspaper, perhaps a few more lines if you are lucky. This is where we start.

Your assignment is to write your own eulogy. What will it say? How will you paint pictures of your life experiences for others to see? Regardless of your age, I want you to fast-forward many years to see yourself as an active senior, enjoying life and sharing your life story with family and friends. What will you say about yourself? Will your eulogy speak of the fine clothes, cars, and jewelry that you owned and the great travels you may have experienced? Will it speak of the pain, suffering, debt, heartbreaks, or emotional roller-coaster rides you took? Will your eulogy describe your perspective on life, the great ideas you dreamed and achieved? Will you remind others in death how unfair your life was, how you never got a break, and how nothing worked out for you? What will you say about yourself? Will you leave a legacy for your children and grandchildren?

Who Are You, Really?

"The eye sees only what the mind is prepared to comprehend."

—Henri Bergson

"People fail to see that their perception of the world is also a confession of character."

—Ralph Waldo Emerson

Perception is not everything! Perception is not truth, and it is not fact; rather, perception is a particular view of something or someone that often requires confirmation. Let me state my case. On a brisk yet sunny Saturday morning, my friend (and writing coach), Judith, and I took a break from writing and went to visit my mother-in-law. We were driving down the road and stopped at a red light in Hurst, Texas. As we waited for the traffic light to change, we looked out the window and saw a CarMax Buying Center. I was intrigued by the presence of the CarMax dealer's location. I had previously lived in a neighborhood not far from the dealer, and I was interested to see how the site had transformed since I'd moved.

The site had once been a 7-Eleven convenience store. This one was an individual store, located on a busy intersection with limited parking. Since there are more than thirty thousand 7-Eleven stores in the United States, it is likely that you have visited one at some point in your life. I grew up buying after-school snacks of Cheetos and ICEE drinks at my local 7-Eleven.

The 7-Eleven that once occupied the same site as this CarMax had been closed for at least three years when I moved into the neighborhood. I took note of it primarily because my husband and I buy and sell commercial real estate. I knew that this property was about 2,500 square feet. (This detail is important, for I want you to think about the many acres of land occupied by any major car dealership, such as Toyota, Ford, or Mercedes, in order to maintain an inventory of several hundred cars.) The location in Hurst had very few parking spaces, and it was clearly not an obvious location to sell cars. Moreover, the parking lot displayed no parked cars with sale stickers, a detail that struck me as strange. This is when my imagination took flight. Of course, I drafted Judith into my conversation and assumptions, as well.

We began speculating about what type of business CarMax was doing. From the sign alone, I began to envision an enterprise that may or may not have had any basis in the reality of the CarMax business. Perhaps they were financing vehicles over the Internet and creating retail outlets to make it easier and more comfortable to secure the business due to the fierce competition in car financing. "If so, what a great idea!" I said. "Maybe that's exactly the kind of business that transpires there." Since we were talking about cars, I told Judith about my experiences of shopping for cars—by searching online and filling out the applications for several companies, I was able to find a local car dealership that would sell me a car at a low interest rate. Maybe this CarMax Buying Center could have assisted me with my purchases.

My imagination was as vivid as ever. Can you see how I was building my perception based on information that had nothing to do with the CarMax Buying Center? Judith was quiet initially, listening to my business scenario, and then she became animated, adding details gleaned by her own perception and processed by her mind. "I don't know why they would do something like that," she said. "People could stay home and look on the Internet themselves, as you did. Why come to this center to buy a car online? Plus, what are they going to do about test drives? How silly would it be to have a center that requires overhead when people could do this kind of search at home?"

Judith had become as interested as I, being fully engaged by my enthusiasm and perceptions of a business that I had conceived purely in my head. I thought briefly about her questions before responding, "I don't know. I guess they're going to send the information about the car over to the retail location and ship the car of your desire to the CarMax location and off you go, having chosen the car and secured the financing in one location." In my mind, I saw a handsome, suave car salesman (thinking of a possible match for Judith, who's single) speeding up to the lot in that beautiful, fiery red convertible roadster Judith just had to have.

It was as if we were picturing the same image. Just as the image had run its course in my mind, complete with an attractive car salesman racing onto the small lot, Judith started laughing out loud! She continued to laugh hysterically while I continued building my business model aloud, making her laugh even more. I was creating a business model out of thin air, a model that I applied to a business on Hurst Road that probably had nothing to do with the actual business model in place. After Judith calmed down, she said, "Can you believe how we came up with every possible idea about this company and we don't have a clue what kind of business is done there?" I joined in her riotous laughter, responding, "Now you know, girl, we're going to have to go in there and ask the people where the cars are!" Where do you think the cars were?

While writing about the importance of developing a right estimation of yourself, I thought about our recent experience and how perceptions are made based on limited knowledge. In my story, I had minimal tidbits of information with questionable validity in my subconscious mind, but in that moment, those tidbits were valid and true to me. Doing a little research on the CarMax Buying Center, however, revealed that my imaginary business model had nothing to do with the true nature of the business.

I had passed the location before and had a logical, analytical conversation with myself before I even passed by the business with Judith and shared my ideas with her. When we were sitting at the stoplight on the corner, Judith saw the new site for the first time. She had never been to this particular area before. But with my assumptions and animations, she was completely drawn in! How long do you think it took that light to change before I came up with my complete business model? Probably not more than ninety seconds.

Perception creates an internal image of external reality in your mind. It consists of pictures painted with a mental brush on the canvas of your mind, and it can also serve as a mirror that reflects who you are. Earlier, I said that perception is not every-thing; being subjective, it is not truth, and it often requires con-firmation. Judith and I had our thinking hats on, and we wanted answers, because the assumptions we made based on our percep-tions demanded confirmation.

I am sure that, by now, you would like some confirmation about what that CarMax Buying Center was all about. The CarMax Buying Center in Hurst was one of the company's first retail sites that allowed customers to sell their vehicles at fair prices. The buying center is in the business of buying cars, not selling them—I was completely off in my thinking. In fact, neither Judith nor I had this perception! Read the company's description, which is listed on their Web site, www.carmax.com:

CarMax Buying Center

The hassle-free way to sell your car. Just need to sell your car? At the CarMax Car Buying Center we don't sell cars, we buy them! Through our unique car-buying process, our appraisal experts have appraised more than 5 million cars nationwide, so you get a fair, free written offer for your car, good for 7 days, and you won't have to deal with the hassles of selling your car yourself.

What are the perceptions others create about you? Do they align with the reality of who you are? Just as Judith and I created our own incorrect business model of the CarMax Buying Center, other people often create incorrect perceptions of who you are based on the images and signals you present to the world. Often, others are as completely wrong as we were about CarMax.

It is important to assess and reflect on how other people perceive you. What images are you projecting? What signals are you sending out? Your perception of yourself is reflected in the world; it becomes how other people see you. I have heard the argument that you can't control someone's perceptions of you, and while I believe that this statement is true, I also believe that you *can* contribute to the reflection of what you create for others to see.

People see only a reflection of you when they make up their minds about who you are. And the size of their screen determines how much of their view of you they retain as truth. How do you perceive yourself? Is it true or factual? How do you dig down to the truth about who you are? Is it based on who you believe yourself to be or what you hear other people saying about you? I would argue that it is based on both. The best way to show the world who you are is a twofold process. First, you must make sure that you are honest with yourself by reflecting the values, principles, and beliefs that are important to you. Then, you must do the work required to become the best you can be—the best you want others to see.

Hans Margolius gave us a good place to begin when he wrote, "Only in quiet waters things mirror themselves undistorted. Only in a quiet mind is adequate perception of the world." Sit quietly and reflect on who you are, as well as on the perceptions other people have of you. In calm solitude, think about who you are and how you best wish to be perceived in the world. The "undistorted" vision of who you are will then be the best reflection, the one that others in the world will see. When this occurs, perceptions will become reality!

Being True to You

"Pursue truth and people will be true to you."

—Arthur Twining Hadley

౪౧

Knowing who you are is only one part of the puzzle. Pursuing the truth of who you are will allow others to see the true you. It is important to be true to who you are so that others will see you with a perception based on truth.

We have already discussed perception and the importance of creating an accurate reflection of who you are for others to see. I will now elaborate on what constitutes or contributes to being true to who you are. In order to do this, I will demonstrate my own daily journey of exercising and executing my values as I create the reflection of who I am to the world.

Being true to who you are means living your life day to day with the evidence of your values and beliefs displayed in your words, actions, and reactions. In our discussion about values, we identified the importance of defining values and aligning our actions with them. I talked about three values that describe the foundation of who I am.

Again, my three primary values are:

1. To represent God in the best possible way as an advocate for the gospel of Jesus Christ.

2. To be the best wife that I can to my husband, Richmond McCoy.

3. To contribute to the excellence of other people.

Identifying personal values creates a framework and a foundation for your behavior and serves as an essential step to being true to you. When you begin your day, what are your feelings about yourself? Are you ready to meet the day with enthusiasm, optimism, and vigor? When I wake up every morning, I am usually expecting something productive to occur that day. But my expectations do not exist within a vacuum. I expect the day to go well based on what I did the day before and during the weeks before. Now, there are many surprises in each day, but these are minimized and managed by prior preparation. I control my daily environment through *preparation*.

How I feel about myself is based largely on my daily actions, and vice versa—my actions are influenced by how I feel about myself, as well. Proverbs 23:6–7 captures this fact of human nature: *"Do not eat the bread of a miser, nor desire his delicacies;* **for as he thinks in his heart, so is he**" (emphasis added).

In order for me to be effective and productive, I must have a detailed road map to direct me. I am a strategic planner, constantly sorting out what is important and unimportant among my ideas and tasks. To create the necessary road map, I think deeply about the things that are important and the people who are dear to me, and I determine the direction I will take based on the objectives that I outline for my short- and long-term goals.

Most people who know me would probably say, "Anna is one of the most productive people I know; she knows how to execute plans, and she gets things done." They would also say, "She does a lot of things, too—I don't know how she gets it all done." Other people usually perceive me as being someone who is versatile, capable, productive, and busy, and my secret is that I always focus intently on where I am going.

Over the years, I have developed an incredible ability to live in the moment. And a part of living in the moment is segmenting my life so that I can be extremely effective in each separate moment. Because being an excellent person is just as important to me as having excellent actions and behavior, it is important that I adhere to my value system. Similar to the mission statement and values of Wachovia, I created my own mission and key operating statements for my life more than fifteen years ago. I am enamored of the ideas of business; I respect systems, methods, and order; thus, my life affects my business just as my business affects my daily life. I view life as a business, and I live the business of life daily. Even though certain challenges are exclusive to business or to life, there is a core value system that is applicable to both realms.

My Mission
I am an advocate for the righteousness of a living God, proclaiming the gospel to all I meet, that they may know about their God-given purposes and work to accomplish them.

Key Operating Values
Dependability: I can be counted on.

Innovation: I will make a difference.

Quality: I will deliver only the best.

Integrity: I will deliver what I promise.

Accountability: I will stand behind my actions.

Teamwork: I am committed to the success of others.

Remember, if you don't define yourself, other people will do it for you. Now that I have helped you to understand my core makeup, let me walk you through an average day in the life of Anna McCoy.

A Day in the Life of Anna McCoy

5 AM–9 AM: I arise with enthusiasm to greet the day and to meet whatever it has in store. I write, read devotional meditations, pray, write in my dream journal (this is exclusively for dreams I have while sleeping). I show love to my husband and affection to our dogs, and I prepare breakfast (usually meat, eggs, toast, and coffee). I exercise, listen to worship and inspirational music, catch the morning news on television, take a walk with my husband and our dogs, center my thoughts, and make myself available to my husband if he has any task he would like me to do.

10 AM–11 AM: I go to work in my home office, read and respond to e-mails, and start moving through my action calendar. I meet with my team members, delegate tasks to others and to myself, and make things happen.

11 AM–2 PM: I schedule my coaching calls and other appointments.

2 PM–4 PM: Lunch; other assorted activities.

4 PM–7 PM: I work on bringing any outstanding projects to completion, reviewing the day's accomplishments, and planning tomorrow's projects and future goals.

7 PM–10 PM: I prepare a substantial dinner if my husband is home. If he is not home, I eat something light: fruit, yogurt—or my favorite, Chipotle (I really could eat it every day). I walk the dogs when the weather is warm enough. Some evenings I spend teaching, hosting meetings, or attending other functions.

That schedule describes my usual daily routine; the only times I stray from it are when I am out of the office, in meetings, speaking, or traveling. And, there is nothing in my schedule that is a burden for me—I do what I love to do, every day of my life. I make certain that my days are filled with tasks that matter to me and align with my mission and values. I may appear to be doing a lot of things, but everything I do is directed toward my bigger picture. To make plans, I use two primary tools. One is my event calendar, which is usually filled with meetings, activities, and things I have to do. Then, I fill in the blanks on my action calendar. I do this by scheduling blocks of time within which I can reach my goals by completing executable steps.

Keeping a date book, whether electronic or paperback, is important—I have used both types. Since I am a visual person who needs to see a more complete picture of what I am doing, I have found personal digital assistant devices to be of little assistance to me. It seems like whenever I enter items or tasks into the Personal Digital Assistant (PDA), they mysteriously disappear into oblivion. I know that the calendar items are there somewhere, but I can't readily see them, and I often ignore the pop-up reminders. Amazingly, I am still considered the "techie" in my group of friends! But I am also smart enough to know which system works best for me. Find the best system that works for you, and don't be afraid to use new technology. It can seem complicated and inscrutable, but if you read the user's manuals and learn to master the basics, certain devices can be extremely useful in helping you to keep your life organized.

I recently stopped using my Outlook and ceased syncing my PDA in favor of returning to a system I used effectively more than fifteen years ago: the Franklin Planner. Because I am so committed to organizing and doing things that matter to me, my assistant and I enrolled together in the Franklin Covey *Focus* class. It was after this meeting that I realized I had defined my life's values but was not effectively aligning those values with my actions—I had a hit-or-miss record of meeting my targets. By readjusting my attitudes about my work ethic, scheduling methods, and family time, I was able to become more effective in every area of my life. Now, I identify the roles I have to play—whether wife, CEO, Web administrator, coach, or momma (to my dogs)—and this enables me to balance my time commitment to each role and the emotional and mental transitions between them.

One thing I have discovered is that being true to you is not always easy when you have to play different roles or shift hats quickly. *The 7 Habits of Highly Effective People* by Stephen Covey, *The Seven Spiritual Laws of Success* by Deepak Chopra, and *Your Best Life Now: 7 Steps to Living at Your Full Potential* by Joel Osteen are three books that encourage success through multistep processes. We read the books and follow a few of the steps, but many of us never complete more than 20 percent of any recommended seven-step process. Rather than trying to present a surefire way to be true to yourself, I have showed you how I align my actions with my values. I hope you can identify with my example and learn from it.

Each of us is usually successful in our mind's eye. What we glean from the experiences and writings of others is a hope to be better, or more like the image of success we and others have envisioned. Being true to yourself is not achieved by making a million dollars or setting lofty goals; rather, it is achieved by taking responsibility for what you love, how you want to be treated, and what you do for others. These are your choices, and you should never be ashamed of what matters most to you, even if you feel that it does not measure up to someone else's standards or point of view. In contrast, I want you to commit to identifying and pursuing what matters to you! Being true to you means living your life based on your discovery of what really matters to you and taking the actions needed to get you where you need to be in life. Ultimately, it's all about your actions—actions that reflect your values and, fundamentally, *you*.

This discussion about discovering and acting on what's important to you reminds me of a phone call I received from a woman named Betty who wanted assistance in managing her finances. Not long into the conversation, I began to realize that Betty was dealing with more than just her issues with fiscal management. As she talked, I was sensitive to the sound of her voice—I detected desperation, confusion, and embarrassment. I listened to her explain her situation, and I could tell that she was disappointed with the choices she had made in her life. She was in her mid-fifties, and the words she used were those of someone who had consistently missed marks and felt ashamed of her choices. In the midst of words laden with disappointment, I sensed that she wanted her life to mean something. I was not in a hurry on this particular day—I was just working through my daily schedule—nor was I under the pressure of any deadlines, so I listened.

It is unusual for me to answer the phone, especially if the incoming call is unexpected or from someone unknown. I prefer to schedule a time for each phone call so that I can devote my entire self to that moment and can focus on assisting a coaching client. My assistant must have been on a break when I answered Betty's call. Betty seemed surprised that I had personally answered the phone, but as she began to talk to me, I knew that we were meant to speak to one another. While my schedule is one that I adhere to routinely, I leave room for unexpected events. John Lennon wisely said, "Life is what happens when we are making other plans." Plan, but always allow moments for the unexpected.

Betty's call came on August 14, 2007. I remember the date because I wrote it down after our phone call so I'd remember in the event that Betty and I ever met in person. As our conversation continued, we talked about some of her concerns, for which I suggested resources that could provide answers for her. When Betty said that she wanted to do something meaningful with her life, her words struck a chord with me because they resonated with my own value system, specifically the value of committing to contribute to the excellence of other people. Being apathetic or impatient would have been completely the opposite of staying true to me. Let me share our conversation:

> **Me**: "Betty, you said that you wanted to do something meaningful in life. So, what do you value? What is important to you?"
>
> *I heard her take a deep breath and slowly exhale.*
>
> **Betty**: "I don't know."
>
> **Me**: "Can I ask you a question? I want you to listen and

think deeply about what I am asking you. Right now, you are blinded by the problems in your life, and telling me that you don't know is kind of like saying, 'I don't want to think about it.' So, here's your question: If you had only six months to live, you had all the money you needed, and your health wasn't a factor, tell me six things that you would want to do before your time expired. Betty, on the last day of the sixth month, when the clock strikes midnight, life will be over—no negotiations, no compromising, and no hoping for one more minute. You would be done and would have made your mark for a meaningful life. Now, think about it. I am only going to give you sixty seconds to respond and no more. Are you ready?"

Betty: *(laughing out loud)* "Okay, but you are not giving me much time."

Me: "Okay, you've had plenty of time, so, on your mark, get set, go!"

Betty: "One—grow closer to God; two—grow closer to family; three—organize my finances; four—reconcile with people; five—travel to visit friends I keep promising I will visit but never do; six—write a book."

Me: "Awesome! You did great! Betty, look at what you said matters to you if time was limited. Well, time *is* limited. It is your life, and every day you have to live it doing the things that matter most. Here are some other questions you have to answer: How will you get closer to God? What are you going to do differently to align your actions with what you said is important to you? What will you do about visiting friends you know you should visit but haven't? What about your finances?"

Betty: "I am going to be more serious about my prayer time with God and read the Bible more. I want to be more intimate with Him. You know, I have a friend who doesn't really live that far from me, and I keep promising her I will visit. This week, I am going to call her and set a date and time that I will go to visit. I will do this; I can do this! My finances? I have to think about that one. The book I know I should write...I just have to do it. I am going to make a list of all the people that I think I need to reconcile with and call them or write them a letter. I will also reach out to my family and let them know I love them and plan to do more with them."

Me: "Betty, how do you feel? What do you think about what you can do to make your life more meaningful?"

Betty: "I can see much better now. I have never been asked that question, and I never really made a list of things I thought were most important to me. I can't believe that I did it in only sixty seconds, but these things are important to me, and I just didn't know that they were inside of me."

Me: "Betty, your life matters, you matter, and I am so happy I took this call today. I don't know where my assistant is, but I am so glad I had an opportunity to meet someone as special as you. Promise me that you will call that friend who doesn't live so far and visit—you can do this, Betty. You are a winner! You are loved and appreciated, and God bless you! Have a great day, and you can do it. I am so proud of you!"

Betty: "Thank you so much. You have really blessed me today. Thanks again. Bye-bye."

The example I am illustrating through the conversation is that my response to that unplanned call was easy for me because I saw it as an opportunity to be and to do what I love. I was able to align my actions with my value of helping others achieve their God-given destinies. Betty and I found ourselves in a life moment together—I was putting my core values into action, and she was benefiting from them. Betty received a treasure she was not seeking—remember, the purpose of her call was simply to receive financial advice—because I had a treasure chest of gifts waiting to share with her! On days like this, I think to myself, *Thank you, Momma and Daddy; I am so happy I was born!* I feel great about having the opportunity to deposit assistance and gifts in the life of another person. When I go to sleep at night, I'm simply obeying my body's pleas to lie down and rest. I eagerly awake the next day, expecting serendipitous discoveries to significantly invade my well-planned thoughts, moments, and days so that I can live up to the values that I have embraced.

Are Your Actions Aligned with Your Values?

Let me ask you to do an exercise similar to the one that Betty did. Take sixty seconds to evaluate whether your actions are aligned with your values. Are you doing the things that matter most in your life? You may not have the opportunity to check off each value application every day, but you need to know what you stand for. Take out a sheet of paper or write your responses in this book—and don't forget to time yourself:

1. _____

2. _____

3. _____

4. _____

5. _____

6. _____

After you have identified your six most meaningful things, I want you to determine how you are going to spend some of your life being, doing, and loving what matters to you. Life is short, so live the one you construct—you deserve to live your life to the fullest. In Christ, we are promised abundance and rich blessings, for Jesus proclaimed in John 10:10, *"I have come that they may have life, and that they may have it more abundantly."* Ralph Waldo Emerson said, "Make the most of yourself, for that is all there is of you." So, start living your best life now!

7

What Do Others Say about Me?

"The LORD has called Me from the womb; from the matrix of My mother He has made mention of My name. He has made My mouth like a sharp sword; in the shadow of His hand He has hidden Me, and made Me a polished shaft; in His quiver He has hidden Me."

—Isaiah 49:1–2

"The unexamined life is not worth living."

—Socrates

I am intrigued by the role of words as communication vehicles. It seems that we have so many words to choose from, but even so, we rarely manage to express ourselves adequately. This chapter will help you examine how the words of others can affect you. What we hear influences what we believe, feel, and think. We have probably all recited the popular idiom, "Sticks and stones may break my bones, but words can never hurt me." I believe that this idiom was ill-conceived, and that its author has deeply misled us in the area of human relations.

We as humans are words housed in flesh. From the moment we develop the sense of hearing in our mothers' wombs, words are on a journey to influence us. A company in Southlake, Texas, called Window in the Womb uses an advanced scanner that detects the yawns, stretches, and even smiles of developing babies and depicts them in 3D/4D ultrasound images for their mothers to see. If an unborn baby responds within the womb in ways similar to human responses outside of the womb, I can only imagine the possibilities that exist inside the womb. An article by Sid Kirchheimer entitled "Mom's Voice Is Distinguished in Womb," published in 2003 on WebMD.com, reports on this newfound phenomenon. Kirchheimer writes, "While it's well established that a newborn recognizes its mother's voice and will change its behavior to hear it, new research suggests that preference actually may begin before birth."

He continues, "Researchers say full-term fetuses can not only recognize their mothers' voices, but also distinguish them from those of other women—and react when hearing them." The supporting research evaluated sixty fetuses in China. Lead researcher Barbara Kisilevsky, Ph.D., of Queens University in Ontario, Canada, conducted the study with Chinese researchers. According to Kisilevsky,

> [The fetuses] get excited when they hear their mother's voice; it is something that they recognize and are aroused by....What this study shows is that the babies had to recognize and distinguish between the two voices in order to respond differently....The experience before birth is influencing language development; perhaps babies are being pre-conditioned to attend to the speech and language cues from their mothers....And it may be setting the baby up to developing social relationships with its mother, which is important for an organism that can't take care of itself. And that facilitates attachment.

From the womb, we continue through life trying to distinguish the right voices and deciding which ones we will believe for our own survival. In the corporate environment, personality tests are often administered to us in hopes of revealing words that give others insight about us, as well as enable them to judge our abilities and aptitude. When I worked for Dictaphone in the early

1990s, it was customary for sales organizations to give potential applicants personality tests to measure their ability to cope with the demands of a sales environment. The scoring on the personality test ranged from 1 to 5, with 5 being the highest. It was rare to find a 4, much less a 5! Most individuals had borderline scores and ultimately didn't make the grade. Although the tests were helpful, they were not conclusive. When we hired a salesperson and she scored a 5, we celebrated!

We always had one applicant who defied the odds and did exceptionally well on this test, usually because she was motivated by factors different from those typical of a personality that will do well in sales. These individuals would do what they were told; they followed the directions, methods, and systems provided for them without being discouraged by the rejections and refusals commonly encountered in the sales business. Believe me, there were frequent rejections! As a sales manager, I had many responsibilities, one of which was to ride along and accompany new hires in order to teach them the ropes. Like many salespeople, I, too, loathed the task of making cold calls. At its core, sales is a numbers business—no matter what you do, you can't avoid the numbers game. You can try to be slick; you can try to improve and make up your numbers; but inevitably, your methods will be exposed, and you will have to produce the numbers, through cold calls or other means. Otherwise, you may find yourself in the unemployment line. For most people, cold calling is one of the most miserable experiences of any profession. Why? Because it hinges on words! In sales, words can help you or destroy you.

Picture this scenario, which actually happened during a training session. One of my trainees entered the office of a doctor or attorney—our primary clients at the time—with me following closely behind. Immediately, a shout came from the woman sitting behind the reception desk: "No, you can't come in here! Didn't you see the sign on the door? No soliciting!" (Salespeople must have a certain look about them that is easily detected by receptionists' radars.) SLAM! Her words were like a solid oak door slammed in our faces. We shuddered on the inside, offered brave smiles, and turned to leave. Even though I was the trainer, I still reacted in the same way as the new hire, though to a less detectable degree; by now, I was a pro at weathering rejection and quickly discarding any feelings of hurt or shame. (This took years of experience, and I never quite mastered it, as my experience with the new hire showed.)

Walking away from the reception desk, I knew my trainee had just taken a big blow. The receptionist's words had hit her like a ton of bricks—she was visibly shaken. On our way out the door, I offered some reassurance: "For every 'no', there's one 'yes' waiting for you." Some hope, huh? A hope that I'm sure was lost on my new hire. We went to the next office and took the next blow. After each blow, dutiful manager that I was, I encouraged the trainee, assuring her that a "yes" would eventually come—but by the ninth consecutive rejection, she was beginning to feel like Dustin Hoffman playing Willy Loman in the movie *Death of a Salesman*, based on the sobering play by Arthur Miller. My response that the next cold call might be "the one" was based on the training and wisdom of the likes of Dale Carnegie and Zig Ziglar: "Keep knocking because one out of ten will need what you have and if you don't knock they don't know you exist."

Although I had experienced some success as a sales manager, many of our new hires could never pass the test of doing cold calls on the front lines. Taking the blows was simply too much; many would back down and give up at the slightest sign of resistance. They quit in order to escape rejection; they couldn't take the negative words that were spewed on them day after day. They would start out strong, doing the required number of cold calls as they visited current clients, but with every passing week, they did fewer and fewer calls, their efforts diminishing until they ceased completely. The same is true in interpersonal relationships—the effect of negative words is not exclusive to the business realm. What other people say about us as we present ourselves every day influences how we feel about ourselves. Some people hear so many hurtful words from others that they retreat from the world, becoming private, withdrawn, and reclusive. What are others saying about you? Have harmful, negative words taken root in your life?

The illustration above enables you to see how words can help you to succeed or fail. In this case, many new hires failed quickly due to the power that negative words had on them. Although the words were not personal, the effect was as if they had been. Most of the salespeople that I trained simply could not handle hearing a constant stream of words of rejection. Have you allowed the words of others, spoken to you or about you, to hinder your success, growth, and sense of self?

You are composed of body, soul, and spirit, but it is primarily words that fuel your thoughts, beliefs, and feelings about yourself. Words that are untamed, unbridled, and unfiltered by your mind can take root in your soul and convince you that you *are* the words spoken to you. In this case, the words become prophetic; they are self-fulfilling.

When I was a young girl, positive words of encouragement were deposited into me. I am convinced that one word in particular actually charted the course of my life. I grew up in Houston, Texas, and my fifth-grade teacher was Mrs. Verna Jones. I loved school and I loved all my teachers, but Mrs. Jones was especially dear to me. I always appreciated the knowledge and commitment of teachers. They were role models who really cared about me. I can recall in detail each of my elementary school teachers. I remember specific moments of growth, nurturing, chastisement, and correction, and, in spite of those times, I loved my teachers with my whole heart. This story is about how a *word* spoken can be so powerful that it etches an indelible mark in the core of your being.

Mrs. Jones had a way of helping her students embrace words. At the start of each school year, she asked her students to bring in a 5" × 7" portrait of themselves from a previous year. She then created a board, bordered in typical colorful classroom paper and covered with bright gold stars. We knew it was a special board. On the board were words that were unfamiliar to many of us. Mrs. Jones didn't teach the words first; rather, she identified the student whose character she thought best exemplified each word, and that student came to represent the word we learned.

Mrs. Jones's method of reward was to post each of our pictures on the board for one month's time with the demonstrated word displayed in quotation marks above the picture. Some of the photo captions included "most exuberant," "most optimistic," "most studious," and "most timorous."

After a few months, those of us who had not yet been picked wondered whether our picture and corresponding word would be next. *Will my picture represent the word chosen for this month?* each of us would ask ourselves. We tried to be overly kind and considerate, focused, careful, or happy—all words we were familiar with and understood how to demonstrate in our actions. Every day, I grew more interested in that board, hoping that I was demonstrating the next new word that Mrs. Jones would choose so that I would be picked and my picture would be displayed. I guess this was an early indication that I wanted to see my name in lights.

One day when Mrs. Jones changed the board, she stood at the front of the class and took down the previous word, "considerate," and then began to construct the new word, adding letters one by one to the board to spell V-E-R-S-A-T-I-L-E. Next, she placed a picture below the word *versatile*...and the picture was of *me!* I could hardly believe my eyes. By this time, several months had passed since the first day of school, and the 5" × 7" picture I had submitted was my school photo from third grade. I was wearing a red dress with a rainbow band on the sleeve. I didn't like that picture at all, for it was on that day that my Nannie Yvonne combed my hair for picture day. She didn't have much skill with hair styling—she had no children of her own to practice on—and it showed. I had a crooked part down the center of my head, my two ponytails were completely askew—one went north, the other went south—and I was grinning from ear to ear. Yet, even though I didn't like the picture, the photo on that board was still me, and that made me happy.

After seeing that *versatile* was the word chosen to describe me, I thumbed feverishly through the dictionary to find its definition. I had no idea what that big word meant, but Mrs. Jones thought that it described me, and I had to know who she thought I was. The definition of *versatile* that I held on to as a fifth grader was "well-rounded, able to do a lot of things easily, and flexible." Every day that my picture was on that board, and every day thereafter, I tried to demonstrate the fullness of that word—it has truly become the core of who I am today. I have to imagine, however, that being the wise person that she was, Mrs. Jones probably chose words that didn't necessarily describe us at that moment but would come to describe us in the future if we worked hard to develop the qualities they conveyed.

Since my initial introduction to the term, I have truly worked on becoming more versatile. Today, as a result, I am more flexible when faced with the opinions and thoughts of others; compromise comes easily to me. It was as if Mrs. Jones sought to build our strengths through word definitions, anticipating the paths that we would take in our lives. Versatility is one of the most important attributes I need in order to coach my growing number of clients. Mrs. Jones, if you're reading this book, many thanks to you. The words that you deposited in me framed the person I eventually became.

Words are like fuel to the human soul, and it's almost overwhelming to think about all of the words you have received from other people, friends and foes alike. Think about pivotal moments in your life when you received words that were eventually woven into the fabric of your soul. You were repeatedly faced with the decision to either keep the words you received, or to sew new words in order to create an entirely new garment of your identity.

Beliefs are like root systems. They are under the surface, deep within our souls, feeding and fueling our behavior and actions. Words are the nutrients that feed our personal root systems. Some of our roots grow deep, while others may lie just below the surface, where they're vulnerable to damage from the sun's scorching rays. When others speak words about us, they either pour life-giving water on our souls or dump toxic waste that causes us to wither. The words of others help us grow or destroy us. Water is necessary, but too much water out of season can be devastating.

I am not much of a gardener. In my last home, my lack of skills was blatantly exposed. We were experiencing a drought in Texas; water restrictions were in effect, and the ground looked like a dried riverbed covered with an endless maze of cracks. Any true gardener would know that the ground was thirsty for water. I had planted some beautiful crape myrtles alongside our backyard pool. They had been flourishing and looked gorgeous, but after a while, I noticed that the leaves had started to turn slightly. However, I didn't adjust the automatic watering system to increase the water supply to the crape myrtles.

When I returned home from a two-week trip, I noticed that two of the crape myrtles were completely brown. I thought for sure that they must have had a disease; they wouldn't just die like that. Wanting to fully inspect the bushes, I broke one of the limbs from the tree; it was so brittle that it immediately snapped in two. I knew that I had a problem on my hands. The tree was dead not only on the outside, but on the inside, too—the branches' marrow had turned into powder. The only remedy for this tree was removal; destroying it was not an option, for it was already dead. If only I had fed it properly and changed its water supply, it might have survived.

Our belief systems are similar. They require the right words in order to make us grow so that we will demonstrate appropriate actions. I want us to take a look at a few of the influences we have in our lives and how they may affect our belief systems. We will look at our workplaces, families, friends, and society in order to assess how they view us and what they say about us. This part of the book will demand your cooperation and willingness to review your world and how you think others see you. Have you heard about 360-degree feedback, a 360-degree life, or a 360-degree financial plan? The idea is to take a 360-degree look at our lives, relationships, and finances to decipher what is important, planned, and most improved.

Corporations use 360-degree feedback to understand employees, analyze systems, and implement change. The feedback we are striving for is for you to do a 360-degree evaluation of yourself based on what others say about you. It is often difficult to know what other people really think of you, especially if you work with difficult people. The only way that you can come close to understanding how others view you is by standing in their shoes, so to speak. To do this, you will need to elevate the position of your thoughts. It's the mental equivalent of standing on a chair—you acquire a sort of aerial view to observe your workplace so that you can think about the people with whom you work and interact on a regular basis. It is important that you identify individuals who have influence or sway in your life, who may be bridge builders and connectors for you to get where you want to go. Although these individuals are important, surprisingly, they are often the ones who sit quietly and observe rather than get involved—people such as an administrative assistant, receptionist, or any number of other colleagues.

I have heard executives say that they don't understand why they need frontline employees, such as receptionists, to participate in surveys about their leadership styles and abilities. The attitude is that frontline employees certainly can't know anything about them. Frankly, frontline individuals can usually speak volumes about attitudes, disrespect, enthusiasm, anger, product problems, customer needs, and many other details that even the most distinguished degree or highest salary couldn't tell them. People are intuitive, and they can sense authenticity.

It is this feedback from individuals at various levels of influence that should give you a balanced understanding of who other people think you are. From my perspective as a visual person, if I were doing this evaluation exercise to find out how others view me, I would stand on a chair so I could get the big picture. I would want to see myself walking in the office, greeting the receptionist with a smile on my face, taking off my coat, and hanging it in the closet while responding to her question, "How are you this morning?" with, "I am excellent and ready to make this day count!"

Join me up on your mental chair, look out at your workplace during a typical day, and answer the following questions:

~What do you do when you go into your office?

~Look at yourself and think about what others are seeing. Describe it.

~Do you like what you see?

~What attitude is reflected in your face?

~What does your walk tell others about you?

~Are you running through the door disheveled, out of breath, and out of control?

When you view yourself as others see you, you can see yourself differently and understand how you contribute to the perceptions others have about you. You may be brilliant as an executive, but are you brilliant in getting along with others? Have you mastered cooperation? Do you value teamwork, or are you apathetic about your coworkers?

Allow me to describe one of the most devastating work experiences I've ever had. The boss called our team together for a meeting and allowed each team member seated around the circular table to take turns expressing his or her view of me. I was a new member on the team, and I thought I had been fitting in pretty well. I had accepted a job in a corporate culture that was completely different from my previous work environment. The culture in my former workplace valued and rewarded tenacity, fearlessness, and assertiveness, while my new company valued a harmonious system of respect and consideration among team members.

Before I listened to each person's response or accusation during that meeting, I was told that I would not be permitted to say anything in my own defense; I couldn't react to their words. I was allowed to say only "thank you" after each comment that was offered about me. Then, the comments began. The words I heard from my coworkers didn't sound like me at all. Who was this woman they were talking about? The only thought I could manage to hold on to was, "They don't know me." I tried desperately to reject their words as they shared them in turn, drowning my soul before rising to exit the room, leaving me alone with my boss and his wife.

As soon as the door closed, my boss asked what I thought about the things they had said about me. I could hardly speak. With my lips trembling and my mouth as dry as if it were filled with cotton, I quietly muttered the words, "They don't know me." I cried deeply like a young child whose best friend had abandoned her for a new best friend, and my boss's wife embraced me. I kept saying through my flooding tears, "It's not who I am. They don't know me. They don't know my heart."

I learned a painful life lesson that day: words can wound deeply. I also learned how much others' opinions and views of who I am matter to me. After further reflection, I determined that while I couldn't control their perceptions of me, I could begin to manage my behavior, which might cause them to alter their own perceptions. I didn't have to give up myself, but I did have to understand myself and be willing to see what they saw. I worked diligently to adjust to my new environment, eventually understanding it and thriving there. Another lesson I learned that day was how to HEAR criticism:

Hear words humbly.

Explore words for insight.

Assess the words' impact.

Receive the truth and discard the rest.

Growing up, my siblings knew exactly how to get my goat with words that seemed not to describe me at all. The neighborhood kids did not exactly know who I was, but as kids often do, they would pick one thing they knew about me and rag on me about it, poking fun at various characteristics or behaviors. Kids may be cute, but they can be mean; they underestimate the power of their words to abuse and cause emotional scars. But many of the children who hear others' taunts and torments are too young to know how to HEAR.

It is sometimes interesting to find out how your friends view you. The very fact that you consider someone your friend should indicate that she understands you in ways that perhaps others do not. If you want to understand how your friends perceive you, set up your own 360-degree analysis using a tool called the Johari Window, which was created in the 1950s to give individuals a view of how others see their personalities. You can set up your own Johari Window for free online at kevan.org/johari and invite family members, friends, coworkers, or anyone else in your circle of influence to participate. You will first select six words you think best describe you, then create a link to send to others who will also select from the grid six words to describe you. You may be surprised at the outcome or your perceptions of how others see you.

You can change the way others perceive you by doing the following:

1. Create your own perception and manage your behavior accordingly.

2. Dress according to where you would like to be.

3. Leave personal worries at the door. Work is not your social network; it is your livelihood. Family and friends are your sources of emotional satisfaction.

4. Demonstrate responsibility rather than blame.

5. Consider what you want others to think of you and communicate in a way that will help them understand you effectively.

6. Say what you mean and mean what you say.

7. Check your own attitude before others check it for you.

8. See yourself through the eyes of others; guessing how others view you objectively will be beneficial.

9. Present yourself professionally in the workplace. Speak with clarity, respect others, and keep your commitments.

8

Why Am I Here?

*"Your assignment is not your decision, it is your discovery.
When your heart decides a destination your mind will
design a map to reach it."*

—Mike Murdock

Of every book written about purpose, Rick Warren's *The Purpose Driven Life* is the most successfully sold. I recall seeing the *40 Days of Purpose* banners hanging on many of the churches in my neighborhood, and I remember thinking that the slogan was catchy. I saw one, then two, then three in various parts of the city, and I concluded that this was larger than a local pastor's marketing campaign to attract believers to his church. Not only did I see the banners, but I also received direct mail from several of the local churches that were undertaking the program. Although I thought it was a great idea, it did not compel me to call or rush to a church to inquire for more information on discovering my purpose.

Soon to follow the church programs was a growing swell of grassroots marketing for the book. People were talking about it in coffee shops and reading it on airplanes. Perhaps the most notable piece of publicity about the book came when Ashley Smith talked the Atlanta courthouse shooter, Brian Nichols, into turning himself in. She said that she read to him from chapter thirty-three of *The Purpose Driven Life*. It was following this incident that I, too, purchased a copy of the book in order to learn about purpose. But, like many others who buy books, read a chapter or two, and relegate them to the shelf, I didn't finish this book—unfortunately, it couldn't keep my attention. I also attempted to listen to the audio version that my husband purchased—it's still sitting on my desk. Nevertheless, I am certain that this book helped millions of people as it did Ashley Smith, who recalled its impactful words in a time of crisis.

The Purpose Driven Life asked a series of questions throughout and after each chapter to help the reader discover, or awaken to, his or her purpose. The questions included some like the following:

~Have you ever wondered about, or felt confused about, the purpose of your life?

~In what ways have you tried to discover your life's purposes but didn't find success?

~Why do you think people try to discover their life's purpose without turning to God, their Creator?

I found this approach difficult to navigate, so I put the book down. I then began to pray and ask God for a definition of purpose that I could understand. I felt that having such a definition would give me clarity in order to answer these types of questions.

In my quest, I did what most of us do: I turned to *Merriam-Webster's* for an answer. The dictionary indicated that "purpose" means "something set up as an object or end to be attained, intention." Well, as you have probably guessed, I didn't understand that definition, either. Back to prayer I went: "Lord, please tell or show me what purpose means." To answer the question, "Have you ever wondered about, or felt confused about, the purpose of your life?" I say, "absolutely," most often because purpose had been poorly defined.

Thus began my quest—I was determined to define "purpose" in order to help individuals understand the *word*! I resolved that if I could construct a definition that would help people truly understand the word *purpose*, perhaps they would have an easier time living lives of purpose.

At 5:59 p.m. on May 8, 2006, I was penning a note of encouragement to a dear friend in her mid-fifties. These are the exact words I used to conclude the letter: "You can spend the next ten to twenty years of your life continuing as the problem-solver to your children—who, by the way, will always have problems for mom to solve—or you can get focused, find balance, and pursue the kingly purpose within you." It was in this moment, as I looked at the words I had written, that God answered my prayer. I was encouraging her to pursue her "kingly purpose," and I asked myself, *What does that mean?* I began to record feverishly on my Tablet PC what I was seeing in my mind's eye and hearing in my spirit.

The words I received that day I now offer to you, in hopes that they'll help you to define and pursue your God-given purpose and destiny. They have helped me to gain tremendous peace, clarity, and direction in my own journey to understand and answer the question *Why am I here?* The words are as follows:

Prayer

Prayer is a means of having a relationship with God. It is the instruction we receive and communication we have with our Maker. Prayer involves us presenting our heavenly Father with requests and petitions, and it offers us the comfort of developing intimacy with Him. Prayer helps us to think deeply and with greater clarity about who we are and what we do. It helps us to meditate and separate ourselves from the noise and clutter of our daily lives in order to enjoy peace in our souls and the presence of God. Prayer helps us to learn humility, so that our self-absorbed egos diminish while at the same time increasing our estimation and appreciation of God's greatness.

By praying, we learn to be humble as we seek God for information we admit we do not know; we request help for ourselves and others. Prayer helps us to develop a steady, faithful relationship to the character of God, and it teaches us how to hear Him. Prayer is my safest place where I experience, learn, touch, hear, and see what I am, who I am, and what I have to offer. Prayer builds my confidence to live, to thrive, and to be!

Passion

Passion is an internal drive that is stimulated by forces that are positive and negative, external and internal. In order to be effective, passions must be intentional. Unbridled passion is destructive; with too much power and too little direction, it causes any plans or pursuits to derail. God is intentional, and when we allow Him to direct our passions and strong emotions, passion becomes the productive ingredient to achieving what we intend to. Passion often breeds obsession, which is good only if directed toward the right targets, and to a healthy degree. An obsession dominates one's thoughts or feelings; it is usually a persistent idea, image, or desire. Passion breeds determination, distinction, and direction, all of which are essential for production and success.

Persistence

Doing what God tells you to do over and over—continuing in spite of opposition and persecution—means that you recognize resistance as a sign to encourage you to move forward. Persistence means directing your actions to an intended result or goal, even in the face of difficult challenges and seemingly insurmountable obstacles. Persist until you succeed in all that you do. Romans 2:7 says, *"To those who by persistence in doing good seek glory, honor and immortality, he* [God] *will give eternal life"* (NIV).

Persistence is similar to perseverance, a quality that the author of Hebrews encouraged believers to exhibit: *"Let us throw off everything that hinders and the sin that so easily entangles, and let us run with perseverance the race marked out for us"* (Hebrews 12:1 NIV). Also, Jesus told His disciples, *"Ask and it will be given to you; seek and you will find; knock and the door will be opened to you"* (Matthew 7:7 NIV). Ask, seek, and knock—the key to these things is *persistence.* Persist and don't give up!

Purpose

One day as I was typing on my computer, I recorded the following words as they came to mind:

Godly instruction I hear when I pray.

Fulfilled intentions.

Reason for existence.

Purpose is not tangible; it is movement, direction.

After I typed these words on my computer, I recalled a familiar quotation by Mike Murdock: "Your assignment is not your decision, it is your discovery," and I added this statement directly above the information I had just typed. I knew I was on to something, because I also know when I am hearing from the Teacher. These words were moving in my spirit and my head like finding that winning word that starts with an X or Z in a game of Scrabble. I had to assemble the thoughts; I was after a definition of purpose that I could relate to and others would benefit from.

I started reorganizing my thoughts about prayer, passion, persistence, and purpose in order to develop a definition of the elusive word *purpose*. As I rearranged my thoughts like pieces of a puzzle, I finally fit them together in a format simple enough for me to embrace, remember, and follow.

Purpose: *Desire of mind and heart directed for the fulfillment of godly instruction.*

This definition encompasses prayer, represented by godly instruction; passion, represented by desire; persistence, represented by the act of directing mind and heart; and purpose itself, represented by fulfillment. No longer am I seeking to accomplish or to be; I want to be fulfilling the instruction I have received through prayer and meditation with God. As I do this, I rely on Him, and my former frustration with trying to discern God's purpose for me is being transformed into a joyful journey of seeking Him for instruction and pursuing my passions.

Based on my new understanding of the word *purpose*, my responsibility has become to direct my passions, and, when I hear or know what I am to do, persisting until I get it done. If I succeed in following the instructions I have received, I am living my life *on purpose.* It is purposeful.

To apply this definition and concept to your own life, consider the following guidelines for living a purposeful life.

Living a Purposeful Life

1. Develop a prayer life. Find time to silence the external sounds in your life—the hustle and bustle of your home, workplace, or vehicle—and escape to a quiet place where you can be intentional about stirring up and sustaining conversation with God. There are many ways to pray. You can speak audibly or silently; you can say short prayers throughout the day or compose long, heartfelt cries to God; you can even write your prayers in a prayer journal. Find the method that is most comfortable for you, making sure to include components of worship, confession, thanksgiving, and supplication at some point during the day. The more you pray, the more your prayer life will emerge as a closer intimacy with God. In time, not only will you pray during the quiet moments you set aside, but you will also find yourself praying in the midst of turmoil, or even during mundane daily tasks. Conversation with God will become almost automatic, ongoing.

Make sure that when you pray, you're not doing all the talking. You must learn to listen, too! One of the statements I make when I am busy telling God about my life—as if He doesn't already know the details—is to consciously say, "Speak, Lord; Your servant is ready to listen." In the Bible, Eli told Samuel that if he heard God's voice, he should say, *"Speak, LORD, for your servant is listening"* (1 Samuel 3:9 NIV). And as I listen, I have pen in hand to make sure I hear and write down my instructions.

2. Proceed passionately based on the instruction you receive. Look for passion, for it rarely hides itself.

It is such a present emotion that it will easily accompany instruction. Recognize your passions by considering what you love—what you say or see over and over again. That which captures and holds your attention is where your heart should be. But be sure to ascertain that your passions are driven by the instruction of God rather than only by your five senses, or by negative external forces.

3. Get moving! Pursue your journey with persistence. Are you moving? Remember, it is not the destination, but rather the journey, that will yield many of life's rewards and the many purposeful moments that you will experience. Purpose is not what you are or who you are; it is what you are *doing* or *completing*, or where you are *going*. Purpose involves aligning your mind with your heart to determine the direction in which you will move. Take it step-by-step as you receive information and instruction.

Your assignment is really a discovery—an exciting journey of developing a life of prayer, meditation, and communication with God. What is truly important is finding peace, fulfillment, and meaning, none of which is accessible without the presence of God in your life. Grabbing hold of what you hear and trusting your God-given passions as you pursue the things you desire with persistence will help you live the intentional life you were born to live.

> *"Quite often we reach that intersection where our gifts,*
> *talents and abilities meet to change the world in ways*
> *we never expected."*

—A. R. Bernard

9

Building Inner Confidence

"As he [man] *thinketh in his heart, so is he."*

—Proverbs 23:7 (KJV)

What does it mean to have confidence? Having confidence means trusting in your own abilities, beliefs, and talents, and being able to project poise effectively, both in private and in public. Confidence is similar to self-esteem; it is how you feel about yourself. How you feel about yourself will also ultimately affect your confidence; it will help you or hurt you. We attain confidence through our personal experiences, culture, parents and familial influences, friends, and education. We demonstrate confidence through the ability to decipher the information that we learn and convert it into meaningful and successful outcomes.

Confidence, and likewise a lack thereof, can come from external and internal victories, failures, pressures, or experiences. Many of us have viewed at least one of the many makeover shows on television and witnessed the metamorphosis in self-awareness when physical appearances improve—the participant's confidence gets a major boost. Before participants undergo their makeovers, we can see that they usually lack confidence—they won't smile; they feel embarrassed, shy, and possibly depressed. The aftereffect is usually a complete turnaround: they feel more confident, their self-esteem has increased greatly, and they believe that others will see them positively. Their new attitudes radiate in their smiles, their confident strides, their more frequent laughter. When the "new and improved" person is presented to family members, friends, and the audience in the studio and at home, we all respond with a similar rush of emotion. We cry, we laugh, we hug, we scream excitedly, we stare in amazement at the transformation the individual has experienced and rejoice in her hope that she will be more successful from this point on in her life journey, which she will approach with a new look and newfound confidence.

I am interested in hearing the stories of people who have experienced internal healing from the external scars of the past. I want to know how long their sense of confidence lasted—did it endure for years, building more and more with every victory, or did it quickly diminish, starting with the first bad-hair day? Confidence and self-esteem are within, and I agree that having the benefit of a great external appearance is helpful—but not always necessary. How we feel about ourselves is embodied in our thoughts, received as words we embrace, based on what others say or demonstrate to us and about us (or based on our own thoughts about ourselves).

Consider these external influences and attributes that may erode your confidence:

~Physical disfigurement (real or perceived).

~Dissatisfaction with height, weight, size, body shape, athleticism, etc.

~Frustration about hair (length, texture, color).

~Dental issues (buck teeth, crooked teeth, cavity fillings).

~Being a frequent victim of teasing.

~Physical abuse (beating, rape, etc.).

~Being the victim of damaging gossip and harmful stories, true or false.

~Receiving threats, either specific or implied, of what someone says he or she will do to you.

~Inhabiting dirty, rundown surroundings (a cluttered house, a neighborhood of poorly maintained homes, a rusty car, stained clothing, etc.).

~Sustaining injuries or permanent disabilities, or suffering from illness or disease.

Most people who know me would probably describe me as being very confident; they would say that I have a strong, positive sense of self. Most of the time, I would agree with them. However, I have had my share of experiences with both external and internal events that hurt or hindered my positive self-image.

As a young girl, I enjoyed ice skating. Once when I was in third grade, I was at the ice rink with my family, and we were having a ball. This was my first time skating, but I caught on quickly. I bravely let go of the rails around the rink and ventured among those who were more skilled. As I made my way around that rink—gliding, laughing, falling, and getting back up, only to do it again—I hoped that when I reached the place where my mother was sitting, I would be skating on two feet. After a few turns, I did make it around to where my mom was. When I saw her, I waved and screamed, "Look at me! Look at me!" I wanted her to see me in all my glory, but just as I passed by, waving and screaming, a male skater flew by me and clipped my feet, sending me flying.

Most of my other falls were definitely results of my own lack of experience and general clumsiness, but this particular crash was not of my doing. My arms and legs failed me completely, and I was airborne. When I came down, I could hardly break my fall, and my face collided with the ice. Being the resilient youth that I was, I hopped up and said, "I'm okay," looking around to assure my mother that what I had said was true. As I proceeded around the rink, the right side of my face felt a little numb from the fall. When I returned again to the place where my mother was sitting, she cast me a suspicious glance and motioned for me to come over.

I made my way over, grinning from ear to ear, expecting her to tell me that she saw the whole incident and wanted to make sure I was not hurt. What my mother saw on my face seemed to disturb her, however. As she looked at me, she said, "Baby, come here, come off the ice, I need to look at you." I said, "What is it?" She looked at me strangely as she grabbed my chin, turning my head from left to right. She asked me to blink my eyes, smile, and open my mouth as she continued her inspection. "What is it, Momma?" I asked, starting to panic. She looked pretty scared, and she said, "Your face is twisted." She could tell that something was terribly wrong, and that my fall on the ice had something to do with it.

My mother did not rush me to the emergency room that evening, but the very next day, she and my dad took me to Herman Hospital in Houston, Texas, to be examined by specialists. They told my mother and father that I had Bell's palsy. Bell's palsy causes one side of the face to pull on the other side of the face so that it contorts; you appear similar to someone who has had a major stroke, but only one side of your face is affected. The nerves that control your ability to blink, taste, and produce saliva are the same. The year was 1974, and there were very few cases of Bell's palsy among children of my age. During that hospital visit there were a half dozen doctors inspecting, touching, and examining me. The specialists prescribed shock treatment, which consisted of applying small bursts of electricity to the neck area just below the ears. These treatments were required daily for several months until the nerve that was affected had healed. Eventually, my face realigned, but not before new words were introduced to my vocabulary—and to my tender heart and soul.

I was a bright and active little girl, cute and full of life and vitality. I was the neighborhood tomboy and the youngest of five siblings: three brothers and one sister. I was known for being intuitive, smart, funny, and full of joy. The incident on the ice rink changed everything. By the following morning, the paralysis had grown more severe. When I awoke, I ran to the mirror, where I was joined by my curious siblings, gawking and staring. The first words I heard that morning were, "You look like the linky-eyed monster." The linky-eyed monster was a figment of the collective imagination of the neighborhood children. There was a wooded area between the path of our busy neighborhood street and the school, and rumor had it that the linky-eyed monster lived in those woods. I had envisioned all kinds of horrible things the linky-eyed monster would do to me if he caught me walking to or from school. But until that day, the linky-eyed monster never had a face; we hadn't determined his appearance. Now, he finally had a face—mine. Through the words of my brothers and sisters, I became, in a sense, that horrible creation of our imaginations. Although I laughed off my siblings' taunts, I was devastated. How was I going to face my classmates, friends, and extended family? What would they say about me? A lot was said, and it wasn't very nice.

Until writing this story, I had long forgotten about my days at Dogan Elementary School. This prolonged forgetfulness was likely the result of a selective recall; I sought to block out memories of this painful time. Maybe that's why my parents transferred me to a different school after that year, giving me a chance to start over in a new place with new people. I am sure it helped me to escape what others knew about me and gave me an opportunity to make a fresh start. By the time I began fourth grade, my face looked normal again, and I had been placed in the classroom of the most loving, caring, and encouraging teacher: Mrs. Sharon Ealy.

Sharon Ealy is still in my life today, and her contribution to my inner healing as a young girl continued well beyond her year as my teacher. She loved me unconditionally, maintaining a close relationship with me. She counseled me through my teenage years, attended my high school commencement ceremony, came to my grandmother's funeral, and bought me my first television set for my college dorm room. We celebrated our birthdays together when I turned forty and she, fifty-seven; we were born on the same date, seventeen years apart.

When I look back on how I overcame the pain of my third grade year, I am certain *now* that Sharon Ealy is an angel who was assigned to help me *become*. Life truly moves in a cyclical way, for now, I have become a teacher of Mrs. Ealy, offering encouragement, support, and assistance as she navigates the decisions and events involved with aging.

My facial paralysis could have caused me to turn completely inward and withdraw from society, hiding from my peers and hating myself. But thanks to the loving support of family, friends, and medical personnel who assured me that although I was experiencing a difficult time, I would not remain that way, I made it through. Even though they filled me with hope and encouragement, my saving grace came when my face healed. I am sure you have your own stories about times when you endured pain, fear, and uncertainty. How did you overcome these forms of adversity?

Confidence is developed by a series of events that occur in our lives that give us the opportunity to respond or react. *Responding* allows us to process information more objectively, even when it appears that the outcome will be neither good nor favorable. One of the lessons I learned after having Bell's palsy was to be aware of—and sensitive to—the differences of others. Although my self-esteem took many blows during that time, I am sure that my confidence ultimately increased. I learned the importance of loving others, withholding criticism of others with physical disabilities and misfortunes, and developing greater sensitivity to the plights of others. Instead of losing my self-confidence completely, I became stronger and more self-assured as I cultivated compassion, empathy, and a recognition that my own situation was less dire than that of many others.

Developing Self-confidence

How do you develop self-confidence? How do you take control of how you feel about yourself? How do you project yourself publicly in a positive way? In order to change yourself, you must change your beliefs and feelings about yourself; different actions will follow.

Confidence is something that can come and go. We see this often in well-trained athletes in various sports. An athlete may have a winning streak, but when he loses a few games or fails to make record-breaking times, commentators try to pinpoint the causes to blame; this may include a drop in self-confidence or a slackening of performance and talent. The key to developing your self-confidence is learning to manage it.

We will achieve some things; others, we'll fail to achieve—but it is how you manage yourself during your experiences, whether successes or failures, that counts. For example, if you lack confidence when speaking before groups of people, you may always lack confidence until you take a class or hire a speaking coach to help you become more comfortable with public speaking. This is a way of managing confidence; it means that you're doing something about it.

BOSS the Movement is a youth training program that teaches young people about poise, professional greetings, and public speaking. Many young people who enroll in the class can, after twenty weeks of training, stand proudly before an audience of adults and speak boldly about their transformations. For many of us, the problem isn't with speaking; it's with standing in front of an audience with everyone's attention focused on us. When we can become comfortable being "on display," and when we've learned to silence the voices in our heads that warn us about the judgments of others, then we can begin to speak more comfortably in front of audiences. Practice and preparation also give us an undeniable sense of confidence. Just imagine what happens when we receive the attention of others when we haven't prepared beforehand. If you have been there, it is truly a miserable experience.

Eliminate Attitudes That Crush Confidence

If you want to manage your confidence, then learn to stop doing the things that destroy your confidence and learn instead to do more of the things that increase your confidence. Learn to let go of presuppositions, and embrace activities that will increase confidence. Some common presuppositions that defeat your ability to develop your self-confidence are the following:

I don't have anything to offer. Breathe in and exhale. If you can do this, you have something to offer to the world.

If only I were more like someone else, then I would do more, be more, and have more. Give up comparing yourself to others, stop binding yourself with a chain of "if only" statements, and start living right where you are in the moment! Make the most of who you are—your talents, your abilities, your life. Maximize your resources to the best of your ability.

What will other people say? If you find yourself worrying about what others will say or think about something you plan to do, do it anyway. Become more discreet in choosing those to whom you reveal your plans; not everyone can celebrate—or tolerate—your success! You can handle what others will say by preparing a ready answer, should your critics request it, or by not answering them at all. Before you know it, you will be what you want to be, you will do what you want do, and those same critics will be trying to jump on your bandwagon and join you. Decide to care about what *you* say and what *you* want to do—and *do it!* Eliminate the barriers and limitations others place in front of you. Other people aren't thinking about you as often as you think they are. Those thoughts in your head are yours, and you alone allow or deny them speech; if they bother you or undermine your confidence, silence them! Other people are wrapped up with their own busy lives, problems, and thoughts. You don't have to make up any for them; you have plenty of your own thoughts to fight off.

I can have it all. *No!* You can't have it all. Having it all is way too much for any one person to desire. What are you after—the universe, matter, time, or space? If you had it all, you would have no need for anyone or anything else. What a boring existence that would be! Choose what's best for you. Set your priorities, follow the direction of your dominant gifts, and you will find your treasure.

Having it all does not guarantee happiness. Even fulfillment, peace, and financial security—great blessings though they are—do not guarantee happiness. Make your choices carefully, focus your attention in one direction, and sharpen your skills; effectiveness will ensue. Effectiveness is essential to building confidence. Chad, a student in my business mentoring class, shared a beautiful insight with me and his fellow students. He came to the conclusion, "Instead of pursuing success, I pursue effectiveness, and success follows."

It's just who I am; this is me. If I hear this from one more woman, I'll want to spank her like my momma spanked me when I was five years old. She held one arm in the air as I ran around in circles, and she got in as many licks as she could before I broke free. Her spanks were usually accompanied by the words, "Girl, wake up! Take responsibility for your actions."

When you make the statement above, you are saying that you are perfect just the way you are. This statement is great evidence that you are not open to the possibilities life has to offer you.

Life is all about change. If you use your personality or tendencies as excuses for substandard performance or unseemly traits, it means you prefer to stick with what you know about yourself, denying yourself the ability to change, improve, and succeed. Open up to yourself and be willing to change. It sounds like you may be afraid of finding your true potential. It's time to move from caterpillar to butterfly; as long you posture with a "this is me" attitude, you have a caterpillar mentality, one that is cramped and confined to its cocoon. But when you break forth as the butterfly, you will never again be limited to a cocoon; the whole world will be your stage. Fly, woman, fly!

అ✧

Increase Your Self-confidence

Pray. Develop a daily prayer life that works for you. Take extended moments of silence, meditating on God's Word and allowing Him to teach, encourage, and love you.

Proclaim your uniqueness. You are rare; you are one of a kind. Refuse to walk in another's shoes; your own are sufficient to take you where you are to go. You can emulate others—wise teachers, role models—but do not imitate them. Be yourself. You are distinct from everyone else. Love your unique self!

Affirm your game. Even on the smaller stages of life, it is important to plan, practice, prepare, and proceed. During a panel discussion at a Black Economic Success Training (BEST) Conference hosted by T. D. Jakes Enterprises, Dr. Cornel West said, "Affirm your game when you are on the bottom." When you get to the top, you will have the skills, talents, and experience to stay there.

Celebrate every victory, however small. If your confidence has been damaged in a certain area, go back to it, set a small goal, achieve it, and set another one immediately afterward. Create cycles of success.

For example, if you tend to procrastinate, the next time you set a goal and hear yourself saying that you are going to do it, stop what you are doing and do it that very moment! Celebrate your victories, acknowledging yourself with affirmative words that other people might use to praise or reward you. Give yourself credit for the tasks you complete, and appreciate yourself for having achieved them. I used this technique while writing this book. For example, after I had finished writing about a certain topic from my outline for this book, I would celebrate in word and in deed. I would shout for joy, call my husband to share the news with him, tell my dogs as if they'd understand, give my writing coach a high five, or rehash the chapter with the help of my executive assistant. Writing this book was not easy, because I had a thousand things I wanted to do other than write. With every small victory, however, I found it becoming easier to write more words, because my confidence grew daily after each topic was completed.

Fail forward. Failure is feedback; it is not your end. Failure provides information from which you can learn. Get back up, dust yourself off, and resume your forward motion. Before you move forward, determine what you need to do differently so that you will get the results you want the next time.

Think about a time you tripped over a rug or other object in your path that you didn't see. What happened? You fell forward, right? After your fall, you probably got up, straightened your disheveled clothing, and looked behind you, trying to figure out what got in your way so that the next time you navigate the same path, you will avoid the obstacle and keep from tripping again. This is a physical example that illustrates how we should mentally and psychologically deal with past failures in order to move on to future successes.

Give! Give more to others than is required of you; go above and beyond what they expect to receive. Be liberal in issuing compliments, encouraging words, and positive feedback to others, and others will take note and give back to you in return. Give, and you will receive.

Keep the commitments you make to yourself. Our greatest disappointments are often self-imposed. We make statements such as, "I am going to do this or that," but we don't. We must try to keep the commitments that we make to ourselves. Take that walk in the park, go on vacation with your family (or simply discover the city you live in, for starters), be kind to yourself (eliminate negative internal feedback), go to the gym, eat health-ily, sever that harmful relationship. Stay true to yourself.

Evaluate your relationships. Assess your relationships with family members, friends, and colleagues, identifying which ones are positive and which ones, if any, are not. Insulate yourself from negative people, period!

Wait patiently for understanding. Don't be quick to jump to conclusions; rather, seek understanding. *"Blessed is the man who finds wisdom, the man who gains understand-ing, for she is more profitable than silver and yields better returns than gold"* (Proverbs 3:13–14 NIV).

Love unconditionally. Practice expressing the love in your heart through your eyes. You don't have to speak out your love; your eyes can reflect it. Learn to appreciate people for who they are, showering them with respect and showing them countless acts of kindness. It really doesn't matter how others treat you—your confidence will soar when you choose to give love regardless of what others give to you.

Master your emotions. Learn to keep your emotions and mood swings in control. Before you speak, chew on the words in your mouth, taste-testing them in anticipa-tion of the effect they will produce on the person to whom you would speak them. Instead of reacting impulsively to a situation that sparks your anger or makes you stressed, wait and calm down instead of spewing forth incendiary words. *"In the multitude of words sin is not lacking, but he who restrains his lips is wise"* (Proverbs 10:19). *"He who is slow to wrath has great understanding, but he who is impul-sive exalts folly"* (Proverbs 14:29). *"A soft answer turns away wrath, but a harsh word stirs up anger"* (Proverbs 15:1).

It is usually best to swallow bitter, unkind words before they slip off the tip of your tongue. Learn and master the art of hearing criticism and using it as a tool for growth instead of allowing your emotions to make it an instrument of despair. Follow the advice of James, being *"swift to hear, slow to speak"* (James 1:19).

Be proactive. Boost your confidence significantly by being proactive and taking initiative in your relationships, personal and professional alike. If you are starting a business and you meet someone who can be helpful to you, don't wait for a phone call that may never come—call that person and invite him or her to join you for a cup of coffee and a discussion about potential business opportunities.

ഹ

So far, you have read about how to create values, build your self-confidence, and understand your purpose. Now that you know more about yourself, I want to teach you how to follow your strengths, establish your brand, navigate change, and execute your ideas.

10 Following Your Strengths

"You cannot be anything you want to be—but you can be a lot more of who you already are."

—Tom Rath

Identifying and following your strengths can catapult you into countless opportunities and great wealth. Failing to follow your strengths can lead you down the path of frustration, disappointment, and sadness. Ten years ago, I picked up my first golf club. I am no Tiger Woods, mind you, but I can hold my own on the green. On the day I swung that first seven iron, I was on the driving range with my friend, Gabrielle. The golf pro who was assisting me showed me how to hold the club, then told me to give it a try. I said, "Sure! All I have to do is swing, right?" He replied with an emphatic, "Yes."

I swung the club and hit the ball effortlessly—and it traveled at least one hundred and fifty yards. The golf pro looked shocked. "Wow, that was easy," I said. As Gabrielle looked on in amazement, the golf pro put another ball on the tee and asked me to try hitting again. I swung the club, and off went the ball, straight ahead about one hundred and fifty yards. He looked at me and asked, "Are you sure you have never golfed before?" I quickly assured him, "No, this is my very first time." He proceeded to tell me that I was a natural. By this time, my excitement was bubbling over. I was on the golf course that day because Richmond, my then fiancé, wanted me to learn to golf, and the golf pro's response let me know that I would do just fine. Richmond would be so pleased! Gabrielle, also a first-time golfer, couldn't strike the ball at all. Still rejoicing over my immediate success, I looked over at Gabrielle and tried to encourage her, saying, "It is really easy; just swing at the ball and hit it." Well, apparently she didn't have a natural knack for golfing, and I didn't know enough about golf to know that few people strike the ball on the first try.

After a few rounds of practice at the driving range, I had the opportunity to golf for the first time with Richmond. He was immediately surprised by my ability, and he was convinced that I had taken private lessons in order to impress him with my skills. However, I had not taken lessons; the truth was that I had a raw talent for golfing. We were married within three months of when I started to golf. In September of that same year, only six months after my first time holding a golf club, I was competing in the Black Enterprise Golf Challenge at the Doral Golf Course in Miami, Florida!

My husband had insisted that I participate in this tournament, and he'd spent most of the time when he wasn't working helping me on the golf course, teaching me the game. So, after only six months of training with my husband of six months, I was a contender for first place in a three-day golf tournament. I was on the leader board from day one of the tournament. I ultimately finished in fifth place, primarily because I lost my focus; on the final day of play, the round exceeded six hours' duration, and I was more than ready to finish. Since that time, though, I have become an even better golfer, beating the fellas on a regular basis and driving the greens. From the ladies' tee box, I can drive the ball to the green in one shot, and my longest drive hitting the green has been 289 yards.

Go ahead and say it: "Wow!" Yes, a "wow" is in order, and that's the response I most commonly receive from anyone who plays golf with me. Even though I don't play very often, my handicap is about a 15, and I have never had a handicap higher than 30. So, from the time I started playing to the present day, I have improved my game

50 percent, and with little instruction (my husband, three professional lessons, plenty of unsolicited advice, and many hours spent viewing the Golf Channel). Imagine what could have happened if I had discovered my raw talent earlier, converted it into a strength, and pursued the opportunity afforded me. I might have been able to compete at the LPGA (Ladies Pro Golfers Association) level, and perhaps I could have even become a famous female golfer!

As I wrote this chapter, my experience with golf clearly illustrated to me the need to identify your raw talent and invest time, energy, effort, and knowledge to convert that talent into a strength that ultimately could lead to great opportunity in your life. If I would have pursued golf, I know I would have succeeded. However, I do not regret that I didn't follow that raw talent, because my life and professional career eventually led me to pursue numerous business opportunities and a higher calling of touching the lives of others through ministering, training, and coaching.

During the same time that I discovered my golfing talent, I was also given a tremendous opportunity to start a business with my husband, Richmond, in 1998. I believed that my talents in administration and operations could better serve in building this business. Collectively focusing our skills, experience, and expertise, we were able to raise ten million dollars in seed capital to start a private equity real estate company. This company has grown in value in excess of five hundred million dollars. It's a good thing I didn't stick with golf as a career!

As we move forward, I want to help you identify not only the strengths in your life, but also the weaknesses, opportunities, and threats (commonly known as a S.W.O.T. analysis). By performing a personal S.W.O.T. analysis, you will be able to analyze your current position and identify the talents you possess that you can develop in order to have the greatest opportunities for success.

Strengths

Identifying your strengths will help you determine the unique attributes and skills that you can convert into opportunities with definite potential for success. There are several especially effective methods you can use to measure your strengths. First, listen to what others say about you. Second, make note of the things others most often ask you to do or to help them with. Third, take one of the many available personality, strength, or behavior assessments, such as the Myers-Briggs Type Indicator. Discovering your strengths will help you move in the direction of discovering and developing your most dominant gift. Another example is Tom Rath's StrengthsFinder 2.0, an online test that uses this well-researched formula to help you identify your strengths:

talent × investment = strength

In other words, **talent** (a natural way of thinking, feeling, or behaving) multiplied by **investment** (time spent practicing or developing your skills and building your knowledge base) equals **strength** (the ability to consistently provide near-perfect performance).

One of my own strengths is public speaking. I am never anxious or nervous when standing before a crowd. In fact, it's when I'm in front of a large group of people that I'm in my zone—there's no other place I would rather be. At a recent conference, I was speaking about the importance of maximizing your strengths and talents, and I prepared a special drama to illustrate the process of developing one's talents. The illustration began when I moved from the podium to the piano. I love the piano—I even have one in my office—but I can't play it. I have no raw talent for playing the piano, nor have I invested much time or effort to hone that particular skill.

When I moved from the podium to the piano, the audience assumed that I had a musical talent based on the way in which I handled myself as my fingers first touched the keys. Because I have a piano, I know how to find middle C, and I can play a basic C-major chord. Now, allow me to digress for one moment. Prior to my taking the stage, an extremely gifted and talented musician had played the piano and sang. Her performance was so impressive that she had received a standing ovation from the audience.

We return to the piano, where my story resumes. After I played that first chord, it was all downhill. Why? Playing the piano is something I hope to do someday; perhaps, when I arrive in heaven, I will have the opportunity to play the piano, but down here on earth, it is just not going to happen. Contrary to my own musical "performance," the young woman who performed before I did had talent, gifts, skills, knowledge, and many hours' practice; therefore, her output was far stronger and more skillful than mine. So, after making the point of my illustration by banging discordantly on the piano keys, I returned to my own strength—public speaking—and received a standing ovation at the conclusion of my presentation. Playing the piano is not one of my strengths, but public speaking is: I have spoken before tens of thousands of people in the course of my career, making presentations to crowds of one to ten thousand people, and I have been consistently effective.

Every assessment of personality, strength, or behavior that I have taken confirms that I am a communicator, speaker, leader, coach, and encourager. Fortunately, I discovered my strength as a communicator early enough to act on it and develop it further. I realized that I must do more than speak, however; I must use every possible medium or outlet to spread my message. This book is another avenue through which I can communicate, as well as a way to leave a legacy of my thoughts for others to benefit from for years to come.

Identifying Your Natural Talents Builds Your Strengths

Let's review the definition of *talent* again. *A talent is a natural way of thinking, feeling, or behaving.* What subjects interest you most? What are you deeply moved by? Do you have strong convictions about any particular issues? What do you do well? What unique resources can you draw on? What do others see as your strengths?

Based on Tom Rath's equation, an investment of time, money, energy, and effort is essential for converting your talents into strengths. How have you invested yourself lately? What classes have you taken? What sports, musical instruments, or other hobbies do you practice? What books have you read in the past six months? If you have many books, check your shelves to see which subjects or genres recur—this will let you know where your primary interests rest. Check your computer, searching your bookmarks or "Favorites" folder in your Internet browser for any interests or patterns in the Web pages you've saved. Look at your calendar to review how you have been spending your time. You might say that you don't have any time to invest in anything, but I challenge you to question that perception. If you are honest with yourself, you will find that there is something important to you—maybe even something that you keep hidden in your heart—for which you make time because of its value to you.

I love the last part of Tom Rath's equation, for it demonstrates that a strength is an ability to consistently provide near-perfect performance. Operating fully in your strength is what I call being *in the zone*. And when we are in the zone, our strengths create values and opportunities for us to live the lives we desire.

Weaknesses

Most of us find it easy to talk about our strengths, but we may feel uncomfortable owning up to our weaknesses. While there are many schools of thought concerning weaknesses, I want to encourage you to remember the Chain Theory: your strength is your weakest link. If you were pulling a heavy object with a chain consisting of twenty links—nineteen links representing your strengths (think of iron) and one representing your weakness (think of an aluminum paper clip)—how strong is your chain?

During a job interview, most people cringe at the dreaded question, "What is your greatest weakness?" Rather than wincing, handle this question with confidence. If you have a weakness, identify it, then share a strength or opportunity that you believe would help you to overcome it. For example, you might respond, "I would say that my greatest weakness has been a lack of proper planning.

I often overcommit myself to too many different tasks, and then am not able to fully accomplish each as I would like. However, since I've come to recognize that weakness, I've taken steps to correct it. For example, I regularly attend time management seminars, and now I carry a planning calendar at all times so that I can schedule all of my appointments and prioritize my 'to do' list."

Your weaknesses can also be viewed as areas where you have not developed strengths—yet. Study my Weakness Formula below and consider how you can turn your weaknesses into strengths.

When assessing your weaknesses, it is important to be honest with yourself. But you don't have to beat yourself up over everything that you haven't done or couldn't accomplish. It is advantageous to identify your weaknesses, for as you become aware of them, you can plan to develop new habits, partner with other people, or learn new skills in order to eliminate, or at least minimize, the threats (explained below) to your success of effectiveness caused by your weaknesses. Let's create our own equation for weakness:

$$weakness = investment / talent$$

In other words, **weakness** equals **investment** (time, effort, energy, and knowledge) divided by **talent** (raw ability, understanding, feelings, beliefs, and behavior). Picture a scale of 1 to 5 to rate your ability to keep your commitments (1 being the lowest, 5 the highest). Your investment (time, effort, energy, and knowledge) can also be measured on a scale from 1 to 5. If you consistently miss appointments, forget what you have told others, take on in one day more than you could possibly do in a year, and wonder why you can't seem to get out of your rut, you're at the low end of the scale. Unfortunately, you have never done the necessary things that could improve your track record, such as take a class in organization, read a book about time management, or practice keeping your word to other people.

Regardless of where you start on the scale of weaknesses to strengths, your investment of time, effort, energy, and knowledge is the only thing that will move you from poor to proficient performance in a given area. We can shift weaknesses to strengths simply by taking small, deliberate steps.

For example, reading an article that discusses techniques to help you keep your commitments can boost your investment score by 1 point if you implement even a few of the author's suggested guidelines. Even a modest investment will alter the equation dramatically, because increasing the frequency of your successes will move you along the scale from weakness to strength.

Ask yourself what value you really place on being a person of commitment, and assign a corresponding numeric value (1 to 5, with 5 being the highest value). Looking at the investment part of the equation, ask yourself how much time, effort, energy, and knowledge you have invested in becoming a person who keeps her commitments. Strengths are important, because they are what we convert to opportunities, income, favor, happiness, and success.

In evaluating your weaknesses, consider these questions:

~In which areas of your life, personal or professional, could you improve?

~In which areas do you seem to have fewer resources than others?

~What are others likely to perceive as weaknesses in your character?

~What activities or tasks do you hate to do?

~What makes you cringe when you are confronted about your personality or character?

After you have answered these questions, apply the weakness formula to determine how much you know about the weakness. Then, determine how much you are willing to invest in order to make the shift from weakness to strength.

Opportunities

> *"Become a possibilitarian. No matter how dark things seem to be or actually are, raise your sights and see possibilities— always see them, for they're always there."*

—Norman Vincent Peale

Strengths are talents multiplied by your time, energy, and knowledge. Your strengths constitute the doorway to your opportunities—the greater your investment in developing your strengths, the greater your opportunity to create value. For example, one of my heroes from the 1980s was Anthony Jerome "Spud" Webb, the third shortest player in NBA history. Despite his diminutive height, Spud won the 1986 Slam Dunk contest against Dominique Wilkins. Spud had many disadvantages as a basketball player, standing only 5 feet 7 inches tall. But Spud had a strong desire, coupled with a natural talent for jumping. Thus, although he was shorter and slimmer than most of his opponents, he could outjump them. His vertical jump was 42 inches—almost four feet in the air!

Spud's unusual talent, focused in the right direction and with years of practice, afforded him the opportunity to compete in the game. His ability to jump made him a striking force against his opponents, many of whom underestimated his skill because of his height. Do the math—67 inches plus a vertical jump of 42 inches yields 109 inches! I remember how awestruck we were as we watched him defy gravity and soar into the air above his 6 foot 10 inch opponents, slam-dunk the basketball, and run back to the other end of the court. He was unstoppable. His dominant gift was jumping, and he further developed this gift by learning to play basketball, practicing, competing on various teams, and ultimately converting his talent into opportunity, earning fame and fortune.

Opportunities arise when you develop your dominant talents and convert them into meaningful outcomes, whether for financial gain or personal enjoyment. Looking at your list of talents, determine which of them hold your hidden treasure, then find the vehicle or conduit by which you can convert your strength into opportunity. Spud had a talent of jumping. The sport of basketball was the vehicle that converted his talent into an opportunity, and the NBA was the opportunity that rewarded him, financially and personally, for investing in and maximizing his strengths.

Answer the following questions to discover what opportunities may be open to you.

~Are there any trends in your particular area of interest of which you can take advantage?

~Identify two specific strengths that you believe you can convert into opportunities.

~List steps you can take to turn these two strengths into opportunities.

Threats

Threats are inhibitors that seek to destroy accomplishments, detour plans, create fear, or erode confidence. The threats that you face are based on your awareness of external events and circumstances, as well as on certain beliefs or feelings you may have. In reality, instead of inhibiting you, fears can become indicators that encourage you to move in the direction of your strengths and to develop your weak areas.

For example, doubt, as a weakness, can expose you to the threat of compromise. If you doubt your decision-making abilities, you may compromise your behavior or follow someone else's advice rather than assessing the situation and making your own decision. Fear, as a weakness, will expose you to the threat of the fear of failure, thereby paralyzing your action. Lack of drive, as a weakness, may expose you to frequent periods of unemployment, because you may not maintain the productivity level required for a specific job; if this is the case, you'll find yourself cycling through opportunities and giving them up.

When you work on eliminating your weaknesses and limit your potential threats, you create an environment conducive to following your strengths and converting them into meaningful opportunities.

Overcoming Your Threats

1. Identify your threats, keeping in mind that they are external and relate to anything that inhibits or prohibits you from reaching your goals.

2. Determine which weaknesses expose you to the threats you have identified.

3. Apply the weakness formula and decide on how much time, energy, effort, and knowledge you will devote to moving your weaknesses up the scale toward the strength end. The intended goal is not to make strengths of all your weaknesses, but rather to emphasize improvement. Even a slight improvement will limit your exposure to threats.

4. Develop a plan of action to improve your areas of weakness. For example, if you lack drive and motivation, look at your strengths and ask yourself if you are in the right profession—do you have the personality, skills, and knowledge necessary to excel in your workplace? If you lack drive, does this lack stem from how you think other people perceive you? Can you improve your appearance or take a class in communication or personal development in order to learn new ways of expressing yourself? Do you arrive at work on time? Do you offer to help others and work well with your team?

5. Ask for help by finding a mentor, accountability partner, or friend to assist you in improving your areas of weakness.

11

Performing a S.W.O.T. Analysis

A s we discussed, a S.W.O.T. (strengths, weaknesses, opportunities, and threats) analysis is a general technique used across various business disciplines during the early stages of strategic and marketing planning. Performing a personal S.W.O.T. analysis will help you identify internal and external factors that contribute to your strengths, weaknesses, opportunities, and threats.

The personal analysis considers those factors for which you may have internal controls (strengths and weakness) and factors external to your control (opportunities and threats).

In the following pages, you will do an exercise for your personal S.W.O.T. analysis. Before you attempt your S.W.O.T. analysis, review the example on the following page to help you. Your strengths are internal and you control them based on your beliefs, behaviors, and actions. Threats are the external factors that your weaknesses, if not improved, may expose you to that may prohibit your ability to convert your strengths into opportunities.

For example, your strength may be a skill in communicating. If you are indeed a skilled communicator, you may want to consider a career that would include a significant amount of public speaking. Let's look at the S.W.O.T. analysis for the talent of being an effective public speaker or gifted communicator.

S.W.O.T. Analysis of a Gifted Communicator

Strengths	Weaknesses
Effective communicator	Negative presuppositions
Gifted public speaker	"No one will like me"
	"I can't speak in front of others"
	"I'm not as good as..."
	Fear
	Low self-esteem
Opportunities	**Threats**
Increase exposure	Failure
Generate revenue	Embarrassment
Join Toastmasters Int'l	Comparison
Reinvent/reposition career	Paralysis
Build communication skills	Insufficient income

Let's take a closer look at this example for an individual who may have a raw talent of communicating effectively and how this strength can be converted into an opportunity. Remember, strengths are developed talents. The objective of performing a personal S.W.O.T. analysis is to look clearly at your internal strengths and weaknesses, which are the ones over which you have control (as opposed to external opportunities and threats, over which you may have little or no control). You can determine your output based on what you do or think.

Looking at this analysis, we see that the strength of communication is developed; however, when we look at the weaknesses, we see that this individual has negative thoughts and feelings regarding how she might be perceived and received by an audience. Although this person is a good communicator, she is filled with fear and has low self-esteem. These weaknesses expose her to the threats of fear of failure, comparison, paralysis, and insufficient income (should she indeed perform poorly and her salary suffer as a result). When we are able to identify our weaknesses, as well as the threats to which our weaknesses expose us, we are able to see clearly the true challenge of converting our strengths into opportunities. Opportunity is always there, but to use a strength most effectively, we must return to our areas of weakness and work on moving toward improvement. Even a slight improvement will eliminate some threats. Consider the weakness of negative presuppositions. If we work on building or managing our confidence in front of an audience by joining Toastmasters International or another public speaking organization, we may be able to eliminate the fear of failure by repeatedly succeeding and receiving positive feedback. Once we have improved our weakness related to a specific strength, we will be better equipped to convert that strength into a meaningful opportunity.

The grid on the following page lists many of the attributes included in most personal S.W.O.T. analyses. Keep in mind the source, or locale, of each analytical component (internal strengths and weaknesses; external opportunities and threats), knowing that these determine the degree to which you can control each one. Your internal strengths—the natural abilities, skills, personality traits, and propensities you possess—must not be taken for granted. It is a blessing to be gifted in a particular way, but that doesn't mean you don't have to work on it. Likewise, our internal weaknesses require work so that we can overcome them. Fears, emotional scars, and other potentially debilitating attributes are not insurmountable. When it comes to external opportunities and threats, your degree of control is diminished, but by drawing from your internal strengths and resourcefulness, you can usually find a way to capitalize on opportunities and minimize threats. To prepare for your personal S.W.O.T. analysis, circle the terms and phrases that best describe you.

Strengths	Weaknesses
Effectiveness	Procrastination
Energy/enthusiasm	Fear
Fortitude	Lack of drive or passion
Competence	Low self-esteem
Dependability	Self-doubt
Resourcefulness	Bad or destructive habits
Integrity	Physical flaws
Credibility	Emotional scars
Confidence	Dishonesty
Expertise	Chronic worry
Flexibility	Perceived limitations
Organization	Feelings of powerlessness
Creativity/innovation	Negative presuppositions
Past experiences	Absentmindedness
Compassion	Lack of foresight
Opportunities	**Threats**
New job opening	Clutter
Promotion at work	Financial strain
Higher educational degree	Unemployment
Consultation with a financial planner	Abuse (emotional, physical, or sexual)
Spheres of influence	Debt
Forgiveness	Illness or injury
New hobby or skill	Negative influences
Healthy eating habits	Substance abuse
Daily exercise	Addictions
Reconciliation	Paralysis caused by past record of failures
Improved organization	
Award or other recognition	Insufficient income
Volunteer service	Persecution
Specific goals	Discrimination

Record Your Strengths, Weaknesses, Opportunities, and Threats

Now, in the space below, make a list of your salient strengths, opportunities, weaknesses, and threats. You may use terms from the chart on the previous page or think of your own. Be honest with yourself, for only then will you benefit from this exercise.

Strengths	Weaknesses
Opportunities	**Threats**

Finally, in this space, choose one specific strength or talent and complete this exercise using the chart below and modeling it after the example provided on page 146 of the gifted communicator. Maybe you have a talent for singing, dancing, connecting with people, writing, event planning, inventing, or interior decorating. Choose a salient strength and perform a personal S.W.O.T. analysis to determine how you will convert this strength into a meaningful opportunity.

Strengths	Weaknesses
Opportunities	Threats

After completing the above S.W.O.T. analysis, answer these questions:

1. What did you discover about the hindrances that may be keeping you from acting on your strength?

2. List three things you can do to shift your weaknesses so that you can eliminate at least one threat.

3. What steps will you take to act on at least one opportunity you have identified?

What Do Others Think of You?

Earlier, I introduced you to the Johari Window, which allows other individuals of your choosing to help you to identify your strengths. You have learned a lot about me as you have read this book, so I invite you to visit my page and share your thoughts about who you perceive me to be at kevan.org/johari?name=AnnaMcCoy. If you would like to find out how others see me, my results can be viewed at results at kevan.org/johari?view=AnnaMcCoy. Also, you may choose to create your own page and invite others to review you. This is a great exercise to evaluate how we open up to others and reveal parts of ourselves as we grow in human interactions with them. It's not a conclusive or clinically proven method of knowing who you are, but it does provide interesting insights about how others view you, and you might just discover something you may not have perceived about yourself. The chart below explains how to interpret your results:

	Known to Self	**Not Known to Self**
Known to Others	This "Arena" quadrant encompasses characteristics or perceived personality traits that both you and others know about you. It is a window that opens only when we come to know others more intimately through relationship building and reciprocal self-revelation.	This "Blind Spot" is composed of perceived traits that you may not acknowledge you possess but others say that they recognize. A teacher or coach, for example, may see abilities and talents you have not yet discovered. Your colleagues may discern qualities you never knew you possessed.
Not Known to Others	This "Façade" quadrant comprises characteristics that you pick to describe yourself but no one else would. It includes things you alone know about youself, whether secrets, hidden hobbies, favorite foods, political or philosophical beliefs, and so forth.	This "Unknown" quadrant is filled with all the traits and qualities that are not used to describe you, whether by others or yourself. You may have a latent passion or undiscovered talent, which, if discovered, would cause that particular trait to move into another quadrant.

Part III

Build
"Brand You"

12

The Makeup of a Brand

"A brand is a collection of perceptions in the mind of the consumer."

—Building Brands Unlimited

*B*randing is a term that has many definitions and is used often in the business of marketing. I want to bring the concept of branding to a personal level. If you will embrace the principles of branding used by advertisers and apply them to your life, they will assist you in achieving clarity, maintaining consistency, and projecting your authentic self. Building Brands Unlimited defines branding as "a collection of perceptions in the mind of the consumer." This definition reflects the effect of branding on the message recipient—the consumer, in this case. I am committed to helping you see the internal meaning of branding, which is more than just an external mark to make something recognizable, as well as the necessity of building your personal brand.

Oprah Winfrey, Martha Stewart, Donald Trump, and Tyra Banks have something in common. Not only are they exceptional entrepreneurs and business professionals, but they have also harnessed and managed to project the purpose, value, attributes, and benefits that embody the essence of who they are. When we think of Oprah, we think, "Live Your Best Life"; we hear Martha Stewart's name and think of the how-to of living; Donald Trump connotes power, wealth, and business savoir faire; Tyra Banks brings to mind a role model for women, as well as the world of fashion.

Each of these individuals has a multitude of skills and attributes, but each chose to develop and "market" one or two in the same theme, projecting them to create a unique brand—an image or concept that comes to mind at the mere mention of their names.

We can think of actors, athletes, and entrepreneurs ad infinitum whose names conjure a brand. For example, Tiger Woods = champion golfer, Jack Welch = business visionary, Mary Kay = beauty and opportunity, Jenny Craig = weight loss. The list goes on. Each of these individuals has created a cohesive blend of qualities and skills that make up a brand in the mind of the "consumer," the general public.

When you shop for various items, you may remain loyal to a specific brand. That's the intended response, for every company's goal is to develop a brand that creates positive connotations in the consumers' minds and instills within them a sense of confidence in all products with that brand's label.

Conversely, you may develop brand disloyalty—the inherent assumption that you will be dissatisfied with a certain product—if you have a negative experience with a particular brand. The sum of your perceptions and opinions about a particular brand, whether positive or negative, will predict your likelihood of purchasing any products with that brand label.

Some brands begin with a significant scope of consumer loyalty only to lose it due to a faulty design or product recall. Other brands manage to maintain their positive image for years or even decades. Still others have what I call "eternal currency"—their influence and image has survived for centuries.

This status can apply to individuals, too. For example, Socrates, Gandhi, Martin Luther King Jr., and others have eternal currency; their "brands," or the impacts of their legacies, are still producing today. Those who have converted their personal values into eternal currency can know that their brands will continue to produce long after they have left the earth and will remain relevant through changing times and trends.

Brand Promise

Jesus Himself has the ultimate "eternal currency." The Bible speaks of Jesus as one who was sent to heal the brokenhearted; that was His purpose. *"The LORD has anointed Me to preach good tidings to the poor; He has sent me to heal the brokenhearted, to proclaim liberty to the captives, and the opening of the prison to those who are bound"* (Isaiah 61:1). Jesus modeled His values and delivered on His promise. He knew His assignment; it was clear to Him what He was to do: He did only what the Father instructed Him to do.

He maintained clarity about His purpose, which was to do the will of God. Jesus said to His disciples, *"I tell you the truth, the Son can do nothing by himself; he can do only what he sees his Father doing, because whatever the Father does the Son also does"* (John 5:19 NIV). Jesus could be the poster child for personal branding. I say this not to belittle His significance but to illustrate a point: Jesus was able to build an effective personal brand by fulfilling four primary goals listed in the above passage from Isaiah.

Your brand is a promise of value that others will receive from a product or service—it is the bridge between two points of reference. The first point of reference is your identity—who you are. The second point is your actions—who you are or what you do with consistency for others. When others think of you, they will conjure a general impression in their minds—this is your brand. What does it convey to them in terms of promised value?

An important part of branding, especially when it comes to products and services, is consistency. Consistency is a key promise of such companies as Starbucks, McDonald's, Wal-Mart, Wendy's, and Burger King. At any location or franchise, you receive consistently what they say you will. I expect the same quality and flavor of a double espresso from a Starbucks in Houston as I do from a Starbucks in Seattle, and I am disappointed when this expectation is not met. Companies can fail when products and services that are supposed to be consistent are not. It is important that you, too, project a consistent brand once you have perfected it.

What will you promise to deliver to the world? When a baby is born, one of the first ways in which his or her identity is recorded is by taking a set of footprints. These inky marks are evidence of that baby's uniqueness as an individual. Identical twins have identical DNA, but their fingerprints and footprints are distinctly different; each twin has his or her own identity and a unique imprint to make upon the world. Your unique footprints and fingerprints symbolize the unique imprint you alone can make on this earth. My questions to you include the following:

1. Where have your feet trod?

2. Have you left an impressionable imprint? Are you leaving imprints in your daily walk?

3. What difference will you make?

4. What path will you take?

5. What promise will others think of when they picture you (your brand)?

6. What indelible mark will you make on this world?

7. Will you represent excellence, commitment, gratitude, hard work, and compassion, or will your brand instead comprise a bad attitude, mediocrity, or the "just enough" principle?

Your brand promise is based on the clarity and the authenticity of who you are and what you promise to deliver or do.

Brand Value

The value of your brand is determined by what is valuable to you. For example, if you value recognition, you will gravitate toward activities and pursuits that afford the opportunity to demonstrate your skills so that others will be able to recognize your efforts and talents. If you value material things, you may work to acquire them through whatever means, whether moral or unscrupulous. If you value relationships, you will spend time honoring, trusting, forgiving, and investing in people in order to maintain them. You demonstrate your values through your behavior, so whatever you choose to value or deem important will be revealed by your actions.

Sometimes values and actions do not align. We discussed the importance of aligning our actions with our values; values are intrinsic beliefs with extrinsic demonstration. Jesus stood for His values—truth, righteousness, peace, the power of God, instruction, character, faith, and so forth—and He demonstrated these through love, compassion, forgiveness, strength, obedience, leadership, and action. How about you? Are your values affirmed by your actions?

1. What will you stand for?

2. What do you consider valuable?

3. Where do you spend your time? This will likely provide an accurate indication of what is valuable to you.

Brand Attributes

Your attributes are the unique features, characteristics, talents, and abilities that you possess and can convert into meaningful actions or contributions in the lives of others. Examples of attributes include dependability, focus, and assertiveness; being short or tall; a sense of humor, intelligence, intensity, compassion, discernment, optimism, and commitment. How will you deliver your message to the "market," or your sphere of influence? Jesus spent much of His time on earth developing His disciples and equipping them to go to every part of the world to spread the Good News. They were representatives who proliferated and popularized His brand.

1. How will you do what you do?

2. What will be your distribution method?

3. How do you work with others?

4. How will you execute your ideas?

5. What will you do to achieve your goals in life?

6. What makes you different, distinct, and unique?

7. What are your strengths?

8. How will you deliver your purpose and value to the world?

Brand Benefit

Benefits are related to how or what you do and the resulting positive effect on others. When we follow the example of Jesus and the Word of God, the benefits we receive include redemption, salvation, faith, righteousness, hope, belief, joy, healing, love, peace, and eternal life.

1. What benefits will you leave with others?

2. How will others profit from knowing you?

Recall my personal mission statement: "I am an advocate for the righteousness of a living God, proclaiming the gospel to all I meet so that they may accomplish their God-given destinies." An effective mission statement defines brand promise, brand value, brand attribute, and brand benefit, as shown below.

My Brand Promise: *Who am I?* I plead the cause of another; I seek opportunities to help others. *I am an advocate...*

My Brand Value: *What are my values?* I value righteousness and living a lifestyle that reflects the character and nature of God. *...for the righteousness of a living God...*

My Brand Attribute: *How do I do what I say I am?* I preach, teach, write, and communicate positive, uplifting messages while holding individuals accountable to reaching levels of excellence and self-knowledge. *...proclaiming the gospel to all I meet...*

My Brand Benefit: *How will others benefit from knowing me and my "brand"?* I am focused on giving others my best and being in the moment as I speak and take action for transformation in their lives, empowering them to identify, achieve, and excel in their purposes. ...*that they may accomplish their God-given purposes.*

Now, take a few minutes to write your own brand mission statement by asking yourself the following questions and thereby defining your brand promise, brand value, brand attributes, and brand benefit.

Who are you?

What are your values?

How do you do what you say you are?

How will others benefit from knowing you and your "brand"?

Personal branding positions you to establish, maintain, and protect your reputation, identity, image, and attitude. You will discover the power of your influence, contribution, and presence. Developing your brand will equip you to remove barriers that threaten your potential. If developed and managed effectively and positively, your brand will secure others' loyalty, drawing them to your side to offer support as you work to accomplish your goals.

13

Building "Brand You"

*"More people will know you than you think know you
primarily because they will know you by your reputation."*

—Richard Parsons

O n a brisk, winter morning, I arrived in Columbus Circle across from Central Park in Manhattan, New York, thrilled that I was about to meet with our friend, Richard Parsons. As I climbed up the steps from the subway, I feared that I would not make it to the meeting on time, having been detained that morning by many unexpected delays and distractions. But when I stepped onto the pavement and looked at the Time Warner Building, I felt like Mary Tyler Moore, marveling at the busy intersection and the fact that I was going to see Dick (Richard's nickname).

Richard Parsons is the chairman of the board at Time Warner, Inc., and he was also the CEO until stepping down in December 2007. Our meeting came a couple of months after the conclusion of his role as CEO. I admire his business acumen, boundless wisdom, and gentle demeanor; this was my moment, and I wanted to make it count. During our meeting, we talked about a number of topics and seven business ideologies in particular. I wanted to question him for suggestions that I could share immediately with the members of Woman Act Now during our weekly calls, as well as with you, my readers. Before we discuss more about the idea of personal branding, let me share with you the seven ideologies Dick and I discussed during our meeting.

Failure: Failure is essential, for if you never fail, it means that you haven't taken enough risks. Taking risks—and risking failure—is necessary if you desire to reach your full potential.

Dream Busters: You must believe in yourself. Belief in self will get you where you are going. Don't quit before you win.

Relationships: Relationships are the stuff of life. The older you get, the more closely your quality of life reflects the quality of your relationships. Life is made up of relationships.

Execution: This is a *sine qua non* without which no success can come about. Execution is where the rubber meets the road—and the road to hell is paved with good intentions. Merely intending to do good, without actually doing it, is of no value. Being successful without execution is impossible.

Women in Business: They're on the rise! Women are smart and intelligent; they're skilled at communicating and proficient at multitasking. Their time has come. Women must be ready for the change. A wave will come, ushering women into leadership positions in all sectors of business and politics.

Leadership: The single most important ingredient in a collective effort is providing vision.

Personal Branding: Take great care to establish, maintain, and protect your reputation, which is also a sort of personal brand. Your reputation is a vital and enduring thing, one that is also fragile and susceptible to the slightest stain. Your reputation should encompass the things that you value. More people will know you than you think know you primarily because they will know you by your reputation.

I was grateful to Dick for taking time to share his wisdom with me. When we talked about personal branding and he used the word *reputation*, I paused for a moment to reflect on his words. Further reflection a few days after our visit confirmed in my mind the necessity of writing more about personal branding in order to help other women understand its importance. We are going to discuss several aspects of your personal brand and how you can be the best in every aspect.

Define Your Reputation

The process of personal branding involves defining who you are so that other people won't do it for you. It means painting the clearest possible picture of yourself for others to see and to know. Your reputation is the shadow of your character that you project on the screen of your life. You must determine what type of reflection others will see. You must create the image that you want to project. Personal branding is not only about what others see—it is inherently related to who you are, underneath the visible surface. What others see must really be a part of your nature, your character, and who you truly are, so that your reputation will be strong and remain intact because of its integrity—its correspondence with who you really are underneath.

I agreed wholeheartedly when Dick identified reputation as an essential ingredient to branding. Your reputation is a treasure that must be protected. Some may say that you can't really control what other people say about you. This statement may be true; however, your reputation is about what you do and how you manage your behavior. Reputation represents the quality of work you produce and are known for producing.

For example, if you are a mother, you create a reputation with your children. Faithfully picking them up from school on time will convey to them that mommy is dependable, punctual, and trustworthy—and these attributes form the reputation that you have among them. In the same way, however, any negative behaviors that you repeatedly practice in relation to your children will form a corresponding reputation among them. If you rarely show up on time and consistently fail to keep your word to your children, your reputation with them will be far from positive.

Children are extremely perceptive. They may lack an ability to articulate what they observe or intuit, but their opinions will usually come across in unexpected ways. For example, your daughter may tell a classmate, "Mommy tells me she is going to come to our school play, but she doesn't really mean it." Children are able to predict their parents' behavior and responses based on consistent patterns. Even if they never say something as clear as, "I can't trust what Mommy tells me" or "Mommy does not keep commitments well," they form an assessment of you, which they implicitly convey to their peers, teachers, neighbors, and so forth.

In every environment in which you operate—at home, in the workplace, among your social networks, or at church—the other people in that environment will likely share a common perception of you, based upon the behavior you consistently demonstrate.

Building the "brand you" requires a commitment to your work product. Your work product tells others whether or not you have capacity to deliver on your promise. Your reputation is a reflection of your name, which is created by your actions.

The Bible speaks of the importance of reputation, saying, *"A good name is to be chosen rather than great riches"* (Proverbs 22:1). Reputation creation and maintenance is your responsibility. As Warren Buffett wisely stated, "It takes twenty years to build a reputation and five minutes to ruin it. If you think about that, you'll do things differently."

Take a moment to fill in the blanks on the chart to the right. The left column is a list of individuals; you are probably familiar with most of them, but some might be new to you. The aim of this exercise is to help you understand that even if we don't know someone intimately, we still form an opinion about him or her, usually based on reputation. In the corresponding blanks on the right side of the chart, record the first few words that come to mind to describe each individual, based on his or her reputation.

Individual	Reputation Key Words
Your mother	
Your father	
Your spouse	
Your manager/supervisor	
Brad Pitt	
Bill Gates	
Oprah Winfrey	
Gail, Oprah's best friend	
Juanita Bynum	
Howard Stern	
Joel Osteen	
Tiger Woods	
Paula Deen	

Now, take a few minutes to describe your own reputation among your family members, friends, and colleagues. List the five characteristics you most often hear others use to describe you.

_____

_____

_____

_____

_____

List five qualities you can express or actions you can take in order to improve your reputation.

_____

_____

_____

_____

Define Your Identity

Identity is valuable because it allows you to find your purpose. When we identify who we are, we gain a clearer understanding of what we are to do—and to be—in life. Most of the struggles we endure in life are fought around the issue of identity. Do you remember the example we used when we were talking about managing self-confidence—the attitude that says, *"This is just who I am"*? We often use this excuse to shield ourselves from the reality of who we truly are, a reality many of us would rather not face. We are constantly trying to figure out who we are. You may search for identity through many avenues—family, culture, education, careers, material possessions, or spirituality.

It is not what we know of ourselves that leaves us in a quandary, but it is all that lies within us that we have yet to discover that keeps us seeking God to learn the great and unsearchable things we do not know. It is in this search that we discover who and what we identify ourselves with, the people with whom we merge our likeness but not at the expense of our uniqueness. Your identity is in your uniqueness as a human being and your specific purpose for being here. The beauty of knowing who you are is freeing—you don't have to pretend in order to be "you," for you are your own, authentic self.

Define Your Plan

Planning your personal brand is twofold: you plan your future in the "now" and look forward to living it, even as you live in the now. Sound confusing? What I mean by this is that even when we try our best to make plans, to map out our lives, we find that life has plans of its own. As we read in Proverbs 16:9, *"In his heart a man plans his course, but the LORD determines his steps"* (NIV). We don't plan the unexpected—that's what makes it unexpected. But something unexpected happens every day.

One of my clients was recently barraged by unexpected events—many of her friends and family members passed away within a ninety-day period. Part of the coaching process I use with clients is helping them to plan their agendas with technological tools, such as an electronic calendar or a personal digital assistant (PDA). This particular client used a PDA, and when she consulted it, she had three weeks' worth of days planned and events scheduled. Three weeks prior to the first death of a family member, though, she had a clear plan of action that left no space for such a tragedy. The weeks following the death were filled with funeral preparations, burial, consoling family members, and dealing with other related issues. More important, the emotional toll of losing someone close, paired with the stress of reevaluating her priorities in order to rearrange her schedule, put a great deal of anxiety and pressure on her. Not only was she saddened and stressed, but she was also not meeting her goals. I told her to review the past pages in her calendar and compare them to the pages that life had dealt her in order to see how well she had actually handled the things that were important to her at the time. By the time I spoke with her that day, her "now" had finally caught up with her current to-do list.

Life has a way of making provision for the now. You will either learn how to take life's moments in stride, or you will find yourself living and rehearsing in your now what you could have done three weeks ago instead of doing it now. Building your "brand you" plan for your life requires forward vision paired with present-day flexibility to reevaluate, readjust, reaffirm, and recommit. Some things in life must be done immediately, in the moment; otherwise, they become dated or overdue. But when life deals you its own schedule of unplanned events, you will have no choice but to make room for them. For example, companies allow bereavement days so that employees may take the necessary time to readjust during times of unexpected hardship, loss, and sorrow. If you have a medical emergency, a household accident, or any other legitimate setback that keeps you from your other commitments, life makes adjustments.

Moving forward is crucial for proactive planning, which creates a road map of future desires, opportunities, or commitments. This is what I refer to as *planning in your now for your future, now*. It involves taking the time to think about what you want to do, where you ought to go, and how to keep your commitments to others. I want to refer you back to the chapter on clarity, in which we discussed S.M.A.R.T.E.R. goals. I will give you an abbreviated example here:

S: Goals Must Be Specific. A specific goal could be to increase sales revenue.

M: Goals Must Be Measurable. How much time, money, effort, or resources will be required to meet your goals? For example, if your general goal is to increase sales, your measurable goal is to make twenty sales calls a day.

A: We Must Be Held Accountable for Meeting Our Goals. Otherwise, our goals will disappear into oblivion. Share your goals with a manager, spouse, or team member, giving that person permission to ask you about how you're coming along and how soon you expect results.

R: Goals Must Be Realistic. Do you have enough prospects to make twenty sales calls a day? Evaluate your resources to make sure that achieving your goals is a feasible expectation.

T: Goals Should Be Time-based. You must carve out a specific time each day to make your twenty sales calls. You cannot set a goal without assigning a time to complete the necessary tasks. Time is movement. You must mark your time to take advantage of moving forward in time; otherwise, time will just pass you by, leaving you with nothing accomplished.

My mother has always insisted that it's best to do things immediately, for never again will you have the same moment or opportunity to redo them. The time you spend thinking about doing something, and even deciding to do it, will often occupy the time that you could have spent carrying out that particular thing.

I was a career student, and I would take occasional breaks from school. But my mother would always say, "If you'd just do it now, whatever effort you put into it, you will be closer to your goal. So, if you don't take fifteen units [credit hours], at least take three units so you can take advantage of this time."

E: Goals Should Be Pursued with Enthusiasm. Enthusiasm is essential for doing things that you may not like to do. As a sales manager, I can't recall one person who was absolutely excited about making sales calls. To be enthusiastic, you have to act *as if you are* enthusiastic; you have to pump up the energy. To encourage my salespeople to be more enthusiastic during sales calls, I would remove the chairs from their cubicles; when they were standing, they had more energy and made more enthusiastic calls.

R: Goals Should Be Rewarding. Learn how to celebrate your success. Think about what you would do to celebrate making those twenty calls. Would you hang a bell in your cubicle and ring it upon successful completion of your task? Could you give yourself a gold star in your planner every time you met your target? Perhaps you could buy yourself a Coke. The reward should be a part of your planning process, even before you start pursuing the goal.

14

"Brand You" Talent

In this new economy of distinction or extinction, as renowned business writer Tom Peters puts it, "you will eventually become extinct if you have no distinction about you." A new day calls for a new you! It is time to reinvent yourself. Living your best life is being the best *you* that you can be, all the time. This new economy's horizon looks very different from how it looked for our mothers and fathers four decades ago. They were encouraged to find their place in the mediocrity of corporate America as line employees or middle managers guaranteed a pension by a loyal company. I cannot imagine going to the same place day after day for forty years. Frankly, we don't have the opportunity or the privilege of doing so anymore. Employees are a company's most productive asset. In the previous chapter, we focused on developing talents and maximizing your strengths. Now, you must use your talents to the best of your ability. You have to view yourself as talent!

Speak this word out loud to yourself: *Talent!* Come on, what are your first thoughts when you say, "Talent"? Like most people who hear that word, you don't think immediately of yourself, do you? If you answered yes, prepare for a paradigm shift; when you finish reading this, you will be thinking thoughts such as *I am a great talent!* Remember, we develop talents by investing time, effort, and knowledge in our abilities or raw talents in order to convert them into strengths. You *become* the talent when you have fully developed your strengths and turned them into opportunities. You might hear others say about you, "She's got talent; she is gifted; she is highly skilled"—all clues that you *are* the *talent*.

Companies are looking for talent. Below are the mind-sets of talent—women who live above the level of mediocrity.

~Talent sees beyond the majority and its herd mentality; it thrives in the minority.

~Talent demonstrates excellence.

~Talent is forever learning.

~Talent is teachable.

~Talent is determined.

~Talent thinks in terms of the big picture.

~Talent evolves and improves.

~Talent contributes.

~Talent leads.

~Talent manages perceptions.

~Talent has presence.

~Talent is influential.

~Talent is courageous.

To be the talent, you can't go with the flow and you can't blend in; you make waves, and you make your mark on life!

15 "Brand You" Attitude

"Attitude is the invisible line between mediocrity and excellence."

—Marc Anderson

L aughter is your heart's way of making your face smile. Attitude is the external reflection of your inward thoughts, beliefs, and feelings towards a person, object, or ideology. If people tell you that you have a great attitude about life, are they saying that you are reacting positively to life's events, or do they mean that you are proactively positive by expecting life to yield the best outcomes possible? How would you respond if someone said that you had a bad attitude? Your instinct would be to defend yourself, stemming from the indignation you would likely feel: *How dare someone judge me about how I react to a situation?*

As I was writing about attitude, I realized that the topic is much more complex than all of the cute clichés would suggest— "Your attitude determines your altitude," "You can go only as far as your attitude will take you," "A winning attitude is essential to success," "Don't let your bad attitude get the best of you," and so forth. What do we mean when we use these phrases? Essentially, attitude is a mental construct. Even as I sit here in Seekers Coffee House in Hurst, Texas, I don't have a positive or negative attitude *about* attitude. I can quote a definition of *attitude* from a dictionary or thesaurus, but rather than consult a dictionary or thesaurus, I want to discover attitude for myself and pass it along to you.

Let's take a journey for a moment. Take out a sheet of paper and write the word *attitude* on it. Look at the word, taste it, see the word in action. First, I want you to write three things that come to your mind when you think of the word *attitude*.

1. _____
2. _____
3. _____

Second, write three things you see when you visualize the word *attitude* in action.

1. _____
2. _____
3. _____

The words you have written describe your beliefs about, thoughts of, feelings toward, and experiences with *attitude*. With these things in mind, look again at the words you listed. Do any of them describe how you perceive your personal attitude?

Let me give you some scenarios that will demonstrate how beliefs, thoughts, feelings, or experiences can shift your attitude.

☙

Scenario One

You are having breakfast at a restaurant, and you placed an order for bacon and eggs, asking specifically that the eggs be cooked as dry as the desert. The server arrives with your plate, over which your eggs are running messily. You bring the mistake to the server's attention, and he immediately acknowledges the error, apologizes, and takes your plate back to the serving window, asking the chef to put the eggs back on the griddle. The chef reacts angrily, accusing the server of making the second mistake on an order that day. The server responds, "No, *you* made the mistake—the ticket says 'cook well done.'"

How would you describe the attitudes of the server and the chef? How will the way that they handled the situation affect your attitude? (Remember, you're still sitting in that restaurant, waiting hungrily for your breakfast.)

_____

_____

_____

_____

_____

Scenario Two

You have a teenage daughter with whom you get along well, but you can't understand why she likes dressing in a "goth" style of clothing. She wears only black, even painting her fingernails and toenails with black polish. You think something must be wrong with her because you didn't raise her that way.

What attitude are you projecting when you disagree with her different styles? Do you feel disappointment, which is reflected in your attitude? Would it be possible for you to see the beauty in your daughter, regardless of her outward appearance, if you had a shift in your attitude?

_____

_____

_____

_____

Scenario Three

You walk into a department store, excited to use a $100 gift card toward a shopping spree. But when you step up to the sales counter, the sales associate does not even look up to acknowledge your presence.

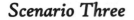

Will you perceive this as accidental or deliberate? How will your interpretation of the sales associate's lack of attentiveness affect your attitude?

_____

_____

_____

_____

_____

Consider each of the four scenarios above, all of which deal directly with your ability to process immediate information you receive and check your presuppositions, which are based on past experiences that have confirmed or validated your attitude. Our presuppositions form a mental construct in the back of the mind that helps us to validate our feelings or attitudes about various situations.

I want you to look at three of the scenarios again with a bit of new information and record if you have any attitude shifts. A significant shift in attitude is also called a paradigm shift—a change in perspective that causes you to view things differently and process information in new ways). Sometimes, learning a seemingly insignificant detail about a person or situation will utterly transform your opinion or viewpoint. In many cases, the more we understand, the more likely we will probably be to exhibit compassion or patience. Take note of any paradigm shifts caused by three revised scenarios.

Scenario One

You are having breakfast at a restaurant, and you place an order for bacon and eggs, asking specifically that the eggs be cooked as dry as the desert. The server brings your plate, and the eggs are runny and slimy. You catch the server's attention, and he immediately acknowledges the error, apologizes, and removes the plate.

He takes it to the serving window and asks the chef to put the eggs back on the griddle. The chef responds that this was the server's second mistake on an order that day. The server responds, "No, *you* made the mistake—the ticket says 'cook well done.'" He then returns to the table and apologizes to you for the exchange you just witnessed, explaining that it's the chef's first week on the job, and he's still somewhat nervous and prone to making mistakes.

Write down how you would respond in this scenario. Is your attitude different from your attitude toward the first version of this scenario? If so, how has it changed?

_____

_____

_____

_____

Scenario Two

You have a teenage daughter with whom you get along well, but you just can't understand why she likes to dress in a "goth" style of clothing. She wears only black, even painting her fingernails and toenails with black polish. You think something must be wrong with her, because you think to yourself, *I didn't raise her to dress that way.*

A friend of your daughter's notices how her fashion style has affected you, and she explains that your daughter is doing a school project that explores parental attitudes and how they are shaped by what their teenagers wear, and, in order to collect objective data, she couldn't tell you about it.

How do you feel about your daughter now that you expect her fashion choices to change back to normal once her school project is completed? Do you feel compelled to let her know you know what she is up to, or will you just play along until she tells you what's going on?

_____

_____

_____

_____

_____

Scenario Three

You walk into a department store, excited to use a $100 gift card toward a shopping spree. But when you step up to the sales counter, the sales associate does not even turn around to acknowledge your presence. Indignant, you pick up your things and are preparing to move to another register when you hear a sniffle and realize that the sales associate is crying.

How has your attitude changed? How are you likely to react now?

_____

_____

_____

_____

_____

⸙

The Truth about Attitude

Attitude is the gap that extends between what you really think about a person or situation and your ability to master your emotions in response to how you think or feel about that person. It is a mental construct that you display outwardly. It is revealed verbally in your words and comments, and it is revealed nonverbally in your facial expressions, body language, and actions. Other people will judge whether your words, nonverbal signs, and actions align with the situation in which you find yourself. Attitude is an engine that runs on emotional fuel and shifts gears to adjust when given new information.

Your attitude is not constant or unchanging, for as soon as you receive new information about a person or situation, your attitude changes. If you change your information, you change your attitude. Individuals who master their emotions can master their attitudes. Your attitude can serve as a lens through which others view you and form perceptions—sometimes perceptions that are completely inaccurate. Attitudes must be adjusted moment by moment.

Maintaining a healthy attitude requires that you do the following:

~Master your emotions.

~Make decisions based on facts.

~Live in the moment, being careful not to judge others without understanding.

~Be positive and optimistic.

~Believe the best in all situations.

~Ask yourself if a situation or problem is really that big a deal. Even if it isn't, try to forgive and let it go.

~Pursue excellence in everything you do.

16   *"Brand You" Power*

The power of your brand has much more to do with effectiveness and influence than brawn. In this chapter, we will discuss several different types of power that characterize any brand, as well as how to develop them in positive ways.

Power of Influence

Influence is measured by your ability to develop, affect, and manage interpersonal relationships. When you are influential, you may cause another person to shift his or her thoughts, ideas, or actions. Increasing your power of influence requires you to be dependable, consistent, respectful, and innovative; it often necessitates being somewhat of a risk taker in your workplace, family, and community. How do you increase your power of influence?

> ~Volunteer to create an agenda for a business meeting. By doing this, you'll position yourself as a person of influence, for you now have sway over what the meeting's content will be, as well as what direction it will take.

> ~Show up! If you want to build influence in your profession, join a trade association and show up regularly for chapter meetings. The more you show up, the more attention you will receive. Contribute, be actively involved, and seek leadership roles—locally, regionally, or even nationally.

~Be an active listener. Pay attention to others. People are hungry for genuine attention, and if you make it a point to engage in the moment with others, your influence level will skyrocket. By being an active listener, you communicate that you care about the person who is speaking. When others know that you care about them, and that you take an interest in what's important to them, they will continue to confide in you and consult you, thereby increasing your sway in their lives.

Power of Contribution

Never underestimate what you have to offer in any given situation. Adding your ideas to a conversation, asking a question, or giving of your talents, time, and treasures are invaluable contributions that you can share with others. I once attended a radio broadcast seminar as one of only two black women in attendance. The other woman's name was TJ. We had some similarities, but it was obvious that we were still completely different. The featured speaker was radio talk show host and political commentator Rush Limbaugh. After he concluded his presentation, he opened the floor for questions. TJ stood and asked a question, and Rush, before answering, commended her for asking such a great question.

When the session ended, several people approached me with congratulations for asking such an intelligent question. After correcting the first few people, telling them that I was not the one who asked the question, I gave up and simply thanked anyone else who approached me. Later, I found TJ and told her that I was living on her contribution. The benefit of contributing a question in front of an audience, as TJ did, is that it gives you a physical platform on which you are visible to everyone else. One woman who confused me with TJ told me that I should contact a radio executive; as an articulate black woman, I was in high demand. I confessed that I wasn't the woman she wanted to talk to.

I learned that day that if you want to cover a lot of ground quickly in a group situation, take the risk and ask a question. You will be known and remembered by all, even if they forget what you look like. Just make sure that you ask an insightful question, and the dividends will pay off well.

Power of Presence

Having a personal presence means being your "authentic" self all the time. It is not charisma or personality; it is being yourself, no matter the situation. More than what you are wearing or how you look, the genuine presence of your true personality will outweigh any first impressions others have of you that are based on superficial details. A first impression is what we make when we size up someone during the first few seconds before we are actually engaged with him or her. Unfortunately, we tend to make judgments of others based on how they look—what they're wearing, how short or tall they are, how much they weigh, the nature of their build, and so forth. But presence differs completely from mere physical attributes. Presence has to do with how you value yourself, how authentic you are, and how present you are in a given moment.

I was enjoying a cup of coffee in a coffeehouse in Palm Springs, California, when a middle-aged woman came in, ordered her coffee, and sat down next to me. Our eyes met, we acknowledged one another with a smile, and I greeted her, saying, "Good morning." As she sat there, I observed that she was reading *Gourmet* magazine. She was flipping briskly through the pages, and she didn't look as if she planned to stay long—she seemed pressed for time. Flipping faster through the pages, she started tearing recipes out of the magazine. I asked her if she was going to make meals from those recipes. Her reply was that someday she would cook the recipes. In the meantime, though, instead of holding on to the magazine, she would tear out the recipes and refer back to them at a later time.

As we talked, I commented on one of the pictures in the magazine that featured some sort of breakfast quiche with a half-cooked egg on top. I said that the recipe would have to be changed because that egg was too raw! She laughed, stood up, looked me in the eyes, and said, "Who are you?" I introduced myself. The woman then said that she had noticed me the moment that she walked into the coffeehouse. She further commented that I had a powerful presence about me. I thanked her, explaining that I enjoy life and people. I told her that I was visiting the area and mentioned that I was writing this book, after which she gave me her regards and wished me the best. I told her that it was a pleasure to meet her, and I wished her a terrific day.

After she left, I thought, *What was this thing she referred to as "presence"?* I think it was my ability to project an awareness of who I am, to be in the moment, and to express joy in my eyes and smile.

Answer the following questions honestly in order to gain a clearer perspective on how others perceive you:

~Do you have a strong sense of presence? What does it say to others about you?

~How do others react to you? Pay close attention to other people's immediate responses to you—your words, your actions, or simply your presence.

~Do you need to unwrinkle your brow and put a smile on your face so that you can reflect your true nature on the outside?

The Importance of "Brand You" Thinking

An essential practice for increasing your power is "brand you" thinking, which starts with what I call "quantum leap" thinking: eliminating any mental boxes, barriers, and presuppositions that threaten to limit your potential. It is the thinking realm of life but without limits. The sky is not your limit; your lack of breath is your limit in this life. As long as you can breathe, you can think without limits. Be a bigger thinker by thinking through the lens of now—what is in front of you? What decisions have to be made? What choices do you have today? How do you become a big thinker?

1. Arrest every intention and thought in your mind, inspect it carefully, and act only on the thoughts that will produce positive results. Destroy any thoughts that will not produce such results. The way to destroy a thought is by choosing not to act on it.

2. Use your mind as the powerful tool that it is. Resist going with the flow. The flow comprises the mass of humanity—most people think that they're out of the flow, but the reality is that they *are* the flow. Being a part of the flow is infinitely easier than standing alone as an independent individual. I am not suggesting that you become a difficult person who questions everyone and everything, but I do want you to expect others to perceive you as someone who goes against the flow, to be someone who thinks, asks questions, and seeks answers to make informed choices. If you go with the flow, you demonstrate an attitude that says, "My ideas aren't important; I don't want to think too hard; the accepted way of doing things is working well, so why rock the boat?"

3. Give your mind permission to see and hear things differently. Approach life with a determination to discover your purpose in each moment. Discoveries are made only by giving your mind permission to look at things in a new way.

4. Think bigger! Avoid filtering your thinking through the limitations of the lens of your past.

5. Adopt an asset-based way of thinking, which starts by changing the way you see things. Asset-based thinking means seeing the benefit of all things. Deficit-based thinking starts with negative ideas, thoughts, and limitations. Visit www.assetbasedthinking.com to learn more about how you can train yourself to be an asset-based thinker. The following are a few examples of the thoughts

and attitudes of deficit-based thinkers versus those of asset-based thinkers:

Deficit-based Thinker

She's too old for the job.

That will never work!

I am too young to start my own company.

Asset-based Thinker

She's experienced and knowledgeable; she can help us get up to speed quickly.

Let's see how we can get it done.

This is a great time to start my own company; I have youthful vitality on my side!

The Importance of Thinking Big

I will close this chapter with a fitting story that I have embellished somewhat in order to illustrate my point. The story was relayed to me by my husband, Richmond, after he heard a sermon by Bill Winston on thinking bigger.

A highly respected businessman went on a trip to the country of Dubai, which is fast becoming a financial hub in the Middle East. The businessman had been hired by a company in Dubai to assist with engineering the tallest skyscraper in the world. As an engineer, he had a reputation for overcoming the impossible. He met with the team in Dubai and shared his strategies with them—and they were elated. The other men asked him, "What can we do for you?" to which he replied, "A golf club would be nice." They shared departing pleasantries, and he went about his business.

Two days passed, and the businessman had not heard from the other men, nor did he give his request much thought. On the third day, the men went to his hotel, called him down, and said, "We want to take you for a ride." They drove along, then pulled into a beautiful, sprawling, palm tree-lined driveway with rock fountains on each side. The place looked like a palace; it was elegant beyond description. The businessman stood there with his mouth open, not able to utter a single word. He had visited palatial golf courses all over the world, but never had he seen anything with this level of grandeur. The men looked at him and asked, "How do you like it?" "It is breathtaking," he replied. "It is yours," they told him. "Wait a minute—what do you mean?" the man sputtered. They responded, "You asked for a golf club, so here you are—this belongs to you." He said, "I can't believe this! I was only speaking of a seven iron."

∞

With whom in this story do you identify more closely—the big thinker (any member of the Dubai team) or the small thinker (the businessman)?

17 "Brand You" Relationships

"Don't let a dispute permanently injure a great relationship, especially if you don't have all the facts."

—Anna McCoy

Relationships are the stuff of life, as Dick Parsons pointed out to me. They are essential to our existence. We are the sum of all the relationships—good and bad alike—that have touched our lives. When I was featured on the cover of *Beautiful One Magazine*, I sent out a few hundred copies of the publication to people I knew. I value relationships, and I am thankful that so many wonderful people have invested themselves in my life. I started thinking of all the individuals who would be blessed if they received a magazine, even if I had not spoken with them in years. I looked into my Rolodex of time and sent magazines to the following women: Rose Norman, the woman who allowed my industrious spirit to blossom for extra money; Maxine Duff, my high school English teacher, who epitomized excellence and discipline in all she did and encouraged me to grow academically; and Senfronia Thompson, whom I admired from the moment I met her, and who eventually embraced me as her goddaughter, teaching me how to speak in front of others, dine in fine restaurants, and be self-assured.

The responses I received from some of these magazine recipients included, "I am proud of you," "Thank you for sharing your success," "You represent the kingdom well," and "The article demonstrates the consistency of your character and work ethic; thank you for remembering me."

Relationships are seasonal. Each of the relationships I mentioned above had an active season in my life. It is important to honor your relationships, both in and out of season. In order for any relationship to thrive and be productive, it must embody the following characteristics:

~Respect for one another and your differences.

~Source of value for both individuals.

~Giving and receiving.

~Willingness to compromise when disputes arise and to resolve disagreements.

Workplace Relationships

Workplace relationships add a whole additional layer of required characteristics. To enjoy successful relationships in your workplace, practice the following guidelines:

1. Observe all four elements necessary for every fruitful relationship, as listed above.

2. Do not assume that your workplace will provide your social stimulation or meet your social needs.

3. Avoid intimate relationships with coworkers, period! The risk is far greater than the benefit of hoping you will meet your soul mate at work. So, don't even have an open mind or heart to the possibility.

4. Meet your agreements, or readjust the deadlines accordingly.

5. Maintain professionalism at all times. Be careful about being too casual in dress or behavior; avoid slang when speaking; try not to speak any foreign languages in the

presence of others who will not understand you, as this is unfair and disrespectful.

6. Be a team player; don't worry about who gets the credit.

7. Give more than required! You will always benefit in the long run.

Family Relationships

A successful family relationship will include portions of the above, as well as the following:

1. Be honorable with your children, spouse, and extended family members.

2. Teach integrity by practicing it. Be a woman of your word at home, first of all, and you will do exceedingly well at keeping your word in the marketplace.

3. Keep commitments to your children, and you will teach them how to keep commitments to others. Unfortunately, many parents view themselves as bosses who don't have to be held accountable for keeping their words to their children.

18

"Brand You" Image

Most companies expect their employees to dress a certain way, to maintain a certain level of sartorial professionalism. Regardless of the nature of your work or the quality of your performance on the job, people will question your business judgment if you have poor fashion judgment. Furthermore, the appropriateness of your attire will directly affect the amount of face time your manager or supervisor will grant you in front of superiors and clients; therefore, the way you dress has an impact on your career path and professional development. Research shows that based on their judgments of your appearance, other people will make assumptions about seven aspects of your life: income, education, social status, sophistication level, success, moral character, and trustworthiness.

We each have several brand images, depending on the role we are playing at a particular time. If you are a mother, your brand look around the house may differ greatly from your brand look in the workplace. It is important that you manage your looks to complement the role in which you are engaged. In this book, we will focus on enhancing your "brand you" image in the workplace, but even if you are a stay-at-home mom, you still must be mindful of your brand image.

Taking special care with your appearance will get you further in the workplace, especially today, when many work environments are becoming casual. Some have even crossed the line to a less than professional sense of casual. In the members area of the Woman Act

Now Web site, we address various subject matters, including business etiquette. An overwhelming number of members expressed how casual dress has added to the decline of professionalism, customer service, and productivity in the workplace. During one of our monthly meetings, I asked the group to tell me what a woman communicates to her colleagues and clients when she comes to work looking as if she's just rolled out of bed. The audience replied that this is offensive; she's communicating that she doesn't care about what others think of her, and she doesn't care about herself. Showing up to work disheveled is disrespectful to one's company, colleagues, clients, and customers. It also shows a lack of respect for oneself.

Creating the Right Impression

What does your appearance say about you? Do you dress to impress, or dress up only by request? How can you know what is appropriate to wear (and what you shouldn't wear) when entering a new work environment, or even when adapting to your current environment? If you are a company owner or president, your apparel should project what you want to see reflected in others. If you are ever in doubt, err on the side of dressing conservatively. Avoid being overdressed or underdressed in your environment. Dress appropriately for the position and the company culture.

There are at least five areas you should consider aligning when planning how you will appear before a company or organization. Most people want their personal styles to reflect who they are. The important thing is to be who you are and not to let your clothing convey a message about you that is not accurate. Your objective should be to find a balance between your own personal style and the style expected of you at work; merge the two together for an ideal outcome. The chart below will allow you to sort through your personal preferences and help you to incorporate them into what works for your company and work environment.

Look at the examples below on how to identify *what works for work* by finding a compromise when personal preference and workplace dress codes conflict. Then, fill in your own chart on the following page.

	What I Like	What's Expected of Me at Work	What Will Work
Attire	Trendy and somewhat wild	Business casual	Business casual clothes that are chic and trendy, too
Jewelry	Extra-large hoop earrings	Anything that fits the category of "understated elegance"	Gold or silver medium-sized hoops
Adornments	Nose ring and navel ring (showing, of course; it's sexy)	No piercings or tattoos may be exposed	Nose ring removed during work hours; no midriff shirts
Hairstyle	Dyed bright colors: purple with streaks of orange, etc.	Natural-looking shades of brown, black, blonde, or grey	Hair dyed one of the preferred shades.
Hygiene	I go natural—no antiperspirant or perfume for me!	Clean and well-groomed	Use natural deodorant and organic products to minimize body odor

	What I Like	What's Expected of Me at Work	What Will Work
Attire			
Jewelry			
Adornments			
Hairstyle			
Hygiene			

Even if you believe that how you dress has little to do with how you perform the job you were hired to do, keep in mind that most companies don't hire individuals just to do specific tasks; they hire individuals in hopes that they will mirror the company's mission, vision, values, and corporate culture.

You must remember that you are hired to do a job, blend in with a corporate culture, and fit within that culture's construct. When you accept a job, you also accept the identity of the organization, and that identity becomes a personal part of who you are during working hours. Many people have problems with being effective in the marketplace because they want their own identities to define the company's identity; unfortunately for them, that's not the way it works.

Learning how to effectively merge the look of your brand with the look of your company's brand will prove the greatest possible enhancement to your personal brand during the time you are representing your organization. I can't count the number of receptionists and administrative assistants who lost their way, conveying one image the day they were interviewed and a completely different image their second week on the job. Something happens to them in the in-between days, and sometimes the change is so drastic that you wonder, *Who's the new temp?* when the woman seated behind the desk is the same one you hired two weeks ago. Seek to understand the acceptable look at your company in order to find a comfortable balance between your brand look and the company's identity (how they hope you will look as you represent them).

Dress for Success: Some General Guidelines

Regardless of where you work and the duties your position entails, the following guidelines are almost always applicable and, if followed, will enable you to make a good impression, not only on the job, but also in society at large.

~**Always be professional** at work, with clients, on company outings, and everywhere. Avoid drinking alcohol, especially if you can't handle yourself under the influence—your actions will follow you to the office on Monday morning.

~**Dress for different levels** when meeting with individuals from different levels of management. If you are meeting with a company executive and the dress code is corporate attire, dress accordingly. Even in a casual dress environment, wearing a suit every once in a while is helpful to let others know what you aspire to be.

~Bring a spare business outfit to the office. Make sure you are prepared to meet with any client or to upgrade your wardrobe at a moment's notice.

~Go easy on the makeup. If others comment on your makeup, then it is too heavy. Seek assistance or call your neighborhood Avon or Mary Kay specialist to arrange a cosmetics consultation or to ask for advice. You might also try hauteface.com, where you can find a great all-in-one makeup color disc for every woman.

~Avoid those memorable hairstyles. I know you have that Friday night club hairdo, but ask yourself if it is appropriate for the office—*before* Monday morning arrives, and regardless of how much you paid for it. Remember, pigtails are never acceptable in the corporate workplace. I was mortified when one of our executive administrators came in on a casual Friday wearing overall shorts, her hair in pigtails. I asked her what in the world she was thinking, then sent her home to change before the arrival of the CEO (who probably would have sent her home permanently).

~Check your skirt length, ladies. Often we forget to think of how others feel when we show off our shapely legs. We think only about how comfortable our clothing style is for us, forgetting that what we wear can have an effect on the comfort level of others. The bottom of your skirt should be no more than one hand's length above your knees. If your skirt is any shorter than that, you have forgotten what happens when you sit down! Try this test: wrap your hand around your knee, and if your skirt doesn't touch your hand, you might want to rethink your outfit.

~**Just say no to crack.** Perform the crack test on your upper chest area and your belt line. If, when you look down, you can see your cleavage, this means that others can see it, too. For those women who are heavily endowed at the bustline, visible cleavage is almost unavoidable in current fashions—low-cut shirts, plunging necklines, V-necks, and so forth. Shop instead for turtleneck tops, boat necks, and other tops that are less revealing. Try this other "crack" test: if, when you bend over, you can feel a draft at your waistline, put on a longer shirt or jacket that will conceal the top of your derriere. You never know when you'll be in a position that might expose it to your colleagues, or, God forbid, your manager. Ask yourself what profit to you there is in showing your crack in the workplace. Most men and women find it distracting, even disgusting. If you insist on showing the crack in the back, get a plumber's job!

~**Avoid eating during your work hours.** Most companies have assigned break times. Honor them. For example, you make a poor impression if you arrive late for work, then sit at your desk and eat breakfast during company time.

~**Turn off your cell phone or PDA during work hours.** If family members or friends want to reach you during office hours, they should call your work number. Consider telling them to contact you only in case of an emergency, or they may just want to chitchat.

~**Do not listen to music,** hum, whistle, or sing out loud when you are at your desk.

~**Avoid slang terms and offensive language.** Showing that you're "in the know" by using terms that are hip or abbreviated will only hurt your image, and it may even cause others to wonder whether you are adequately articulate, mature, and sophisticated to handle clients, responsibility, or leadership.

Your "brand you" image reflects the image that you want others to see and the impression you want them to form about you. It is not just what you wear, but it is also how you speak and handle yourself in various situations. Be the best brand you can be!

❧

19

"Brand You" Money

"Your word is your currency!"

—Richmond McCoy

During the first few years my husband, Richmond, and I were developing a new business, UrbanAmerica, I learned an important principle: your word is your currency. This I discovered by observing Richmond in his business dealings. Richmond received a phone call from a broker who was negotiating a real estate deal for him and said, "This seller must really like you because he required that the buyer pay a $100,000 non-refundable deposit to secure the offer." When the seller found out that the broker was representing Richmond McCoy, he said, "I know Richmond! Never mind that deposit; he is a man of his word." Richmond's word was his currency; because he is known as a man of integrity who fulfills his promises and keeps his commitments, his word was enough to act as a deposit. Favor and a good name are far greater than all the money you have. (See Proverbs 22:1.) Richmond's word had become his currency; it was as good as gold and allowed him to proceed with the transaction without having to use cash.

At the time of writing this book, the U.S. economy was in a tailspin from failed financial institutions, increasing oil prices, job losses, and a meltdown on Wall Street. Witnessing great companies like Bear Stearns, Lehman Brothers, Washington Mutual, Merrill Lynch, and others falter left me in a quandary, and the importance of investing in the stock market and planning for retirement seem difficult topics to write about, as pertinent advice changes with every twist and turn of the economy. However, I want to share with you a few principles about money that will help you survive difficult times and flourish during easier times.

Be a Woman of Integrity

The foundation of building your "brand you" money is being a woman of your word. I am convinced that many of the difficult situations in which we find ourselves, often due to poor or ill-informed choices we have made, stem from a lack of integrity or a lack of self-credibility. This chapter will teach you how to use money as a tool in order to become a money manager who converts her word and its credibility into wealth.

Money Is a Tool

Money is a tool that we can use when negotiating our needs and wants in the marketplace and maximizing opportunities to build wealth. The primary function of money is transactional, meaning that you will give or receive something in exchange for value. In itself, money is neutral; it acts at the discretion of those who possess it and direct its flow. Your financial success depends largely on how well you give instructions to your money; you, not your dollars and cents, are in charge. Your money will never tell you, "Buy this dress" or "Splurge on that trendy purse"; rather, your mind generates instructions of this sort. Mastering your money requires that you become an expert at keeping your word, exercise common sense, practice discipline, and make sound financial choices that will benefit your future.

Be a Money Manager

Deuteronomy 8:18 says, *"And you shall remember the LORD your God, for it is He who gives you power to get wealth, that He may establish His covenant which He swore to your fathers, as it is this day."* We are money managers, or stewards, of the money we earn or receive. It is our responsibility to ensure that we manage our money well. Think of it this way: money has no value unless it is converted into goods or services by way of purchasing, or exchanging. You probably have coins lying around your house that you think little of, but if you collected and counted them, you would place a higher value on them if they were your sole source of gas money. As long as they are scattered around the house—a quarter here, a dime there—they do not serve a valuable function. We must collect, count, and convert them into purchasing power.

Think like a money manager. Think like a steward. Accept the responsibility of making wise decisions about what to spend and what to save. The fruits of sound money management are the reproduction, duplication, or increase of what you have. Poor money managers come up short; they tend to make decisions that are detrimental not only to themselves, but to others, as well. Some centuries-old financial companies have demonstrated poor money management and unethical practices; their greed and excessive executive compensation comes at the expense of stockholders, shareholders, taxpayers, and so on. The rise in bankruptcy, foreclosures, and credit card debt are evidence of consumers' poor decisions regarding money management.

The key to avoiding such pitfalls is properly managing what you have, not making excuses. I have heard the stories before: "Well, I don't make that much money anyway," "I am robbing Peter to pay Paul," "I have to do anything I can in order to make ends meet," "I am going to get my children the best of everything, no matter the cost," "I don't know anything about finances; I'm just doing the best I can." These are sorry excuses for poor money management and financial ignorance. Remember, you do know a lot about money, starting with what you've read in the Bible. Let's look at a familiar parable about investment, found in the gospel of Matthew:

> *It's also like a man going off on an extended trip. He called*
> *his servants together and delegated responsibilities. To one he*

gave five thousand dollars, to another two thousand, to a third one thousand, depending on their abilities. Then he left. Right off, the first servant went to work and doubled his master's investment. The second did the same. But the man with the single thousand dug a hole and carefully buried his master's money. After a long absence, the master of those three servants came back and settled up with them. The one given five thousand dollars showed him how he had doubled his investment. His master commended him: "Good work! You did your job well. From now on be my partner." The servant with the two thousand showed how he also had doubled his master's investment. His master commended him: "Good work! You did your job well. From now on be my partner." The servant given one thousand said, "Master, I know you have high standards and hate careless ways, that you demand the best and make no allowances for error. I was afraid I might disappoint you, so I found a good hiding place and secured your money. Here it is, safe and sound down to the last cent." The master was furious. "That's a terrible way to live! It's criminal to live cautiously like that! If you knew I was after the best, why did you do less than the least? The least you could have done would have been to invest the sum with the bankers, where at least I would have gotten a little interest. Take the thousand and give it to the one who risked the most. And get rid of this "play-it-safe" who won't go out on a limb. Throw him out into utter darkness."

(Matthew 25:14–30 MSG)

Principles of a Money Manager

~Take responsibility for what you earn or receive.

~Manage according to your ability.

~Put your money to work immediately.

~Don't neglect opportunities to use your finances productively; you will miss out if you bury yourself deeper in debt rather than reproduce, like the third servant.

~Give an account for what you have done with your money, whether to yourself, your spouse, or your family.

~Avoid careless expenditures.

~Exchange your money for things of value, even if it means you earn only 1 percent interest in a savings account; make your money productive.

~Take responsible risks that will yield the greatest rewards. Invest in the stock market, invest in enterprise, invest in moneymaking partnerships, reproduce, and avoid consuming all that you have.

Eschew Consumption Behavior

Consumption behavior is like the last servant who buried the money because he was afraid something would happen to it. Instead of burying our money, we bury ourselves in the debt graveyard by purchasing depreciating assets such as cars, clothes, and furniture, which immediately start to lose value. On the inside, we feel great; on the outside, we look great to others. But if the truth is that we have no savings, then we have little or no ability to reproduce the money we have earned or have received, and then we neither look nor feel so good.

Eliminate Your Excuses

Enough! Stop making excuses for your poor financial choices. It's time to face the consequences. The excuse "I was never taught about money" is a myth that you can no longer use to justify poor choices. If you can add and subtract, you have 75 percent of what you need in order to manage your money well. You have a passing grade, and you can achieve the remaining 25 percent by working to make better choices, investing, and saving for a rainy day. It's simple math, really. You don't need to be a mathematician to figure out that you shouldn't spend more money than you bring into your household. Whenever possible, use cash rather than a credit or debit card; when the money you're spending is tangible, you will be less likely to overspend. If you are paying with cash at the grocery store, you can spend only as much as you have. If you are using a credit card, overspending is easy; one swipe and you're covered—until the bill arrives. Start resisting some of those purchases you know that you can't afford; stop relying on credit cards and delaying payments. We must become smarter about what we buy and how we pay for it. Remember: income minus expenses = cash flow! What this formula means is that if you have any cash leftover after you pay your expenses, you may have just enough to flow over into the following month; you may have more than enough to flow into creating something of value.

Convert Your Word into Currency

Convert your word (intellectual and spiritual capital) into something of value. Convert your talent into something of value. Convert your faith into spiritual capital, which is far more valuable than talent and intellect. Spiritual capital, when converted, brings favor with God and man, and favor is always more valuable than money. Managing your money effectively requires that you grasp the necessity of conversion. Like the coins I mentioned earlier, mere objects—not just dollar bills or personal checks—must be converted to more valuable use. In the process of managing your money, your intention should be to convert what you have as many times as you can in order to produce the most fruitful results possible.

I want to explain how we can begin to convert our word (our talents and gifts) into currency. The following explanation describes the process by which we convert our word to wealth.

Your Word Yields Human, Intellectual, and Spiritual Capital

You have three valuable assets to start with, and how you develop them determines the way in which you will move through this process of conversion. To convert something means to transform it into another form. This conversion process takes what you have and transforms it into something of even greater value. *Human capital* encompasses your raw talents and gifts. *Intellectual capital* includes how you think and process information. And *spiritual capital* is what you believe; your eternal inheritance as a child of God. Maximizing your spiritual capital is in your ability to convert God's Word into practical application.

Strengths Yield Opportunities

Earlier, we discussed the importance of following your strengths and converting them into opportunities. As you build your human capital, intellectual capital, and spiritual capital, you must work on converting them into strengths by executing your talents and gifts in the marketplace. Your strength is manifest when you invest time in practicing your talents, developing your skills, and building your knowledge base. When you are able to achieve nearly perfect performance, your strengths can be converted to opportunities.

Opportunities Yield Income

Converting your strengths into opportunities yields income. Many people stop at this stage and become complacent with their levels of achievement, but complacency does not generate additional opportunities. I hope that you have read at least one book by Robert "Rich Dad" Kiyosaki, *Cashflow Quadrant* in particular. In this book, Kiyosaki instructs readers about such tactics as leverage and expansion while trying to encourage them to move from the position of employee, living on earned income, to that of an investor, living on passive income.

The stage of converting our talents into opportunities and opportunities into income is just the beginning. We must go further. Some will reach the summit of wealth before others, but what keeps us all from moving forward is consumerism. America's financial system is driven by consumption, and although consumption fuels the economy, some people consume so much that they are unable to climb up the pyramid of wealth generation. My message to you is this: Woman, take the leap! The average savings of single women in this country is a mere 1 percent of their incomes. If the average median income is forty thousand dollars, the typical single woman sets aside four hundred dollars in savings each year. This does not build wealth at a significant rate.

As my friend Brooke Stephens, an author, speaker, and financial adviser, points out in her book *Talking Dollars and Making Sense*, "Making money is important, but saving it is more important." She cautions that while the African American community can be proud about having contributed hundreds of billions to the nation's economy, it is crucial for them not to lose sight of the importance of savings in creating economic empowerment and building personal wealth. "You're not building wealth if you use all your money for consumption," Stephens writes. "Real wealth is being able to say, 'I have the freedom to do what I want with my life, and I don't have to stay in this job if I don't want to.'"

Many of us would like for that last statement to ring true for us, but few are really willing to sacrifice the "get now, pay later" mentality in order to invest in things of value. This attitude of impatient consumption is another way of saying, in essence, "I would rather live the debt-ridden life than the debt-free life." Debt-free living comes only to those wise enough to build their cash reserves, invest in assets that appreciate, and resist spending money on wants rather than needs. So, in order to convert your income into capital or appreciating assets, you will have to hold on to adequate cash rather than spending it.

Income Yields Capital

Before your income can be converted into capital, or assets, you must acquire the right types of assets. There are four types of assets that we can acquire:

Personal property: *Personal possessions of value, such as cars, clothing, jewelry, and furniture.*

Liquid assets: *hard cash and money stored in checking, savings, and money market accounts.*

Real property: *Houses, tracts of land, etc.*

Investment: *Retirement plans, stocks, bonds, annuities, business, enterprise, pension.*

Three of the four types of assets will get you closer to converting than the first, personal property, which, though it's considered an asset, includes items that are called "depreciating assets." As stated earlier, these items depreciate in value from the moment you purchase them; they become true assets only if you pay them off or sell them and thereby increase the value of your liquid assets. In order to increase the other three types of assets, we must curtail our personal property expenditures, buying only what we truly need.

Look around your house and take an account of your personal property, then estimate how much cash you exchanged for all that stuff (not forgetting about all those things piled in your garage or packed in the storage space you had to rent). Your detailed inventory should examine such details as the number of television sets you have, the varieties of video games you own, and the dozens of shoes you wear (or don't wear but bought and kept anyway). You should be getting the picture. It's time to stop amassing personal property like a squirrel hordes acorns for the winter so that we can save more and invest more in our dreams.

Your Capital Converted Yields Enterprise

Stop the money bleeding induced by materialism (a preoccupation with purchasing things but never to the point of satisfaction) and start investing in your dreams, whether of starting a business, running for office, writing a book, recording an album, or pursuing some other meaningful endeavor. In doing this, you take the first step toward creating wealth. When you create wealth, you give yourself the freedom to focus on dreams rather than survival; instead of "just getting by," you just fly!

While we cannot all attain the same level of wealth, we must keep in mind that wealth is not our ultimate goal. We are all capable of taking the necessary steps to make this climb and to pursue wealth through responsible financial habits. And each of us has a limitless potential for spiritual wealth—salvation is for all, regardless of financial resources. If we convert our spiritual capital into faith, we receive God's favor and climb higher than our wildest dreams could ever conjure. If it comes down to seeking God or increasing your salary, you know where your loyalties must lie. As Jesus told us, *"No one can serve two masters....You cannot serve both God and Money"* (Matthew 6:24 NIV).

The process of converting your word to wealth is not a get-rich-quick scheme but instead a strategy for successfully building your "brand you" money. Converting your assets into value and investing resources in your ideas are yours by right as an American citizen. Your rights include the ability to participate in free enterprise. The foundation of our country's economy still operates on our word. We transact business with other individuals or entities based on an agreement of words regarding the exchange of products and services in the marketplace. Exercise your right to participate in free enterprise by saving more than you spend and acquiring valuable assets you can exchange in order to build an enterprise or business that will yield you profits.

Enterprise Converted Yields Profit

Successful execution of your business plan, project proposal, book manuscript, or other dream will yield a profit, whether monetary or in terms of self-esteem, recognition, renown, or gain in another arena. These profits, if monetary, can then be invested in other enterprises, or stocks, bonds, or other long-term investments. If your profit is a boost in self-esteem, invest time in the life of another individual and offer encouragement so that she, too, may experience a similar boost. If your profit is increased recognition and renown in a particular community, use this recognition as a means of generating more opportunities to promote yourself, your product, or your book. Even if your profit is nothing more than a line added to your résumé, that increase is not insignificant. Every step counts!

Profit Converted Yields Wealth (Passive Income)

Passive income is income you acquire when you have invested in opportunities that do not require you to exert time and effort. Your invested money works for you, usually by earning interest. Passive income allows you to spend time doing what really matters to you rather than working 24/7 to amass wealth. When you reach this level, you are building wealth not only for yourself, but also for generations to come.

The chart below will help you to visualize the flow of the conversion process we just discussed.

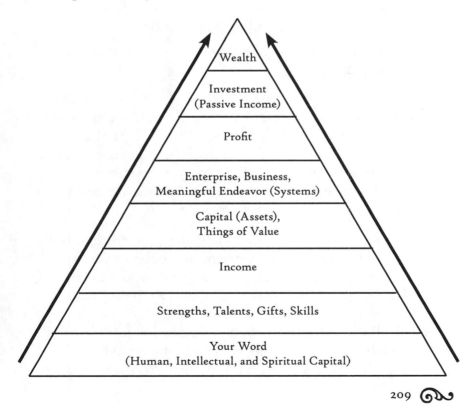

Plan for Your Financial Future

It is crucial to manage and eliminate debt. Managing debt is twofold. First, we want to live our lives free of debt, owing nothing but love to anyone. (See Romans 13:8.) Being debt free is important because it allows you to live a life of purpose and destiny; the chains of debt will choke you and keep you from breathing freely and living in your "now." Debt is one way that your past catches up with you in the now. All those purchases you made with plastic come back to haunt you. Debt is the evidence of choices you made that still follow you in your now and will often limit your outlook on the possibilities that exist for you.

Prepare a budget.

~Develop a needs-based budget that enables you to buy what you need and be disciplined with your spending.

Strive to eliminate debt.

~Stop the fiscal bleeding by limiting credit card use. Pay with cash instead.

~Keep track of your spending so that you can create a realistic budget. I suggest carrying a small notebook in which you can record your expenditures. At womanact-now.com, you can take advantage of the expense tracker, an automated system that records your purchases and expenditures every time you call in. You can access your up-to-date balance online at any time.

~Pay down your debt. Make a list of all your creditors, due dates, and interest rates. Start paying off your accounts with the highest interest rates. Pay a few low balance, high interest-rate bills first so that you can make progress and experience some success. Then, take the money previously allocated for the account balances you just paid off and apply it to another bill until each one is paid off. The average family has about ten thousand dollars' worth of debt, and it takes a lot longer to pay off than to accumulate. You cannot afford to pay the minimum balance; it is far too costly in the long run. Paying off your debt as soon as possible not only gives you freedom, but it also gives you the opportunity to become a debt convertor. The more you pay consistently over the minimum amount the faster you will pay down your debt.

Increase cash flow.

~Create different revenue streams. Often, more income is required for us to be able to pay off debt, which is usually why people find themselves living from paycheck to paycheck. The only way to change the equation is to increase your income and reduce your expenses. Don't expect a miracle or a life-saving lottery check; you must take responsibility and cut back accordingly on your spending. If you cannot meet or exceed your expenses with what you save by cutting back, your only recourse is creating more income. This can be achieved by a number of means, including the following:

~Check your payroll deductions. If you find that you consistently receive tax refunds, your withholdings are excessive. If you receive twelve hundred dollars or more in refunds, you can increase your cash flow immediately by talking with someone in your human resources department at work and asking that person to adjust your withholdings.

~Start that business you have been putting off.

~Get a part-time job.

~Organize a neighborhood garage sale.

~Sell your unused or valuable collectors' items on eBay.

~Consider a network marketing or multilevel marketing opportunity. Do your research and choose a product or service that you believe in, and make sure that it does not require you to carry any inventory in order to be an active member. Be wary of elevated signup fees, keeping in mind that most businesses can work, but your success depends on your commitment to working the business.

~If you have a Web site, consider adding links and joining affiliated sites to earn extra money. If you enjoy reading books, for example, you can add a link to amazon.com recommendations and receive compensation for doing so.

Manage expenses.

~Resist using your credit card and use cash instead whenever possible.

~Save money on your household utilities. To reduce your electric bill, for example, diligently turn off lights when you leave a room; to save money on your gas bill, lower the heat in the winter and wear an extra sweater or two.

~Take care of household maintenance tasks, if you are able, or try to find a friend or family member who can help so that you don't have to hire a professional to do the job.

~Barter and trade your professional services, if possible, with family members and friends.

Create emergency and rainy-day funds.

~Set aside three to six months' worth of income. Some experts say that six to nine months' worth is more likely to be needed due to the length of time it often requires an individual to find new employment. For every ten thousand dollars in income replacement, you should allow one month of unemployment. For example, if your income was seventy thousand before you were let go, it may take you as long as seven months to replace your income.

~Prepare for a rainy day. The rain always comes, regardless of the financial season in which you find yourself. Plan for it; be proactive. A rainy-day fund is in addition to an emergency fund. Make sure that you always have a few extra hundreds to take care of unexpected expenses.

~Open a savings account or credit union account. The first step is to start making regular deposits into your account. If you have direct deposit available to you, this is a good way to deposit money into your account before you receive the cash. You want to keep this money in a liquid account should you need access to it in an emergency.

Ensure proper protection.

~Protect against loss of income. Life insurance, disability insurance, and long-term care products can protect you during times when you cannot earn an income.

~Protect family assets. Write a will. It doesn't matter how much or how little you believe you have, especially if you have any real property (real estate or businesses). Without a will, your family could lose the majority of your estate to probate taxes.

∽

These points and pieces of advice are by no means an exhaustive primer on fiscal management. My chief concern, though, is that you understand the importance of sound money management, especially as it bears on your reputation as a woman of integrity. Paying your bills punctually, tithing faithfully, and earning enough so that you can donate to charities are actions by which you prove yourself a woman of her word—someone who converts income into valuable outcomes. Make your word your currency. Show yourself a responsible steward of the financial and material blessings you have earned and received, and you will create positive, "brand you" money that inspires confidence in others.

Part IV

Execute

20

Innovation into Execution

"Every minute you spend planning saves ten minutes of execution."

—Brian Tracy

Every day that you wake up, you are doing something to survive—to get life done. But are you doing what really matters? This chapter will teach you how to become a woman of action. You will discover your execution type, overcome inhibitors that keep you from taking action, and learn how to close the execution gap—the overwhelming expanse that exists between your dream and its successful execution. As you learn the principles that propel people who execute successfully and leap across the gap, your life goals will materialize and your ideas will be realized.

Execution is, first of all, a mind-set. To be an effective woman of execution, you must embrace it as a way of life, part of your daily lifestyle. You were created for productivity—the capability to produce is encoded in your DNA, and execution is what you were born to do. *Execution is action; it is producing; it is getting life done.* Having the mind-set of execution means that you examine whether you have the ability to get things done when you plan your dreams and visions. It means that you ask yourself if you have what it takes, including, *Am I doing what matters? Do I have the skills necessary to achieve my dream? Whom do I know who can help me?* If you have the mind-set of execution, you believe in the existence of a solution, method, or process that will help you leap across the gap of your ideas to action.

An execution mind-set is not developed automatically or passively; it can't be absorbed. Instead, it comes to those who develop the intentional habit of getting things done. To meet your goals, you must develop patience and perseverance, putting off instant gratification in favor of working harder—and longer, if necessary—to pursue worthier opportunities whose results that endure. As you increase how often you take action on your ideas, the act of taking action will become easier and easier.

Execution is a systematic way of exposing what is real and then acting on it. When you fail to face reality, execution will be impossible for you. The fruit of your life will be evidence of where you have executed successfully. You may be a highly productive saleswoman whose fruit—increased sales and loyal customers—is evidence of the consistent action you have taken in those areas. Fruit can be negative, however. You may be known as a gossip whose fruit— filthy rumors and damaged reputations—is evidence of what you have spent your time producing.

You may be a highly motivated individual who sets goals and achieves them. If so, this evidence is the fruit of execution. We are all executing, on some level; however, prioritizing important goals and objectives and delaying gratification of less important goals makes the difference in your ability to execute the plans that matter most.

Innovation and Execution

To be effective at achieving what matters, you need both innovation and execution. Innovation involves creative thoughts, ideas, and dreams. Innovating involves discovery and problem-solving, and the process includes developing new ideas that transform individuals, communities, cultures, economies, or other spheres. Google, Microsoft, and Dell are considered innovative companies, primarily because they have introduced new and useful things to society. In just a few years, Google has changed our lives—how we perform research, find information, and make decisions. I recently met a young woman who told me that she "Googled" my name and found a lot of information about me. This novel term that started as a company name is now a verb!

Google is innovative because the company has revolutionalized advertising and improved user interface of a basic Internet search engine. Other companies existed before Google, but Google's process is more efficient and powerful, enabling millions of users to search for information and retrieve it instantly. Prior to Google's advent, Microsoft created software that made personal computers easier for the average person to understand and use. Dell's innovative contribution to our lives was streamlining the delivery method of building and selling computers.

Okay, so you are thinking, *I'm not Google, Microsoft, or Dell—I may have set the bar too high. How can I come up with something that's remotely innovative?* Have you read *The Dip* by Seth Godin? If you haven't, I recommend that you pick up a copy at your local bookseller or borrow one from your local library. *The Dip* is one of my favorite books because its message is simple: Winners know when to quit and when to stick. Godin discusses how you can be the best in your world, which is relative to you and to those who believe that you are the best in their worlds. Your world is defined not by geographical boundaries but by what you have access to, as well as what—or who—has access to you. I mention this book to help you understand that you can be innovative in your world— you can introduce your own ideas, methods, thoughts, and innovative processes to your family members, friends, coworkers, or clients, thereby making a difference in your "world," or sphere of influence. Your innovation is realized in the lives of others by your ability to bring your ideas to life. Thus, innovation is a new way of thinking, a creative concept or novel mind-set that is open to originality.

In addition to being a mind-set, execution is an act—the act of converting innovation into action by turning your ideas into concrete realities. Dr. Edward de Bono, the world's leading authority on conceptual, parallel, and creative (lateral) thinking, teaches on "operacy," his term for the skills that are necessary for doing, or the act of doing. Acquiring knowledge does not guarantee that we will acquire the skills needed to act on that knowledge. Dr. de Bono teaches that acquiring the skills of action is as equally important as acquiring knowledge. Execution is action, and to execute fully, you must be able to convert your thoughts, ideas, and dreams into concrete reality. A good place to begin is to identify the execution type that best describes you. Doing so may help you improve your innovation skills, as well as the skills needed to take action and execute your innovative ideas.

21

What Is My Execution Type?

In assessing how you pursue and accomplish your dreams, it is useful to examine what I call your *execution type*. There are four execution types, each distinguished by varying strengths and weaknesses in terms of innovation and execution. Innovation encompasses ideas, thoughts, or dreams; it is the capacity to create something new and useful. Execution is the ability to convert one's ideas, thoughts, and dreams into actions and outcomes.

The diagram below illustrates the four execution types: the Wisher (weak in both innovation and execution), the Wanderer (strong in innovation, weak in execution), the Zombie (weak in innovation, strong in execution), and the Doer (strong in both innovation and execution). As you read the more descriptions of each of the four types, recognize that they relate specifically to doing what matters most when you are fulfilling your dreams in life.

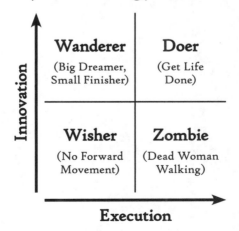

The Wisher

The wisher is the person I described in the first chapter of this book when we discussed dreaming versus wishing. Wishers lack forward movement; they do the same things, day in and day out. I am reminded of a wisher I met during the holiday shopping season at a local hobby shop. I was buying festive fabric to decorate my buffet area for the Woman Act Now holiday gathering. As the clerk measured and cut the fabric, I shared with her why I was purchasing the four yards of green and red satin material. I explained that Woman Act Now was an organization where women mentor other women, helping one another to achieve their dreams. I had barely finished my sentence when she looked up from her task and said in a sarcastic voice, "Well, that's not for me! I don't have any dreams. I just work here, but I wish I didn't have to—then I could retire and have all the money I need!" I responded, "You are just the lady that should come to this meeting, because I am sure you are kidding— you must have something you want to do!" She looked me square in the eye and said, "No, I really mean it—I don't have any ideas or dreams, and I just wish I had some money and didn't have to work here."

At that point, I realized there was no talking her through this or changing her mind, especially as one of her coworkers chimed in to echo her point of view. I said I was sorry to hear her response but was certain that if she thought about it, she would find a dream. Then, I politely took my material and headed for the checkout counter. Although my interaction with the hobby shop clerk may have been too short to truly judge her intent, my impression was that her attitude about her dreams was really a reflection of her dislike for her job—discontent with her current situation clouded any hopes for her future.

Often, if a wisher is dissatisfied with her current situation, she is unable to dream or execute because of the apparent inescapability of her circumstances, which weigh heavily on her mind. She wishes for what she does not have and feels powerless to do anything to obtain it. Wishers are weak in innovation and weak in execution. A wisher is a lazy thinker; she lacks creativity and does nothing that requires too much effort. She responds to what she sees and to what exists instead of imagining a brighter future filled with what *could* exist.

A wisher does not set goals, preferring instead to follow instructions from others. She does not see time as an investment; as long as she can get through the day, she thinks she is doing well. She is quick to take from others, and, in the process, she whines and complains about the difficulties life has dealt her. She does not take responsibility for her choices, and she hopes that things will work out in her favor, even when she consciously makes poor choices.

When you find yourself working with a wisher, be sure not to ask her to commit to anything of substance, because she won't be able to carry it out. She may seem willing to help you, but the reality is that she routinely overcommits and lacks the self-discipline necessary for getting things done. Treading water in the ocean of life, wishers tire easily and sink without leaving as much as a ripple or bubble to signify their imprint upon the earth.

The Wanderer

The second execution type is the wanderer: a person who is a big dreamer but a small finisher. She is a great innovator, full of ideas and dreams, but she is a poor executor. A wanderer may start many projects, but she rarely completes them. She takes many paths, but they lead to nowhere. She is filled with drive and passion, but she directs these aimlessly, failing to achieve any meaningful goals. She is smart and talented—a Jane of all trades and a master of none. The wanderer begins many projects, businesses, books, and hobbies but bores easily and abandons them. She is a breakthrough thinker, but she breaks down when converting ideas to action.

At every event where I speak or present, I meet wanderers. I can spot them a mile away; I can pick them out of a packed crowd as I scan a room from my position at the podium. A wanderer is enthusiastic about life; she is positive; she gets a lot done—just not the right things. She is a big picture thinker. She looks like she's got it together, but underneath her façade, she knows she's off track. She desperately wants to fulfill her destiny, but her passion keeps her searching for the right idea, opportunity, or connection—and it's never satisfied with what it finds. She is hardworking but easily distracted.

The Zombie

The zombie is essentially a dead woman walking. She is weak in innovation but strong in execution. She lacks vision, drive, and motivation. She does well in environments where she is expected to do as she is told. She does not initiate projects or take risks, but she executes with precision the plans that other people construct. She can be counted on to do her part, but don't expect her to do anything more—she has little motivation to go above or beyond what's expected. She is methodical, willing to help others but never envisioning or pursuing her own dreams.

A zombie is protective of her territory—she will confront anyone who threatens her systems or processes. She expects to do what she does forever and is usually surprised when changes are made that affect her. She prides herself on being able to carry out instructions, but she's befuddled and confused when called upon to provide input or new ideas. She may suffer from lack of confidence, feeling that her ideas are insignificant and her contributions are unrecognized.

A zombie looks at life from the "if only" or "what if" attitude: *If only I had a better job, if only I had more money, if only I had a degree, if only I were thinner, if only I were liked more,* and so on. "If only" and "what if" keep her in her comfort zone. She prefers to go unnoticed, and she's the poster girl for the "good enough" principle, which says: Do good enough to keep others off your back, keep customers happy, or keep your job. The problem with following the "good enough" principle is that it makes her think she is good at what she does, and she grows complacent, comfortable to keep listing the "if onlys" and "what ifs" that life deals her in generous portions.

The Doer

The final execution type is the Doer. She is a woman who approaches life proactively and gets life done. She does not wait for life to happen—she is strong in innovation and strong in execution. A doer is moved by inward vision, believes in her abilities, and has a strong sense of who she is. She is committed to her word and is character-driven. She is teachable, always looking to sharpen her skills and develop her talents. She is purposeful, passionate, and powerful, and these characteristics describe how she reacts to what life deals her in her now. She is forward-moving and effective; she eliminates rhetoric by doing.

A doer makes meaningful change through execution. She responds to life by choice rather than by passivity or reaction. She values systems and processes, makes the right choices, and falls in love with the results. She respects others and instinctively knows when to insist and when to back off. She aligns her actions with her values and meets life with a sense of urgency, eager to live and act in the now. She knows when to say yes and when to say no. She is a servant leader. She honors and appreciates the gifts of others, and she knows without a doubt that with God, all things are possible. (See Matthew 19:26.)

What Is Your Execution Type?

Which of the types above is most similar to you? As you read the descriptions, you probably related to one primary type, but you also may have related to traits of other types. The reason for this is that we all exhibit a little bit of each of the execution types in various seasons of our lives.

Regardless of the execution type you related to the most, to increase your effectiveness in life you must become more and more like the doer. Since the doer has the ability to execute, or convert ideas to action, it is important that you understand some specific attitudes that make doers successful. Implement some of the following suggestions in order to become more like a doer.

Characteristics of a Doer

~Many of us know what we should do but don't do it. A doer bridges that gap by knowing what to do and actually doing it.

~A doer has a propensity for action rather than passivity.

~A doer knows that the cure for procrastination is to "do it now."

~Poor execution is the death of anyone who delegates authority to someone else who fails. A doer never delegates responsibility to someone to do something that she herself should do.

~Life is full of opportunities that require problem solvers to take advantage of them. A doer solves big problems.

~A doer finds better, faster, and smarter ways of doing things.

~A doer has a healthy disregard for the impossible. She is optimistic about possibility.

~In a doer's life, execution is a way of thinking.

~Discipline is a lifestyle choice for a doer. She routinely delays self-gratification—delaying the less important pleasures so that the greater things may be achieved.

~A doer develops habits of execution. She silences the voices of doubt and discouragement through consistent and persistent action.

~A doer has an insatiable drive to pursue quality and excellence.

~A doer values training and learning, and passing knowledge on to the next generation.

~A doer has personal standard operating procedures. Similar to a corporation's standard operating procedures, she sets standards for how she will operate in her life, her relationships, and her finances.

~A doer develops and implements quality control procedures. She is accountable for her actions.

~A doer gives more than is asked or required.

~A doer has the same attitude as Robert Winship Woodruff, who said, "There is no limit to what a man can do or where he can go if he doesn't mind who gets the credit."

~A doer repositions herself when doing so is necessary. For example, in 1994, the *Oprah Winfrey Show* repackaged itself from sleaze programming to "change your life" TV. To date, the show has continued to be in a category all its own.

~A doer develops values to guide behavior. Like Jack Welch, former CEO of General Electric, she is willing to destroy existing systems, create new ones to replace them, and insist on qualities and values that can be implemented in her life.

~A doer embraces innovation. Like Sam Walton, founder of retail giants Wal-Mart and Sam's Club, she understands the value of innovation and doesn't underestimate how her thinking can contribute to the world of opportunity.

~A doer follows her instincts. She trusts in her personal GPS (God Positioning System), using it to be in the right place, and to take action at the right time, in order to fulfill her purpose.

~A doer routinely does things that have a positive impact on her world—her sphere of influence, relationships, and community. Anita Roddick, founder of The Body Shop, once said, "If you think you are too small to have an impact, try going to bed with a mosquito."

~A doer is willing to pay the price for opportunity—even if the price is high!

~A doer knows that some of the best deals in life are the ones she walks away from.

In the words of Michael Dell, "Ideas are a commodity. Execution of them is not." Doers are the consummate executors. They can go unrecognized because they are not always the ones out front—they are just disciplined people who love living life to the fullest as they intentionally make their marks upon the world.

22

Crucial Qualities for Successful Execution

Once you discover your primary execution type, it is important to make a commitment to execution in your life. As you do so, recognize that there are personal qualities and knowledge you must possess that will help you to become an effective doer. The first of these qualities is *character*. Executing your ideas, staying true to who you are, and living your best life require a depth of character.

In essence, character is who you are, not what you do. Character interlocks your values and beliefs, helping you to determine what is truly important to you. Character is a necessary component of the ability to execute your ideas, for it is the glue that will hold you together as you give your all to accomplish what you believe you were created to do. Your character will remind you why you were born, reveal that you can do many things, and hold you accountable for being your best.

The intention of character—the demonstration of character in action—is *integrity*, the next important quality to possess. Without integrity, it is impossible to be the best you that you can be and to reflect your true character to others.

As you execute your ideas, it is important to understand that *change* is a constant. Change is a powerful force that will occur with or without your permission. Because you are changing at every moment, it is far better to embrace change than to try to resist it.

Crisis Change

Unfortunately, change is most visible when you suffer a crisis and are forced to change. Your crisis might be the death of a spouse, the receipt of a pink slip at work, the rejection of a lover, or any number of other hardships. Crisis brings a time of testing, usually when you least expect it. This type of change makes you deal with the issue at hand, calling upon whatever preparation you may (or probably don't) have. Even though testing due to a crisis is usually temporary, it may bring with it permanent impact and change in your life. Crisis usually causes or calls for immediate change.

Evolutionary Change

A second type of change is evolutionary change, which implies that you change gradually as your circumstances evolve. For example, the evolution of cassette to compact disc to mp3 files describes the process of change in audio media. If you desire to continue listening to your favorite songs, you are obligated to change concurrently with the technology, purchasing a portable CD player to replace your Walkman, an iPod to replace your portable CD player, and so on. Eventually, like it or not, you will be forced to upgrade your equipment, discarding outdated equipment for new equipment that supports the latest format.

Visionary Change

The final way in which you can change—and the most productive form of change—is visionary change, in which an individual is motivated from within to change. Visionary change is necessary for people of execution. It is the vision within you that drives you to take the next step, to try it again, and to execute your dreams. Executors initiate visionary change.

As you change, you must *imagine your success*. Review our discussion about the I-FACTOR Zone and think about what you want to do and who you want to be. Walk out your success by taking each step and repeating it over and over in your mind until you can see and experience each detail. As you confirm your convictions and affirm your actions, *use your words carefully and clearly*. One major hindrance to execution is poor communication. Execution requires you to find the right words that convey what you desire from others, as well as what you desire from yourself. Using words effectively will help you to establish a foundation of execution in your life.

I teach a business mentoring class and usually give my students a simple assignment that deals with execution and communication. I instruct them to set aside thirty minutes before the next scheduled class and answer certain questions about their business plans. The second part of the assignment requires each student to schedule a time to call a fellow student in order to verify that he or she fulfilled the first part of the assignment. After explaining the assignment, I ascertain that the students have a clear understanding of what is required. Even though all the students insist that they understand the assignment, they sometimes have trouble fulfilling it. One time, when I taught the class and gave this assignment, the students all said they understood. But when we met again two weeks later, and I checked to see if each student had fulfilled the assignment, I was chagrined to discover an awful mess of confusion. Read some of the excuses my students gave to explain why the assignment was not completed according to my instructions:

~"I wrote the assignment on my calendar, but my information was incomplete."

~"I wasn't sure whom I should call."

~"I was two hours late making my call, but I called anyway."

~"I forgot what I was supposed to do and whom I was supposed to call."

~"I forgot the time I scheduled for my thirty-minute assignment, so I wasn't ready when she called to verify."

~"I called the wrong person."

Clarity Is Crucial for Successful Execution

~Clarity gets the assignment right.

~Clarity helps you to honor your commitments.

~Clarity keeps you focused on the task.

~Clarity eliminates confusion.

~Clarity expels excuses.

Finally, understand that *the valley of execution is inevitable*. The space (gap) between your ideas and your concrete actions is also known as the valley. The valley is the low place between the mountains that are your goals, whose peaks are your successes. Unfortunately, the low place can quickly become an emotional dungeon filled with internal repercussions if you fail to push through and execute your goals. You must learn to push through the valley and ride the waves of your choices in order to produce actions that will help you achieve your goals. The valley is similar to the gap of execution, and bridging it requires you to remain fully focused, asking yourself if you can push through it. Pushing through the valley involves determining the answers and refusing to give up, even when you are faced with difficult choices and find it hard to answer the questions required for closing the gap of execution. It means that if you believe that your solution is on the next mountaintop, you can see it on the horizon and keep pressing forward until you can climb that mountaintop and achieve it.

Ten Keys for Successful Execution

1. Choices are everything in life. Choices and decisions connect the dots of execution. You must become a master of right choices and actions by choosing carefully what to execute. When faced with two options, weigh them carefully. Choice is only choice when two or more possible paths exist. Never take the easy path just because it is easy—take it if it is the right choice.

2. Value differences in methods of execution so that you can avoid doing things one way all the time. Most of us envision how we want to accomplish a task and, if it involves others, are prone to getting stuck in the valley of execution because we do not value the methods or systems that other people may use to reach the same desired result. Execution focuses on the results, and we must remain open to various ways of achieving the outcome.

3. Overcome internal struggles. Positive self-talk will help you to excel in execution. Spend your time focusing on what you can do rather than on what you can't do. Be your own cheerleader and chant your own victory song. When you don't hear encouragement from others, let your encouragement speak loudly from within—you are your own greatest fan.

4. Vision is seeing plainly and clearly where you are going. Effective execution plans are well written. Write your vision, complete with each step you are going to take to complete every related task. Many tasks add up to finished projects, and finished projects become milestones, points of verifiable completion along the way to the bigger goal. Write your vision so that you can convey your message clearly to others who are assisting you to get where you want to go.

5. Verify and follow up. These two principles are the essence of execution when delegating tasks to other people. Dreams die when crucial tasks are delegated to people who don't have the capacity or commitment to complete them. Most of us can avoid this tragic end if we follow up early and consistently with those to whom we delegate tasks. It is useless to delegate responsibilities unless we verify that what we have asked others to do is being done.

6. "Patience and diligence, like faith, move mountains," in the wise words of William Penn. Patience and diligence will carry you through the gap of execution. The more obstacles you meet with patient diligence, chipping away at them, moment by moment, with perseverance, the closer you will come to eliminating obstacles altogether.

7. Performance is a requirement of execution. Being a passive person of inaction is antithetical to execution. You must be willing to evaluate your personal performance in order to determine if it aligns with the performance and action required to achieve your desired outcome. Performing over a prolonged period of time is a lifestyle choice that comes from a commitment to honesty, integrity, and character. Value your performance and work to the best of your ability to execute consistently over time.

8. Don't assume. Ask. Clarify, clarify, and clarify. Make sure that you have clear directions before, during, and after completing your goals, personal and professional. Always remember that questions applied at the right time will save you from pain and suffering, as well as assist you in delivering what is expected of you the first time.

9. Always be honest. Honesty is the best policy. Avoid trying to cover up your mistakes, especially when other people are involved. In time, the mistake will be exposed, and it might cause the entire project or system to derail. It is best to reveal mistakes immediately after they occur, for if they are handled right away, you allow yourself a greater window of potential recovery time. If you cover them up until it's too late, it may be impossible to correct the issues. Taking responsibility for your actions will always earn you respect; even if it comes at a price, do it anyway. There is usually a bigger price to pay later for cover-ups.

10. Keep your word. Be a woman of your word. Your word should be the thread that weaves together the fibers of your life. Your word is your bond; without it, nothing can bond to you, nor will it want to. Your word defines what you can execute. It is the precommitment to your actions, and it paints a picture for others to see what you expect to deliver. Mean what you say and say what you mean.

23

Closing the Execution Gap

*"I am an executor of my ideas and I master closing the gap
between my thoughts and my actions."*

—Woman Act Now Covenant

xecution is important only if you have defined a desired outcome. The execution gap exists between your ideas and your
ability to convert them into material reality. The diagram
below shows the various questions (which are elaborated later in
this chapter) that you must answer in order to close the execution
gap and get things done. Closing the execution gap involves gathering, eliminating, and preparing different pieces of information
in order to implement your ideas. Noted in the diagram are seven
areas that, if not addressed properly, may cause you to become par-
alyzed in the process of striving for your goals.

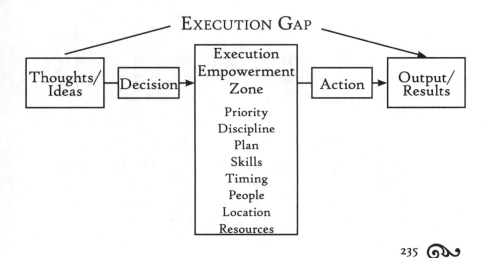

Execution comprises the systems and processes by which you will take action on your ideas. Your thoughts must move from mere thoughts to decisions. Once a decision is made, you can then proceed to the empowering stage of execution. During the empowering stage, you ask questions and seek answers to help you clarify who, what, when, why, where, and how you are going to accomplish what needs to be done. Most people who fail during the empowerment stage do so primarily because they lack clarity, they are misinformed, or they don't get answers to these questions to empower them for action. Instead, they move forward, taking action but disregarding details that could keep them moving steadily through the gap. The process of closing the execution gap will empower you to do more with less. The key is that the more information you gather, the more you equip yourself to take action while eliminating distractions and inhibitors that might keep you from meeting your objective.

To close the execution gap, start with an idea and make a decision to act on it. Next, review the systems and processes that will help you to bring your idea to fruition. This Execution Empowerment Zone is the stage that will help you overcome any doubt about your abilities, giving you confidence and equipping you to succeed. The diagram's components represent ten questions you must ask yourself in the Execution Empowerment Zone in order to be best equipped to move forward into action:

Question 1: Idea – *What is my idea or goal?*

Question 2: Worthiness – *Is this idea worth pursuing?* If the answer is "yes," continue execution to empowerment zone. If the answer is "no," scrap the idea or store for future use.

Question 3: Priority – *Why am I doing this? Is it a priority for me?* Are you compelled, convicted, or committed to your idea? If you cannot answer this question with conviction, it is highly probable that you may not have enough passion to move through the gap of execution. Answer this question honestly, admitting if you are really not committed to the idea or task. By assessing and acknowledging your level of commitment, you make the most efficient investment of your time, energy, and resources. If it is a priority for you, continue to question four to determine if you have the will to do it.

Question 4: Discipline and Sacrifice – *Am I willing to set aside all other activities and goals until I have fulfilled this idea?*

Question 5: Plan – *What steps do I need to take to make this happen?*

Question 6: Skills – *How do I do this? Do I have all the skills necessary to do this?*

Question 7: Timing – *When should I do this?* (Remember, S.M.A.R.T.E.R. goals must have a time frame attached to all required actions.)

Question 8: People – *Do I need anyone else to help me do this, or can I do it on my own?*

Question 9: Location – *Where should I do this? Is the environment appropriate?*

Question 10: Resources – *Do I have all the tools I need to do this?*

Action comes after you ask yourself the questions above and gather all the necessary information. Only then can you make the appropriate choices that move you toward your goal. The empowerment stage gives you the clarity you need to close the gap, so practice staying in the zone until you are fully empowered to act. Remember, decision, clarity, and action reside in the valley of execution (the gap), and moving into action eventually gives you the output and results you desire.

You can apply the execution process to anything you do. Break your ideas down into manageable parts rather than trying to tackle the big picture as a whole. Your desired outcome will be easier to achieve if you think of it as the sum of many small, manageable goals.

Below is an example for you to follow when thinking through a project you would like to undertake. Big picture: Build a women's organization that will empower women to succeed in business and personal life. Instead of trying to execute everything about creating a women's organization, I am going to start with the execution of the corporate structure of the organization.

1. What is your idea? *Choose and detail the corporate structure of the organization.*

2. Have you decided that this idea is worth pursuing? *Yes, this idea is very important to me; it is my life's purpose to empower others to fulfill their destinies.*

3. Is this idea a priority for you? Where does it fit on a scale of one to ten, one being most important? *My decision is based on committing the next five years of my life to building an effective organization that will impact thousands of women worldwide. It is my number two priority in life.*

4. Are you willing to delay all other activities and goals in order to fulfill this idea? *Absolutely—defining the structure of the organization is the first step in establishing what it will be. I need to make sure the legal steps are taken before I launch my idea.*

5. What are three steps you will take to execute this idea?

~I will decide whether the organization will be a nonprofit or for-profit corporation.

~I will contact www.legalzoom.com to research and file my incorporation papers.

~After I file the corporate papers, I will obtain a local business license.

6. Do you have all the skills you need to execute this idea? *I am able to use my computer to access the tools and Web sites I need to research in order to register my company.*

7. What makes right now the right time to do this? *This is the right timing to establish this organization after soul searching and identifying the need of women for mentors in their lives.*

8. Do you need help from other people, or can you do this on your own? *I will contact my accountant to make sure that I am choosing the right type of organization and structure for tax purposes and requirements. I will also meet with my team of advisers to ensure that we are in agreement on the type of company as it relates to our long-term objectives.*

9. Where do you need to do this? Do you have the right environment that will allow you to be as effective as possible? *I can do this from the comfort of my home or office, but I must set aside a specific time to accomplish it on my computer.*

10. Do you have the necessary resources, such as funding, equipment, transportation, and supplies? *I have my computer; I am not yet sure about the cost, but I will determine that during my research phase. I have everything I need to take action!*

Close the Gap

Execution closes the gap that gets you to the finish line. Finishing is hard work. Let's review the entire process. First, we dream; then, we believe we can do it; next, we execute to the finish; and, finally, we connect with others to distribute our ideas to the world. Finishing means that we have started, our action is in progress, but we are not yet done. What do you do when you fall off the wagon of execution somewhere in the middle of the valley? It is inevitable that you will fall off the wagon of execution at some point in your life. Believe me, I have fallen off a few times. But you don't need to lie there in the dust; you can get up, brush yourself off, straighten your clothes, and climb back on the wagon, taking the reins. Here are some steps that will help you.

Set an allotted time in which to tackle the task.

Keep an execution calendar in addition to your event calendar. Most of us mark our calendars with places we have to go and people we have to meet. We write out unending task lists, but rarely do we set appointments with ourselves to execute our ideas. If you are trying to get everything done at the end of the day, only after the phone stops ringing, then you may be guilty of being places and meeting people rather than doing the things you have made a commitment to do. If possible, start setting a time to execute the details during your workday, and you will make use of your time rather than finding yourself feeling overworked and under-paid. For example, perhaps you want to write out a business plan, but instead of beginning the task, you merely talk about it, feeling that you'll never get it done. Schedule a time on your calendar for research, planning, and writing. You can start small, but if you assign an execution time, stick to it, guard it, and don't give it up for less important matters. It is highly probable that if you have scheduled the time, then you will find it easier to excuse yourself from invitations, lunch dates, appointments, or phone calls that might interfere. Value your allotted time as an investment, just as you would value meeting with a customer or closing a deal. If you don't put the time in, you won't get the results later.

Develop a habit of doing.

If you are tackling a project for the first time, or even if you're tackling one you've done before, start by making a concerted effort to develop the habit of doing. You develop habits by doing the same thing over and over until it becomes natural, automatic. As it becomes easier, it will be a pleasure to do it. Let's say that you want to write a book, for example. Usually, you start by fleshing out an outline. Once you have completed your outline, however skeletal it may be, it is time to get to work. Books are rarely written in a single setting—rather, they are compiled over extended periods of time. I have found that the best way to get the stream going is by committing to write during a specific block of time each day. When I began the writing process, I found it very difficult and frustrating to move in a linear fashion through my outline. I wanted to jump all around from topic to topic, and I wanted to write when I felt inspired, not according to a disciplined schedule. I found the latter to be much more effective, for when I became more serious about the task of writing, I was able to produce more material in shorter periods of time.

Regardless of what you are trying to achieve, if you practice consistently over a protracted period of time, you will become better and more effective with each time period of practice. Enjoy the process. Learning to enjoy the process is half the battle. We all look forward to the results, but it is the process that we must endure to get us there. Changing your attitude about the process so that you are able to find enjoyment, even in the midst of challenge, will help you finish it.

As I developed the discipline of writing, I began to enjoy the process rather than viewing it as a dreaded chore. I also relished the time I spent writing, because it became my measure of productivity. Time began to validate my talent, and I couldn't wait to experience the discovery of new information that came each day. I have enjoyed the entire process of writing this book. I must confess that there were many times when I could not produce as much as a word, and I avoided writing altogether. It is important not to obsess about the entire project during the execution phase, for this will overwhelm you. Focus instead on the steps required, which are easier to manage one at a time.

For example, when I thought about the task of writing a book of more than 50,000 words, this staggering end result was overwhelming and immobilizing to me. It made me obsess about the number of words I needed to write. When I set a schedule to write for a certain amount of time, it became easier to do. I focused only on the time, during which I would write between one hundred and five thousand words. The words added up, day after day, and before

I knew it, I had exceeded the required amount by 20 percent! The minutes became hours, and the hours became words put to paper.

Don't sweat the small stuff.

Try not to be tripped up by fastidious details during the process; rather, give yourself time afterward to review and redo. Many surprises will veer you off course, but don't tire of doing what you know will get you where you want to go. Make sure you develop relationships with others who will encourage and support you, as well as hold you accountable for getting through the small stuff in order to reach the big finale.

At some point in the process, you may get stuck. Getting unstuck requires recommitting to your goals, then stepping away to review your progress, to refresh your energy, and to reposition yourself. Getting unstuck requires repositioning, because whatever you are doing cannot be continued in the same faulty manner, and an adjustment must be made if you are to move forward.

Many of us have seen motor vehicles stuck along the side of the road—maybe we've even been in one of those vehicles. One night when I was seventeen, I wanted to go to a friend's house to pick up a book that was circulating around the school. I insisted on going to her house, in spite of the thunderstorm that was raging outside that evening. The problem was that my friend lived on a dirt road that became impassable when the dirt mixed with the water. Being independent and somewhat rebellious, I was convinced that I could drive that car safely and successfully through the mud.

My older sister, Sonya, came along with me, and she tried to persuade me not to drive through the mud, warning me that I would get stuck, and, when I did, that my daddy would get me. I ignored her warnings and drove right into the mud. Not only did I get stuck, but the new 1983 burgundy Lincoln Continental slid into the ditch several yards from my friend's driveway. Getting stuck in any situation is no laughing matter—unless, of course, you're my sister, who kept saying, "I told you so," and moreover refused to help me extricate the car. "You got it stuck, so you have to get it unstuck," she said matter-of-factly. "I am just going to sit here and wait."

The rain was coming down in torrents, and I was wearing a red denim skirt and red leather strap clogs—not exactly the best clothing to wear in the rain. I got out of the car and walked fifty yards, which seemed to stretch for miles, and showed up on my friend's doorstep, soaked to the bone. Mr. Pina, my friend's father, looked at my guilt-ridden face and asked, "Anna, what have you done?" With trembling lips, I replied, "I got Daddy's car stuck. Please promise me you won't tell him. Can you get us out of the ditch?" Mr. Pina responded quickly, pulling his tractor out of the garage and driving it down the street as I walked alongside in the rain.

Remember, the key to getting unstuck is changing your position, changing your behavior or actions, asking for help, and adjusting what you are doing. I had been trying hopelessly to get the car out, only to realize that I was causing the car to sink even deeper into the ditch. Mr. Pina put pieces of wood under the tires, attached the car to the tractor with a chain, and slowly adjusted the car's position as he pulled it out of the ditch. Once we were back on the road, I asked Sonya if she wanted to drive home, and she refused, insisting that I was going to have to drive us out of there. I drove back down the road, through the same conditions that got us stuck in the first place. This time, however, I followed the tracks that I had made on the drive in, and I was able to drive the half mile to the paved road safely, making my way home with the infamous book in tow.

Develop a network.

It is crucial to develop a network of trusted advisers—friends, family members, or coworkers whom you can run your ideas by and ask for feedback. During the process of writing of this manuscript, I had several instances of getting stuck. To get myself unstuck, I hired writing coaches to put me back on track. My husband was also a tremendous resource, as he would speak the right words at the right time to help me get back on course. One word can open an avenue that you didn't know existed, enabling you to continue moving in the right direction while you are still musing on your ideas.

Develop your execution state.

Develop a routine or state of execution for getting things done. The state of execution can be observed most clearly in athletes, singers, or musicians who develop a definite and specific routine before exercising their talent. This state of being helps the individual to visualize success and to align his or her thoughts with bodily actions. Take golf, for example. In order for you to learn to be a successful putter on the green, golf professionals will teach you to develop a pre-putt routine that you execute precisely each time before you putt the ball, whether it is three feet or thirty feet from the hole.

Think about a time when you felt great—when you were filled with confidence, awareness, and assurance that you could do something. Visualize that moment and memorize how you felt. Then, conjure up those same feelings each time you need to get something done. For me, my state of execution (what I call *getting my mind right*) happens when I visualize the beloved children's book by Watty Piper, *The Little Engine That Could*. Remember how the little engine took on the challenge of transporting the toys and food to the children on the other side of the mountain? He kept saying, "I think I can, I think I can" as he huffed and puffed his way to the top of the mountain. As he came down the other side of the mountain, he said, "I thought I could, I thought I could."

The detail of this story that encouraged me the most was the fact that the little engine had never been to the other side of the mountain. Do whatever it takes for you to get to that place where you have never been. Some people carry things in their pockets, rub their hands together, do jumping jacks, listen to music, sit quietly, or speak self-affirmations in order to build up the courage to do something.

Finish it.

Focus on the results. Starting something is always easier than finishing it. Yet finishing a project does something for the soul.

Being determined, focused, committed, and purposeful in completing what you start provides nourishment for your soul.

In John 4:31–34, Jesus was speaking with His disciples about eating natural food versus spiritual food:

> *Meanwhile his disciples urged him, "Rabbi, eat something." But he said to them, "I have food to eat that you know nothing about." Then his disciples said to each other, "Could someone have brought him food?" "My food," said Jesus, "is to do the will of him who sent me and to finish his work."*
> (NIV)

For Jesus, fulfilling His purpose on earth—finishing His assignment—was as necessary as eating. Finishing is not only rewarding, but it is also mandatory when it comes to reaching your destiny and fulfilling your dream on the earth. Let's apply 2 Corinthians 8:11, which says, *"Now finish the work, so that your eager willingness to do it* [start] *may be matched by your completion of it* [finish]*, according to your means* [your priorities, discipline, plan, skills, timing, relationships, location, and resources]" (NIV).

24

Execution Self-assessment

A s we conclude this part of the book, I want you to take a short execution assessment. This assessment is designed to help measure your execution effectiveness. The only answers that are important are the ones that you can honestly assess.

1. How often are projects significantly delayed or completed below your standards of excellence because of poor execution?

__Never __Seldom __Sometimes __Almost always

2. How often do you change your vision because of poor execution?

3. Where do execution problems usually occur in your life?

_____	Job objectives	_____	percent of the time
_____	Personal goals	_____	percent of the time
_____	Finances	_____	percent of the time
_____	Business	_____	percent of the time
_____	Relationships	_____	percent of the time

4. How many other people are responsible for your inability to execute?

_____ Family members

_____ Spouse/partner

_____ Boss/coworker

_____ Project team members

5. Which factors are most frequently linked with execution problems in your life?

_____ Unplanned-for "emergencies"

_____ Time availability for necessary activities

_____ Consistent clarity of expectations

_____ Cooperation from others

_____ Effective communication

_____ Motivation/morale

_____ Procrastination

6. In your personal life, what have been the effects or consequences of poor execution?

_____ Devastating

_____ Quite serious

_____ An area of concern

_____ Somewhat serious

_____ Not at all serious

7. Estimate the total annual cost of execution problems in your life (productivity, efficiency, profit, or opportunity cost).

_____ Interest paid

_____ Late fees

_____ Income loss

_____ Relationship loss

_____ Job loss

_____ Cost of starting over

_____ Customer loss

Making Sense of Your Assessment

Question 1

If you answered "never," you are not being honest with yourself. Go back to the mirror, take a close look, and apologize to yourself. Then, answer the question again—transparently. Rarely do we execute 100 percent of the time. If you answered "seldom," you are doing great, and you understand how to close the execution gap. You also value excellence and are able to communicate that value to others to produce fruitful results. If you answered "sometimes," then you have more work to do. You may need to review "Closing the Execution Gap" and work to become more skillful and mindful of exercising all the steps necessary to get you through the gap. If you answered "almost always," you are not alone. There have been many others who, like you, recognize that they are truly not the best that they can be due to poor execution. You are on your way to becoming exceedingly great, though, because you recognize that being better at execution will make you a better you.

Question 2

This question should provoke you to understand that if you can't decide on the direction of your vision, find yourself changing the vision every other month or year, and lack clarity, it may be that you simply don't execute well. Improving your execution skills will help you stay the course.

Question 3

Where do execution problems usually occur in your life? By thinking carefully about your response, you can determine where you need to put more time into understanding the challenges you face in getting through the gap. Some people have more skills with execution in the professional realm than in the domestic sphere. Learning to transfer your skills in execution and applying them to all areas of life will help you to increase your effectiveness.

Question 4

Identify specific people who may prohibit you from executing successfully in your circles of influence. When you are able to identify these individuals, you can more readily determine the methods you will need to use to get through the gap. For example, if you are in the workplace and your job requires you to work with other people as a team, how will you achieve successful execution if you fail to get full participation from your fellow team members? If you can identify the individuals who tend to keep you from executing, you can develop systems to adapt accordingly, or you might choose to confront those individuals and discuss the issues.

Question 5

Be completely honest as you respond to this question, because it is a serious clue to the areas you must address, as they are likely keeping you from executing your ideas. For example, everyone encounters an emergency or an unexpected crisis every once in a while. But if you find that a great percentage of your time, whether at work or in the home, is dedicated to addressing unexpected emergencies, this requires some investigation. Ask yourself why you have become the designated problem solver. Were these emergencies genuinely unavoidable or could they have been prevented by better management of your time? If this is the case, you should consider enrolling in a time management class to equip you to prioritize your schedule.

Question 6

Do you understand the implications of failing to execute? Perhaps you had a presentation scheduled for months but procrastinated, waiting to prepare for it until the last possible minute. You finished it just before the meeting, but you had no time to review or redo, and your boss found critical mistakes. If this situation really happened to you, what would the consequences be? Think of the most recent situation in which you failed to execute properly and suffered the consequences.

Question 7

What was the impact of your lack of execution on yourself and others? The one thing that gets most people's attention is loss—loss of money, belongings, relationships, or careers. How much have you lost as a result of poor executions in life? Have you lost a job, a career, a relationship, or money? What will you do differently to execute more effectively in the future?

Part V

Make the Connection

25

Relationships with a Greater Reason

"For waging war you need guidance, and for victory many advisers."

—Proverbs 24:6 (NIV)

H ave you ever been a spectator at a sporting event where you were seated in the nosebleed section of the arena? The nosebleed section is so high that no matter how piercing your scream, how loud your yelling, or how high your jump, you may never be noticed by the players on your favorite team. Although there are many sections in an arena, your access and the price you are willing to pay will determine how close you get to being recognized as a devoted and supportive fan.

Relationships work in the same way. How much you are willing to give determines how devoted and supportive others will consider you. I share this analogy primarily because I want you to understand that the right connections don't just occur by accident; rather, they occur through a series of serendipitous events and deliberate relational opportunities.

Each of you has friends, coaches, cheerleaders, and other supporters—even some you have yet to meet—who are in the nosebleed section of your life. They have been watching from high up in the stands, far enough away from you that they don't know you personally, but at least they know *of* you. Many of them have watched you grow, many want you to keep growing, and many know that you have what it takes to succeed. Some will be strangers who may have seen you from a distance, but when you eventually make contact with them, you will know that you have made "the" connection.

I am amazed at the number of people who saw me speak from platforms throughout the nation and, many years later, sat in my living room or across the table from me at a restaurant. Many of these individuals were necessary connections I needed to make in order to reach the next level of my life, and I was a necessary connection for many of them, too.

I recently met a woman who had seen me in Los Angeles when I was speaking to several thousand women. This particular woman had worked behind the scenes of that event. We never spoke during the conference; she simply observed my behavior offstage and determined in her heart that we would meet again someday. "Someday" came four years later when she was introduced to me at my home by a member of Woman Act Now. This woman is an incredibly gifted speaker, a savvy businesswoman, and an honest, transparent person. We have many similarities regarding vision, purpose, and passion. I look forward to seeing where our relationship will take us in the future.

I am reminded of the meeting with Dick Parsons that I discussed earlier. He said, "Relationships are essential to life." I have come to realize that knowing the right people and maintaining relationships with them is absolutely necessary for us to achieve our destinies. I can think of countless moments, connections, and relationships that I have developed along my path in life, and many of them flow continually in my memory, if not in my life.

Senfronia Thompson

Let me share with you one of the most incredible connections I have made. I first met Senfronia Thompson in 1972. My seven-year-old eyes widened as I sat in the children's choir and looked down the aisle as she strode into Greater Oak Grove Baptist Church in Houston, Texas. She was one of the most beautiful and professional women I had ever seen, and I knew in that moment that I wanted to be whatever she was. She exuded confidence and assurance like no woman I had ever seen or admired, other than the women in my immediate family. She walked up to the podium that was situated just below the pulpit, for at that time women were not permitted to stand in the pulpit, and she began to speak about her desire for change, something that would be achieved if she was voted into the office of State Representative for our district.

I did not have the opportunity to meet her that day, but a few weeks later, my mom, who was politically active in our community, took me to Senfronia Thompson's headquarters. I had seen her picture on plenty of *Vote for Senfronia* posters, so I knew who she was right away. I was nervous and excited at the same time, imagining what she might be like up close. I was shaking in my shoes, but I told my mom that I wanted to meet her. She was larger than life—certainly a giant in my perspective, given my mere three-foot height. But I vividly remember what I felt the moment that I saw her: the conviction that I must get to know her.

Immediately upon being introduced to one another, Senfronia and I both knew that each of us had won the other's heart. I could see in her eyes that an eternal connection had been made, even though I was only seven years old. My mother acted as the connector, due to her path of political activism, but I was the executor who actually developed a relationship with Senfronia. I would bug my mother to take me along with her to Senfronia's headquarters—whatever it took to spend time in her presence. I would listen to her conversations, paying attention to the way she treated her workers and volunteers; I would help her and do what she asked of me. I didn't want anything to ruin my chances of being involved with her and her campaign.

I am not sure exactly when it happened, but she soon embraced me and my sister as her goddaughters, and she started taking time out of her busy schedule to love, nurture, and mentor us. We were always on our best behavior with Senfronia, for we hoped this would ensure that she would want to spend time with us again. As the years passed, I would call to talk with her, spend time with her when she was out of session, and then work on her campaign during election years. Over the next twelve years, she taught me many things, from the etiquette of fine dining to the art of speaking with people of great renown. She sponsored me when, as a high school student, I served as an honorary page in the House of Representatives in the Texas Legislature. This experience exposed me to everything from the process of lawmaking to developing relationships. Senfronia was an especially instrumental influence during my senior year in high school. She worked with Senator Lloyd Benson, who appointed me to attend the United States Air Force Academy. At this time, few women were accepted to the Air Force Academy, much less appreciated there. I was honored to be appointed, but I chose to attend Spelman College in Atlanta, Georgia, instead.

Fast-forward twelve years to 1996 when Senfronia paid me a visit in Los Angeles, California, with concern about my future. During those twelve years, we had maintained contact, and I would see her as often as possible, visiting her whenever I came home to Texas. When I was a young girl, she would always talk about my running for political office one day. This was probably one major reason why I pursued political/governmental interests in college, where I was involved in student government, and why, after college, I became involved in community politics. Senfronia's purpose for this particular visit was to determine if I was on track with my life, as well as to find out if I would return to Texas to work with her, attend law school, and later pursue politics, perhaps even replacing her in the house of representatives someday.

Today, Senfronia is more than seventy years old. The year 2008 marked her eighteenth term in the house of representatives, and in 2009 she will run for Speaker of the House, the third most powerful position in the Texas State government.

After that visit in 1996, Senfronia was put completely at peace about the journey I was on, but she still encouraged me to make some immediate changes. Those changes included leaving my current corporate job to pursue a full-time ministry opportunity and serve my future mentors, Al and Hattie Hollingsworth. She told me that they would teach me how to be a businesswoman. They taught me more than that; this couple prepared me to be the wife for my husband, Richmond, whom I would meet while under their tutelage. Senfronia met Al and Hattie briefly during that visit, and she could tell that they would be significantly instrumental in my life journey and direction. Again, I followed her leading, and it was the greatest decision I have ever made. Because I took her advice and launched a relationship with Al and Hattie, I ended up meeting, through them as my connectors, the most awesome and incredible man in my world: my husband, Richmond.

Human nature often causes us to question our decisions with "what ifs" about various situations. I often think, *What if I had opted not to enter into a relationship with the Hollingsworths? Would I have eventually met Richmond?* Maybe I would have met him somewhere else along the way, but who knows? What I do know for certain is that meeting Senfronia more than thirty years ago, combined with all of the love, patience, discipline, and wisdom she has shared with me throughout the years, remains a positive influence on my life today.

The Necessity of Connections

Connections are essential to who we are and integral to what we can become. The story of my long and fruitful relationship with Senfronia Thompson is not unique, however. I have dozens of stories of wonderful people I have met whose presence has proved a necessary connection for me to get to the next level, to make an important decision, to find peace, to accept salvation in Christ, to discover love, to bury a deceased loved one, to touch and feel deeply, to unleash the beauty of immediate friendship, and to step into my destiny. It is often the people we least expect whom God uses to lead us to life-changing connections, decisions, events, and experiences. Earning a college degree, meeting a spouse, starting a career, and beginning a business are all significant life events often directed or determined, at least to some degree, by the people we know—people placed in our lives for a reason. We should never underestimate the blessings and connections other people have to offer us—or the blessings and connections we have to offer them.

The organization Woman Act Now (WAN) encourages women to dream big, to believe in their abilities, to execute their ideas, and, of chief importance, to connect with other women—supportive women who applaud creativity, believe in hope, and affirm opportunity. We are largely the sum total of all the people we encounter in our lives, each one making a unique and indelible mark upon us. We can do many things alone, but we can accomplish far greater feats with more power and widespread impact when we call upon good, wise counsel from many circles of influence.

26

Don't Network, Connect-work

As I stated earlier, connecting with someone else requires giving of oneself. Connections occur through, and because of, many different vehicles. In this chapter, you will learn how to maximize your relationships, position yourself for making connections, and act as a connector for others.

Enlarging your circle of influence requires more than attending a few networking events. The WAN method of enlarging your circles of influence is to adopt an attitude of generous giving and free sharing. In order to recognize the right connections, make them, and act on them, you are encouraged to shift your thinking away from the networking mentality that focuses on passing out business cards and pitching your idea, service, or product to a potential partner or market.

Instead, adopt what I call a connect-working mentality. Networking is driven by the question, "What's in it for me?" Conversely, connect-working operates by the question, "What's in it for others?" These questions have a direct impact on your attitude, as well as on the quality and duration of relationships you will develop.

The concept of connect-working centers around five major attitudes and goals: *The Giving Mentality, Marketplace Space for You and Me, Be Your Authentic Self, Listen with Intention,* and *Connect Others with Your Resources.*

The Giving Mentality

The WAN way involves an attitude that's enthusiastic about giving to others. The idea is that you will always have an abundant inventory in your life—of relationships, resources, tools, and so on—and having an attitude of openness and generosity will propel you forward faster than the fear of losing a customer, product, or opportunity.

Marketplace Space for You and Me

If you embrace a giving attitude toward your connections, whether they are partners or competitors, you recognize that there is always room in the marketplace for dual existence. The WAN way looks at each rival or competitor as an opportunity for collaboration. Learn how you can work together to maximize your opportunities, to learn more about each other's strengths, and to support one another. For example, most business associations have referral groups in which only a select number of businesses of different markets can participate so that competing interests do not coexist. I find that these types of organizations continue to promote the competitive interests of business while promoting this added value for their services. However, I also find that it tends to limit the interaction of competing businesses, which keeps them from understanding each other. Industry classifications and career groupings are so broad that people often assume that two people in real estate are doing the same thing and are therefore rivals. In reality, two people in real estate may have completely different—and often complementary—positions or tasks. Being in the same field does not necessitate rivalry.

Be Your Authentic Self

In any given situation, you may have the opportunity to connect with other like-minded individuals, and it is important that you project the true and authentic person that you are at all times. For example, many of us masquerade in a disguise comprising what we have accomplished in life, whether through toil, sweat, or education. We project an identity composed of what we do, not who we are.

I often host WAN meetings at my home. These meetings give women the opportunity to connect with others in a relaxed, informal atmosphere that reduces pressure and facilitates easy, free-flowing conversation. At these meetings, I can usually spot the women who have not yet understood the benefit of connect-working rather than networking. The woman who focuses on net-working displays obvious self-promotion. She talks more than she listens, she introduces herself with all of her titles and accolades, and she is often interested in getting to know others so that she can tell them about herself. Rarely is she willing to invest time and effort in other people, especially if doing so won't benefit her in some way.

Listen with Intention

Connect-working is driven by the desire to empower others and the belief that you can make connections with them. The beauty of listening with intention is that it is free from the pressure to solve problems and the obligation to agree. By listening, you might provide what the other individual needs in order to move to the next level in the process of achieving her dream. Moreover, listening with intention enables you to learn more about the individual and truly discover if you have anything in your arsenal of resources that would be helpful to her.

When I meet new contacts, I often write down specific comments they have shared on the backs of the business cards they provide me so that I can remember small details when I see them again. They are usually surprised if I mention any of those details upon future meetings. The benefit is simple—you earn trust and gain access.

Read what one of our members had to say about learning how to connect-work after listening to a WAN 15 Minutes to Destiny Call on Connect-working:

Hey Anna, I hopped on the call today just in time to catch your new "connect-working"! I love changing the way I think and having a new perspective on connecting with intention. The thought of helping others and having a plan prepared can break some really awkward moments. Since the monthly WAN meeting in February, I have remembered what Maya Angelou said: "It is how you make others feel that they remember." That is such wisdom! It keeps replaying in my mind and now I just want to walk that wisdom out in my life not only for business, but in all relationships!

—Sandi

Connect Others with Your Resources

Listening with intention prepares you to understand the needs of others. It also empowers you to reach into your bag of resources and retrieve a helpful Web site, book, or relationship that can be the bridge to benefit for the person with whom you're connecting. If you have exchanged business cards with a new acquaintance, you should note on the back what you recommended to the person so that when you connect again, you can refer to the information you offered and ask whether it was helpful.

For example, I once met a woman who needed someone to help her complete the incorporation filings for her company, and I recommended an attorney I know. I also suggested a few alternatives, just in case she preferred to complete her forms online rather than hiring an attorney. She decided to call the attorney for assistance. A few days later, she phoned me and left a message about how delighted, appreciative, and grateful she was that I had made that particular recommendation. She was overwhelmed by the professionalism and generosity of the individual to whom I referred her. I had told her, "If you call him, he will help you with everything, I am certain." Connecting other people with your own resources may not sound like a generous or giving act at the time, but when a person has a roadblock removed or a problem solved because she acts on your recommendation or takes your advice, you gain immediate credibility and favor with her.

27

Maximize Your Connections

A s you learn to connect with others, there are several key principles that will help you to maximize those connections. Below are fifteen such principles—basic, simple truths that make sense and, if implemented, will help to keep your relationships fresh and fruitful. Think about your current connections and determine if they conform to each of these principles.

~Connect with others who affirm who you are.

~Connect with like-minded individuals who have interests similar to yours.

~Connect with others who appreciate and celebrate you.

~Connect with others around whom you can be your authentic self.

~Connect with others who are where you want to be in life.

~Connect with others who are doing what you want to do.

~Connect with others who can mentor you and hold you accountable.

~Connect with others who can teach you new things.

~Connect with others who challenge you to be better.

 262

~Connect with others who respect differences.

~Connect with others with whom you can love, laugh, and live your best life.

~Connect spiritually and emotionally to what makes you whole.

~Connect with the activities that refresh, regenerate, and restore your balance.

~Connect with others who value friendship.

~Connect with others whose values are similar to yours.

Conclusion

A Dream Fulfilled, a Dream Deferred

As we come to the end, let's go back to the beginning, where you found out that my intent in writing this book was not to reach the wishers. I told you that I was writing this book for the dreamers—for those who believe their ideas are significant and worth pursuing. If you are a dreamer and you read on to reach this point, you are clearly serious about releasing your untapped talents and fulfilling your dreams. Like the women whose testimonies told how they were influenced and inspired by various aspects of the Woman Act Now organization, you can appreciate this book as a useful resource to help you clarify your dreams and discover how to turn those dreams into potent realities.

You entered the place in your imagination I identified as the I-FACTOR Zone, and you realized the importance of values, clarity, and vision—three things that can either derail or capture your dream. You now understand how to build inner confidence, you know your true self, and you've identified your strengths by performing a personal S.W.O.T. analysis. You were introduced to the concept of developing the "brand you" by focusing on reputation, identity, talent, attitude, power, thinking, relationships, and image.

Later on in the book, you explored your personal execution type, learned about the qualities that are crucial for successful execution, witnessed how to close the execution gap, and came to understand the importance of relationships, connect-working, and maximizing your connections.

This book bears the subtitle *Learn, Launch, and Live Your Dream.* By reading this book, you accomplished the *"Learn"* component of the subtitle. My hope is that you are convinced that your dreams are valuable and worth pursuing. My hope is that you have discovered more about who you are as a woman and have begun to process and perfect the "Brand You." You now have considerable book learning, but you can't put the book down—or, worse, tuck it away in a dusty corner of your bookcase—at least not until you have accomplished the *"Launch"* and *"Live Your Dream"* components, too.

Take what you learned in Part IV, which dealt with execution, and use it to create a plan detailing how you will launch and live out your dream today. Also, connect with other like-minded women who can surround you, support you, and encourage you to make your dream a reality. If no one currently falls into this category in your life, please don't hesitate to contact my office so that we can connect you with a chapter of Woman Act Now, which has chapters across the country. New chapters are forming even as you read this. We are here to help you make it happen! As your coach, newfound friend, and fellow dreamer, I commission you: *Woman, Act Now!*

Just before this manuscript was about to go to print, one of my dreams was realized. I wrote this book over a ten-month period, before which I visited Dreamland. During this particular visit to the I-FACTOR Zone, I envisioned what the next twelve months would have in store for me. Among my primary goals for that period was to visit the *Oprah Winfrey Show.* I wanted to go to Chicago and get a firsthand look behind the scenes at this popular show in order to cast my vision for a talk show that I have been thinking about launching for several years now.

Fast-forward to September 2, 2008, when my husband, Richmond, told me that we would be going to Chicago to visit some friends. I initially resisted, knowing we had made plans to visit friends in Sacramento that same weekend. I had even confirmed our reservations! But when your dream nears materialization, you can count on a bit of confusion to come and threaten to get you off course. I quickly realized that going to Chicago could be beneficial, so I said, "Okay, if we are going to Chicago, I know only one person, albeit by her reputation, whom I must see while I am there." Oprah was the only person I could think of who was in Chicago, and I had to see her. When we write down our visions and goals, we don't just write them on paper, but we also write them with indelible ink upon our hearts. They reside in the quiet place of our hearts until a catalytic moment comes and stirs us, telling us that this is the time to act! When my husband changed our weekend plans, I knew it was time to put my thoughts and ideas into action. I became intent on getting to Chicago, and I told Richmond about my vision, adding that I intended to stay in Chicago until Monday, September 8, because I needed to see Oprah.

Although Richmond was supportive of my plans, he had his own agenda, and having been on the road for several weeks, he was intent on returning home on Sunday, September 7. In fact, he had made reservations and scheduled our tickets for a return flight on Sunday. When I received confirmation of our flight reservations, I thought to myself, *He can go back, but I am staying in Chicago until Monday, September 8*. I am convinced that when we sense that we are getting closer to our dreams, it is often the case that everything in the atmosphere begins to move on our behalf. My case is no exception. I continued explaining to my husband that I needed to go to the Harpo Studio, have my picture taken by the sign out front, and visit the Oprah Store. He said, "You could do that anytime." He had no idea how strongly I believed in my vision or how persistently I would determine to be at the *Oprah Winfrey Show* on Monday, September 8.

As the week progressed, Richmond shared with me that he was trying to get me tickets to Oprah's show on Monday. From former attempts, I knew this was no easy task. Earlier in the year when I had returned from Dreamland with sights set on going to the *Oprah Winfrey Show*, I hung a note on the wall above my assistant's desk that read, "Call Oprah today!" On the note was the phone number of the audience ticket line. I instructed her to call every day until we procured tickets to the show. Well, she didn't call every day, but she did call quite often. The morning of Thursday, September 4, she called as usual, only to find out that the audience request line would be closed until the next available opportunity for ticket hopefuls to call. I did not know that she had called that morning, however, and at the inner prompting of the Holy Spirit, I visited Oprah's Web site, www.oprah.com. The urge to visit the site came on suddenly, and once I reached the Web page, I was filled with an even stronger spirit of urgency and search. I wasn't sure what I was looking for, but, being a frequent visitor to Oprah's online community, I noticed that the Web site had undergone a few changes. Intrigued, I began to look for a few things I read habitually, but I couldn't find them; however, it was this spirit of search that allowed me to see a link located in the lower right-hand corner of the screen, tucked discreetly between two other links. It read, "Tickets available for September 8 show."

Now, you can imagine how excited I was—and how nervous at the same time. I thought to myself, *This can't be true; it can't be possible for me to get last-minute tickets.* Nevertheless, I clicked on the link and filled in the necessary information. My personal message read something like this:

> Hi, my name is Anna McCoy, and I am supposed to be at your show on September 8. I have followed Oprah for the past twenty years and have been a student of hers. A year ago, I posted a sign on my assistant's desk to "Call Oprah today" to get tickets. We have been unsuccessful, so if you have tickets for the show, I will be in Chicago on Monday, September 8.
>
> Here are my four people: (I listed the names of three people in addition to myself for whom I desired tickets to the show.)
>
> PS: If you have only one ticket left, you can forget about those other three names; I will still be in Chicago on September 8.

A Dream Fulfilled, a Dream Deferred

When you are attempting to fulfill your dream and have begun to move forward, taking action is paramount. Think about what would have happened if I had not taken action and sent this message. This is the place where most people become discouraged because they do not have a healthy disregard for the impossible. I have said that doers believe in the possibility of every event they dream. I knew at this moment that I was acting on my idea and pursuing my goal of attending Oprah's show, and this was the closest I had ever come to seeing it as a possibility.

After I submitted my ticket request on Oprah's Web site, I had to pack for a trip to Baltimore, Maryland, where I was headed the following day. As I packed my suitcases, I thought about what I was going to wear to Oprah's show. I chose a bright yellow-colored satin jacket, which I dubbed my "Oprah jacket." Again, I was preparing myself for success, even though I had no official confirmation that I would be attending the show the following Monday. Part of believing is seeing yourself in your desired future moment. As I placed my Oprah jacket in my suitcase, I saw myself in the audience of the Oprah Winfrey Show, wearing that very jacket and sitting in the front row.

As my assistant, Shonna Stallworth, and I prepared to leave for Baltimore the next morning, she shared with me that she had called Oprah's audience line and had been informed that tickets for Monday's show were no longer available. Brimming with excitement, I told her that I was going to get some tickets to see Oprah, for I had sent my message the night before, when the Web site still had a link posted for people to obtain tickets to Monday's show. The two of us agreed in prayer that someone would read my request and would call me back.

When we arrived in Baltimore, I checked into my hotel room, where I needed to use the landline phone to call in for a radio interview in New York. While I was on the phone, my cell phone rang. The area code of the incoming call was 312, which I didn't recognize, so I pushed the ignore button and continued with the radio interview. My cell phone rang again, and I thought, *Who's blowing up my phone? I need to call this person back.* After my radio interview,

I redialed the number, and the woman who answered said, "The Oprah Winfrey Show." I screamed, "Oh, my gosh, you got my tickets?" She laughed and said, "I am sure we do, but do you have the name of someone to whom I can connect you?" I told her that I had no names or extensions, but that I would check my voice mail for a message and then call again. I immediately checked my voice mail, then called back and asked for the audience coordinator, as instructed; in order to confirm your tickets, you must speak to this person. I was transferred to the audience coordinator's voice mail, where I left a lively message asking her to call me back because she had my tickets and I was going to be in Chicago on September 8. I told her not to give away my tickets; I was waiting to see the 312 area code on my phone and would answer her call immediately.

My cell phone rang a few minutes later. I answered, and before she could even get my name out, I let her know that she was talking to Anna McCoy and then asked if she had my tickets. She said, "Mrs. McCoy, I have your tickets," then proceeded to explain the rules of the show and to confirm my guest list. I told her that my husband would be joining me, but I would have to retract the two other names because I had not spoken with those individuals, and I wanted to make sure that I confirmed only those who could come so that my opportunity to attend would not be jeopardized.

After confirming my tickets, I shared the news with Shonna, and we celebrated together. Next, I called Richmond, but he was not answering either of his two cell phones, so I left voice messages and sent a text message. When he called me back, he said, "You must be kidding! I cancelled everything; we are not going to Chicago." I said, "You don't understand. I got tickets to Oprah, and this is my opportunity. I am going to Chicago, and I must be there on Monday, September 8." He said, "Honey, you won't be able to get to Chicago because of Hurricane Hanna, which will hit the East Coast on Saturday."

Now, this was where the rubber met the road. I reminded myself what I had written about being a woman of execution. Seeing the *Oprah Winfrey Show* was one of my dreams, and my determination to be in Chicago on September 8 was incredibly strong; I was not about to let Hurricane Hanna deflate it. My mind kept turning over the idea that an executor is someone who always believes that a solution exists. I knew that although Hurricane Hanna was threatening to derail my dream, I would not let that happen. I asked Shonna to find out how long it would take to get from Baltimore to Chicago. She told me that a twelve-hour drive would cover the distance, and at that moment, I knew that I would make it to Chicago, even if I had to drive (which would be my last resort). I started singing Oleta Adams's song "Get There If You Can." I researched every possible vehicle that could convey me to Chicago and looked into different reservations, including everything from train tickets to rental cars. I was determined to get to Chicago no matter the cost.

It wasn't yet clear what my journey would bring, but I knew that my passion and my goal were coalescing to a dramatic fruition. I was about to see one of today's most admired women, Oprah—a woman of execution who has taught me much from afar, a woman whom I have watched realize her dreams—and I would have the opportunity to witness one of her dreams in action.

As I reflected on what was happening to me, I was convinced that I was walking out the principles and practices I had just finished writing about for this book.

An hour after my phone conversation with Richmond, I had prepared a plan of action that would get me to Chicago with or without him. When he called me back, I told him my plan. He agreed with me and suggested that I stay in Baltimore until Sunday, when the skies were expected to be clear and sunny enough for airplane travel without threat of delays. I took his advice and stayed an extra night in Baltimore, but I was prepared with a backup plan of driving to Chicago on Sunday in the event that the plane did not leave the terminal on time the next morning.

It turns out that Shonna had her own dreams of going to the *Oprah Winfrey Show*, so we were two crazy, excited, and faith-filled women who were in agreement about everything that would result from this journey.

We boarded the plane on Sunday morning and were off to Chicago. In our excitement, we told everyone we met that we were going to see the *Oprah Winfrey Show* the following day. When we arrived in Chicago, we were sure that nothing would keep us from getting to the show. Our first stop was Harpo Studios, where we made sure that we knew exactly where we were going so we wouldn't get lost on Monday. We took pictures, then made our way to the Hyatt Hotel near Lakeshore Drive in downtown Chicago.

From the second I decided I was going to Chicago, I started making a list of the things that I wanted to do there. The weather was beautiful on Sunday, and stopping by the studio gave us the opportunity to take pictures and take in the sights. We rented bikes and rode the seemingly endless path of Lakeshore Drive while reveling in the beauty of Lake Michigan (which looks like an ocean) and all the activities a warm beach day can bring. We strolled along the Navy Pier and toured other sites in the downtown area. I am not much of a shopper, so we didn't venture to Michigan Avenue or State Street, where most people flock for the city's finest shopping experience.

We did eat at Bubba Gump Shrimp Company for fun, even though we were still full from the meal we had eaten earlier. We took pictures with our cell phones and sent them to our husbands, wanting them to experience every moment with us.

We talked with strangers who were happy to hear that we were there to attend Oprah's show. Many of them were native Chicagoans who said, regretfully, that they had never been in the studio audience themselves. What made us different from them? The difference was not luck but execution. The link that I followed on Oprah's Web site was available to anyone, anywhere; but timing, passion, desire, and action made it accessible and effective for Shonna and me.

On Monday morning, we awoke with excitement and expectancy, in spite of the early hour. I left the room and found a quiet place in the hotel lobby where I could pray about the coming hours. I reflected on how much this experience meant to me and wrote my thoughts down in my journal. The tapestry of my life was being weaved together with the lives of hundreds of others in Chicago— mostly people I didn't know—and one of these individuals would be Oprah! I determined to be intentional about making the most of this opportunity, just as I had been with every decision I had made on the trip thus far. I called four people that morning to request agreement for favor in any serendipitous events that happened during the day. Each of these individuals prayed for favor and for open doors. Three of the people I called were the women whose names I had submitted in my online request for tickets to the show almost one year earlier. I told them that I had originally chosen them, but that God's plan was for Shonna to be with me instead as a witness to my living out all the principles I had been teaching the members of Woman Act Now about execution.

Just before leaving for the studio, Shonna and I made our regularly scheduled 15 Minutes to Destiny Call with a group of members from Woman Act Now, and we told them about our exciting journey. They were elated.

After the call, we were off to the show. We arrived early, hoping to beat the rain that was starting to pour down. We were certainly thankful that we had come the previous day to take pictures; as much as I wanted to get photographic documentation of our trip, I wasn't about to get wet in the process! Shonna and I prayed that the Lord would provide a break in the downpour so that we could make a run for the building without getting wet and claim our places in line. Once we made it inside, our bags were checked and secured; no promotional items, cameras, notebooks, or pens were permitted in the studio. The only items we took with us were lipstick and powder compacts—we had to look our best for the cameras! After coming in and passing through security, we were directed to an audience holding area upstairs.

As we were passing through the halls on our way to the holding area, a few studio employees commented on my jacket, quietly telling me that it was beautiful and that I would probably get a seat in the front row. Each time someone made a positive comment, it was a confirmation of my reality. I knew that my choice of attire was intentional, and it appeared that it might just get me in the front row after all. While we were waiting in the audience holding area, we talked with several other women and found out how they got tickets to the show. Many of them had stories similar to ours—they, too, had procured last-minute tickets by going to Oprah's Web site and following the same link I had. I figured that this show might be a last-minute addition to Oprah's lineup, which would explain why we were able to get tickets.

The audience coordinator announced that studio seating would begin shortly, and she instructed us to be careful, assuring us that there was no need to rush down the stairs, for we would all be seated. We received sheets of blue paper with numbers printed on them; by signing them, we authorized the show to film us and to publicize our identities on the program. As our numbers were called, we were to proceed to the studio. The coordinator started by calling specific parties by name, then began calling numbers 1 through 25. Our numbers were 233 and 234, so we figured that we would be waiting a while. But after numbers 25 through 50 were called, the coordinator called the McCoy Party downstairs! Shonna and I proceeded coolly down the stairs. As we approached the studio door, the woman who was seating the audience members saw my "Oprah jacket" and was captivated by the bright shade and satin fabric. She said, "Please wait a moment," then, "How many in your party?" "Two," we replied, and she said, "Follow me."

Where did she lead us but to two front-row seats situated no more than five feet from where Oprah and her guests would be sitting? We were brimming with excitement! As soon as we took our seats, Shonna and I joined hands and prayed for favor. What were we hoping and praying for? We were praying for an exceptional experience that would create an opportunity for relationship and maximize our moment to the fullest.

I am certain that many of the other guests were equally passionate about being in the audience, but the difference was in our intention. Shonna's mother had prayed that her daughter would be on Oprah's stage; I had prayed that I would be positioned to be seen by Oprah so that one day, when I am a featured guest on her show, she will remember me and make the connection. When we sat down, the realization hit us: *Hey! We just walked on Oprah's stage!* In order to reach the front row of seats, we had to walk across the stage.

The walk to our seats wasn't just special—it was also anointed. Right before we had gotten out of the car after arriving at the studio, Shonna had pulled out a vial of anointing oil and started applying it to her feet. I thought to myself, *I need some of that, too*—my heels were somewhat calloused, and I figured it might help. Shonna looked at me and said, "Momma said to anoint my feet before we go in there because one day, I am going to sing at the Oprah show." I quickly agreed and asked her to give me some oil, and I, too, anointed my feet. We had walked with anointed feet to the front row.

So, here we were at the *Oprah Winfrey Show* in Chicago, in spite of cancelled plans and inclement weather and a scarcity of tickets. The odds had been against us, but we took action and executed our goals with determination. God had truly heaped favor upon us—and He wasn't done yet!

Before Oprah makes her entrance, a stage manager informs the audience members about show protocol, tells them what to do, and warms them up. During this warm-up time, the stage manager asked to know who among us could sing. I pointed dramatically at Shonna, which drew her attention. She asked Shonna to name her favorite artist, and she responded, "CeCe Winans." The stage manager responded, "She's my favorite, too!" Then, Shonna sang a song by CeCe Winans. We were certainly excited now! I knew that I would have my chance, too—I was just waiting for my moment because I knew it was coming.

Sure enough, the stage manager asked another question: "What show would you like to see Oprah do?" Several women in the audience raised their hands to share their thoughts, and I raised my hand, too. When the stage manager called on me, I said, "I think Oprah could do more shows on how to help women execute their dreams successfully." She responded, "We do that." "Yes, you do," I said. "However, you make dreams come true, and I am speaking about helping women learn how to execute their own dreams." The stage manager looked around and asked the audience members whether any of them had a dream; few responded. Then, as I had done for Shonna, a woman raised her hand enthusiastically and spoke up for a friend seated next to her, saying, "She has a dream!" The stage manager asked her, "What's keeping you from achieving your dream?" But this woman was shy, so her friend replied, "Fear!" The stage manager turned back to me and said, "We are going to put Anna to work," and she handed me a microphone so that I could coach this fearful woman. It was an amazing opportunity to help her discover how to execute her dream. It was clear that she wasn't ready, and it's always scary being put on the spot, but I told her that I would help her if she would reach out to me to birth her dream.

After the show, this woman sought me out. We exchanged numbers and hugs, and she gave us her umbrella to keep us from getting wet in the rain. I hope that she will connect with me before she reads this book and that she will soon birth her dream. I have faith that she will reconnect and will offer a featured WAN testimony in the future. There were other women who also asked for my information, and I am certain that I will reconnect with them.

In chapter 16, "'Brand You" Power,' you read about TJ, who executed the same principle: like I did in front of the audience at the *Oprah Winfrey Show*, she took a risk and let her idea live in the presence of a crowd of people. This was my moment, and I made the most of it rather than letting it pass me by. Our experience in Chicago was exceptional, and while the other women there contributed to our experience, I am certain that we also contributed to their experiences. It was the culmination of everything discussed in this book. As Shonna and I made decisions and pursued the fulfillment of our dreams, we were continually reminded of the principles we have learned and internalized from being members and leaders of Woman Act Now.

We hope that you will learn from our example, as well as from the tools and resources in this book, and that you will be compelled to go after your dreams—dreams written with indelible ink upon your heart. The moment you recognize an opportunity, take advantage of it and move with intention, expectation, faith, and God's favor. The story I just shared with you still isn't over, for I still expect to achieve my goal of being a featured guest on the *Oprah Winfrey Show* and contributing to her dream of building the Oprah Winfrey Network, where the same principles embraced and taught by the WAN organization will come alive in the lives of women all over the world as they strive to fulfill their potential and live the best lives possible!

Start executing your dream today, no matter how small or large it may seem. You owe it to yourself. Take the risk of telling others what you will do and then do it! It's time to act!

~It's time to launch and live your dream!

~Set aside your daily "15 Minutes to Destiny"!

~Go after that new job!

~Start a business!

~Ask for that sales order!

~Expand your product line!

~Volunteer for community service!

~Be a political leader!

~Preach, woman, preach!

~Say "yes" to your significant other!

~Develop that new connection!

~Bake your cake and eat it, too!

~Apply for a passport!

~Write your book!

~Speak about your vision to others!

~Formulate an action plan!

~Adopt a child!

~Sing, woman, sing!

~Go to a developing country!

~Buy a computer!

~Say "no" to unproductive and unfruitful relationships!

~Live the assignment you were born to do!

~Follow the healthy diet and exercise plan you have avoided!

~Build the prototype of the invention burning inside of you!

~Design jewelry, clothing, or a new makeup formula!

~Trust your instincts, believe in yourself, and speak up for destiny!

~Let your dreams live again!

~Engage life with the best of who you are! You can do it!

Woman, Act Now!

Afterword

Real Women Who Made the Connection

Women across the country are connecting with one another and helping each other reach their destinies through Woman Act Now. Through personal coaching, the 15 Minutes to Destiny calls, Start Your Business E-learning Center, Business 101, Monthly WAN meetings, Online Community, Financial Learning Center, and online videos and podcasts, women just like you are learning to live out the principles that we have explored in this book. Here are the powerful testimonies from a few of the founding members of Woman Act Now.

Community
LaShawn Amires, Training Consultant
McKinney, Texas

One of the main lessons that I learned from Woman Act Now is that although we may have a plan that is set in place, complete with goals and objectives established for the year, things may take an unexpected turn beyond our control. So, I have learned persistence and due diligence to stick to the golden dreams that I have established, even when it does not feel good or when I cannot see the light.

I have benefited from a number of the tools of the Woman Act Now program, specifically the 15 Minutes to Destiny call on Mondays. Wow, what a great way to get my week started, especially if the morning has not gone so well. The 15 Minutes to Destiny has empowered me to press forward and to turn any negative into a positive.

I have also been a participant in the awesome Business 101 class. We may think that because we have been in business for many years we know a lot. But then, you really evaluate your current situation, and you wonder why you are not further along than you are. This class showed me that although I did have some things in order as an entrepreneur, there were a lot of things that were not in order.

I have also benefited from personal coaching. What an awesome blessing to receive personal coaching from Coach Anna McCoy. The personal coaching included the WAN Community, where we can go online within Woman Act Now and communicate with one another. I personally use the online community to reach out to other members who are currently in the same field that I am in, but are located in other states across the country.

The monthly WAN meeting is also another powerful tool. At this meeting, you come together with other women who also have hopes and dreams and are looking to partner with others in order to make their hopes and dreams come to life. I had an opportunity to meet one of the young ladies I communicated with online at one of our local Woman Act Now meetings.

Coach Anna has influenced me and inspired me as a woman to act in my now. I often tell her that she does not know the impact that she has made in my life. I thank you, Coach Anna, for hanging in there with me, encouraging me, and empowering me to keep pressing forward.

I would advise any woman to join Woman Act Now if you desire to own your own business or if you simply need to be empowered with the tools and resources to assist you in corporate America. I cannot wait for the worldwide launch as we go international. Coach Anna, you have truly been a blessing. I thank you. God bless you. Keep up the good work.

Acting in My Now
Leslie Denman, Life Purpose Coach
Dallas, Texas

I joined Woman Act Now because I was inspired by the concept, and I was looking for such an organization to partner with as I prepared to take my life to the next level. One of the numerous principles that I have learned that really stands out in my mind, and that I have begun to practice every day, is to make sure that my behavior is in alignment with my values and beliefs.

The 15 Minutes to Destiny Call gives me a boost. The beginning of the week, Monday, is not always my favorite day of the week, but the call helps to keep me refocused and recharged, as well as to think of my week in a more positive way.

The monthly Woman Act Now meetings have become my official girls' nights out, and Coach Anna provides a positive and warm environment for sisterhood, promoting accountability and empowerment.

Coach Anna has really influenced me to make sure that I am a woman who acts in my now. Whether I am thinking or praying, all of those things, in one form or another, really help me to act in my now. Her energy and willingness to share are inspiring, and she really makes me feel that I can have whatever it is I desire out of life. She shares her resources and her wisdom, and I absolutely love her openness.

Coach Anna, you are a godsend. I thank God each and every day that I have had the calls. You are truly a woman who acts in her now, and it is so refreshing to see that there are still women who are sincere about reaching out to empower other young women. The world has yet to be blessed with the wealth of favor and talent God has bestowed upon you and within you. I am honored to know you, and I know that the best is yet to come. Coach Anna, you are loved and appreciated.

Inspiration and Technology
Judith Ellis, CEO, JDE Consulting
Detroit, Michigan

I joined Woman Act Now to connect with other women in business and to share experiences, secrets of success, and pitfalls to avoid.

Anna's online videos always seem to arrive at the perfect time. Sometimes, it is just a few sentences of encouragement—her belief in others, telling them that they can indeed do the grand things they set out to do, is all that's needed. Anna has given such encouragement to me. Empathy and sympathy are hallmarks of a good coach. Anna has these traits in abundance, albeit sometimes in a forthright way that propels you to action.

Among the most thoughtful words that Anna has spoken to me, words that have changed my life, were, "Take care of your opportunities." This thought has reverberated in my spirit to become a guiding light in developing relationships of all kinds.

I have always been a calculated risk taker and a woman of action, having built many careers in the now. But Anna inspires me to move further, to accomplish more, and to embrace technology wholly. I have called her many times about this or that new technology, and she has always responded by giving me the pros and cons of more than a few different brands.

There are many tools available to encourage and inspire women to act in the now. With Anna and Woman Act Now, there is something for everyone!

Thinking and Acting Big
Phyllis Hayden, Owner, Transitional Woman
Mesquite, Texas

I joined Woman Act Now because I wanted to be part of an organization for women being challenged and motivated by a variety of techniques to be successful in moving forward in their personal and business lives. I have learned how to identify my goals and to use a plan of action in order to get the results I want.

Since I have been a member, I think big and act big in order to execute my thoughts, my vision, and my passion so that I can walk in my destiny as an entrepreneur. On a daily basis, I make sure I use my time wisely in order to get the results I want by the end of the day. I have learned to be a doer and a woman of my word.

I am always so eager to get on the 15 Minutes to Destiny calls. They have helped me on a weekly basis to be rejuvenated with my plan of action for my business. The topics addressed have been instrumental in assisting me to go in a better direction when dealing with a variety of issues. It is like the blueprint for the week. The calls have provided fifteen-minute blessings that help me to evaluate or elevate my business with strategies that help me to be a woman of action.

The Business 101 class is all about choices. It has taught me how to plan my success, execute the tasks on my calendar, and remain conscious of time. This class taught me a lot about how a business plan works, as well as how I can execute my plan in order to be a better business owner. It has taught me discipline. It has taught me how to be accountable for my business and how to be a better thinker. It has caused me to focus on the results and to realize that I have to learn to fall in love with my passion. It also has taught me how to be credible with myself. It is all about the choices to be better and to move forward.

Coach Anna has been a magnificent mentor. She has a heart for women who are striving to be successful in business. She believes in you and challenges you to move forward in your now. She holds you accountable for what you say you will do. She is such a motivator. I am always eager to hear the next statement that comes out of her mouth. My thought is, *Give me more; feed me more knowledge.* I am hungry for wisdom in order to move forward and be a woman who acts in her now. Thank you for giving me this opportunity.

Empowerment and Confidence
Trina Geter, Lifestyle Solution Planner, Connect and Go Concierge Services
Arlington, Texas

I joined Woman Act Now for its phenomenal support and time-sensitive information. I believe that every woman needs to be a part of a group that feeds her mentally, spiritually, and physically. Women have an innate desire to belong and to love. Woman Act Now not only radiates love, but it welcomes diversity with open arms.

I have learned several key principles from Woman Act Now. They are: (1) Do not let people or things steal your time. If you value your time, so will others. (2) One minute of planning saves ten minutes in execution. Once you have obtained ideas, plan out the steps and move in your now. (3) Think: ideas in, action out. (4) Learn to move in your now, and do not allow procrastination to immobilize you. I use these principles as a daily affirmation.

The personal coaching has benefited me tremendously. Prior to being coached, I was not as confident as one should be when starting a new business. I frequently defeated myself due to fear of rejection. Do not get me wrong: I am an optimistic person, but I would always figure out the end result as being negative, not positive. During the first meeting, I did not know how in the world I would be able to accomplish all that was laid before me. You know how it is when you know what to do, but for some reason, procrastination just immobilizes you. Not only do you fail without trying, but you talk yourself into failure without realizing it.

The fact that I had no education in the areas of graphics and building Web sites really caused me to believe that I could not build my own. This was a major factor that kept me from moving forward in my vision. I had placed the responsibility in the hands of another person who had promised to design it for me. Since there was no payment involved, I felt like my hands were tied, and I figured it would get done when it ran across his mind.

After the conclusion of the first and second meetings of Woman Act Now that I attended, I felt empowered not only to build my own Web site, but to create my own flyers for marketing. Now, I am more disciplined to do all that I know to do in my now, as well as to ask for help and guidance when needed.

Coach Anna has influenced me to become a woman who acts in her now by living the words she sows. Many people share profound words of wisdom but never live by them. If the words you share are truly profound, they will become you. If you are a woman looking for support, embarking on the search for your dreams, seeking lessons about business, or needing another chance at life, join Woman Act Now today! Make a decision to move in your now and begin living again.

Making the Relationship Connection
Carla Freeman, Air Traffic Control Specialist
Fort Worth, Texas

Anna has influenced and inspired me in many ways. On a personal level, she has really put the fire under me. I started acting in my now to make right decisions. Anna gives you the personal touch. If she does not see you for awhile, and if you come across her mind, she will send you a personal, encouraging, and thoughtful video message via e-mail. When I moved to Fort Worth, I didn't know anyone, and yet there is somebody who cares about me, who says she is concerned about my well-being and how I am doing. There are very few other people who have that hands-on approach.

The monthly Woman Act Now meetings are a treasure. Every month, I look forward to meeting Anna, Shonna, and the other women who attend. It is a great group of women with diverse backgrounds who are eager and willing to sit at the feet of wisdom to learn and gain from Anna. You will have fun, you will learn, and you will walk away with something you can use in your personal life, as well as in your business.

The Business 101 course is a small, intimate setting of entrepreneurs and future entrepreneurs. I learned a lot from everyone, as well as from Anna's teaching, and I felt that we had a close connection. It was something that I believe anyone can benefit from, whether you have a thriving business or you are just getting started. The class offers a wealth of information that will help propel you into your destiny. I encourage you to participate in Woman Act Now. You will gain useful tools that will equip you for your journey as you dream, believe, execute, and connect. I guarantee you that the relationships you form with Anna, Shonna, and the other women of Woman Act Now will leave you excited about your journey, invigorated about life, and empowered to carry out your lifelong dreams.

Stepping Outside the Box
Margie Stewart, Financial Coach
Tyler, Texas

I joined Woman Act Now because I was searching for a mentor/coach who would hold me accountable. I have worked in the corporate world for over twenty-five years and am transitioning to owning my own business. However, changing my mind-set from employee to employer/proprietor has been challenging. I attended an enrichment program where Anna shared how God gave her wisdom and knowledge of the subject matter in a unique way. I gained respect for her and trusted her enough to be my coach. Anna is a selfless godsend with a giving heart. She gives us so much helpful information, exposes us to great resources, and helps us to be all we can be by stepping outside the box. The podcast, videos, and other online resources have helped me to act in my now.

I share this information with many people who can benefit, as well as with all my teammates. Woman, are you ready to go to the next level? Are you searching for a mentor or coach? Well, you can stop searching, for you've got the right one, right now. Woman Act Now is a great tool to help you to walk in excellence in life, whether it is on the job, in your church, owning your business, being a wife, or being a mother. I highly recommend joining Woman Act Now.

The Benefits of Coaching
Jeraldine Patterson, Assistant Pastor,
Crusade Christian Faith Center
Los Angeles, California

I joined Woman Act Now because I wanted help in focusing my life, and also in focusing my energies, my potential, and my capabilities in order to get the best results in life. I have been a member for several months now, and I have enacted a number of principles that have had a great influence on my life. A concept that is particularly important to me is the one conveyed by the well-known statement of Socrates: "The unexamined life is not worth living." In 2 Corinthians, Paul discussed the importance of examining oneself. He wrote, *"Examine yourselves to see whether you are in the faith; test yourselves"* (2 Corinthians 13:5 NIV). That is what Woman Act Now and Coach Anna have meant to me. Anna has given me the opportunities and tools to examine myself and my life, to discover what I am doing with my energies, my capabilities. To know that I am exerting my best efforts in the right direction is so powerful, and it is probably one of Woman Act Now's greatest benefits to me.

Personal coaching is the aspect of this program that has been the most meaningful. Coach Anna is a person who is a conduit—she connects me with knowledge and with other people. Recently on the Woman Act Now radio broadcast, we were discussing personal service as it relates to the church. It was a tremendous connection, and it gave me the opportunity to have my thoughts challenged and examined. It also validated and affirmed that I was going in the direction in which I wanted to go.

In addition to giving me guidance, Coach Anna has provided me with knowledge for various aspects of life and business, specifi-cally the technological field and problem solving. Many times, the answer has been in me, the knowledge has even been in me, but to have it stirred up and challenged, to have a personal coach say, "No, you can do this; no, go back and look at this again," has helped me to hone my skills.

We have just completed the world championship in basketball. I think about coaches like Phil, who coaches the Lakers, or Doc Rivers, who coached the winning team, the Celtics. They are working with capable people who have skills and knowledge, but the coach is there to bring it all together. That is what Anna has done for me.

I cannot say enough about what Coach Anna and Woman Act Now have meant to me. I have to admit that there are many more aspects of the program than I am taking advantage of. Just this morning, I was listening to the Word of the Day. I am going to take more advantage of the 15 Minutes to Destiny.

And again, I have been strongly encouraged to press my way into the Internet and to grow familiar with using this great technology. Because of Coach Anna, I have been truly blessed, and I can say that the people who are connected to me and who work with me also experience the fruits of that blessing. Many thanks to Coach Anna and to Woman Act Now.

Personal Encouragement
Linda Wallace, World Evangelist
San Dimas, California

As a founding member of Woman Act Now, I joined the organization to be part of a network of progressive women with vision. It has given me the opportunity for accountability, to enlarge my personal development, and to meet other women in the marketplace with whom I can interact and grow, and from whom I can learn.

I have received one-on-one coaching and personal encouragement from Anna that has been invaluable. She is a wealth of resources. Every time I hang up the phone after talking to her, I know I have discovered something new that will help me to grow and develop my business and ministry. I have participated in the 15 Minutes to Destiny phone call, and it was beneficial simply to chat online with women who share success principles that they are applying and using daily to work in their businesses.

The accountability provided by my personal coaching relationship with Anna has been most beneficial. She is always probing my mind and provoking my ideas. She asks the hard questions that help you to continue on with your vision and goals. I love Anna very much. She is a great influence, someone destined for great things. I am excited about her upcoming book and looking forward to a continued relationship with her—of friendship and mentorship. You just go, Anna! Thank you very much for starting Woman Act Now. I look forward to being more connected in the future to other women in the network. God bless you.

Checking Off the Goals
Sandra Gonzalez, Artist/Owner, A Work of Art
Keller, Texas

I joined Woman Act Now because I saw great value in a community of women who were like-minded. I also saw the opportunity to network with women who had great passion and tenacity for what they were doing and where they were going in life.

One principle I have learned from Woman Act Now is acting in my now—to find clarity by thinking through various processes rather than acting before I achieve clarity. By following that principle, I was able to achieve clarity and refine a few of the things I was already enacting in my own business. It helped me to put it down in a formula. I have also learned to choose wisely the people with whom I allow myself to be in business, seeing if we have the same type of mind-set, the same goals, and the same work ethic.

I love the 15 Minutes to Destiny phone calls. I do not always get on them, but I have enjoyed every one that I have been on and the little nuggets that we get during the week. If I cannot get on the phone call, I can always log onto my computer during that day when I get home from work. It's another little thing to keep me focused and moving forward.

One of the things I loved learning about was business etiquette. I have often wondered what to do with my fork if it falls on the floor. Am I supposed to discreetly pick it up? Does it make me a bad person if I leave it there, or is it better if I just go ahead and leave it alone? That is one of those things that Anna shared with us in a business etiquette seminar. It just pulled me to freedom— answering questions on simple, small things regarding how to conduct myself in business settings for which I never had answers before.

I love the monthly WAN meetings. I think they provide a great way to meet other women and to network, and I appreciate Anna's teaching on connect-working, because it's really not about handing out tons of business cards. To me, whenever I have done that, I have felt like my time and my resources were used in vain.

I have several personal and business goals that I wanted to reach. What Anna has presented through Woman Act Now has kept me and other women on track, moving forward. As I accomplish items on my list, I can check them off; when I look back at my life ten or twenty years from now, instead of saying, "Man, I gave nothing!" I will be able to say, "Look what I gave. I accomplished those things that were so desperately desired in my heart and weighing on my mind." This is how Anna inspires me to move forward and to become the better me that I have already established.

If your heart has a passion that is just burning inside of you but you don't know what to do with it, get connected with women who think like you, who have similar goals and desires. Figure out your own purpose and destiny, and move forward to pursue them.

Woman Act Now is the right place to do it, and Anna McCoy is the right woman to propel you forward.

I Have Something to Accomplish
Catherine Karingith, Certified Public Accountant
Dallas, Texas

I joined Woman Act Now at a point in my life when I felt there were things I wanted to accomplish that I could achieve only with the help of a mentor.

I had heard a lot about the value of mentors. When I finally met up with Anna McCoy at a conference, I was privileged to speak with her, and I told her point-blank, "I am looking for a mentor. Would you mentor me?" It just so happened that she had recently launched Woman Act Now as a mentorship organization. I became the first member, and it has been such a blessing in my life.

As a member of Woman Act Now, I have learned many valuable lessons and principles. I think that Anna's most fundamental teaching is to act in our now. Time is precious and fleeting; therefore, you have to decide to act on your dream, your desire, your business, or whatever it is that you want to accomplish. You have to work on it now—not tomorrow, not yesterday—because now is the gift that you have.

Then, you must commit to doing something every day to work toward your dream. It does not matter whether you work as little as fifteen minutes, but you have to do something every day, for that is what gets you closer to your goal. To be a doer, you have to execute your plans. You can have an idea that you break down into plans and goals, but ultimately, you must execute to accomplish results.

One thing I like about 15 Minutes to Destiny is that it gives me a weekly reminder that I have something to accomplish. It keeps me on track. It keeps me focused. At the same time, 15 Minutes to Destiny teaches you many useful things about business, life, execution, and more. Every week, you are increasing your knowledge, being continually reminded that you have a goal that you need to work toward accomplishing.

I went to Business 101 with a broad, vague idea of what I could do and what I could accomplish. I walked out of Business 101 with a precise idea of what I wanted to accomplish, having worked on a big chunk of my business plan. We went over the process of putting together a business plan. We also acquired a lot of useful basic information about business that we had never known before—information related to bringing together ideas about business and actually creating that business. Business 101 was a phenomenal experience for me. It helped my diverse ideas to converge into a couple of executable business ideas that were much more feasible to manage, and I am very thankful for that.

I enjoy attending WAN meetings because they give you the opportunity to interact with other women, and I have actually been able to make business contacts whose services I have used. Other women have picked up my contact information, too, and I have offered them services. So, these meetings are definitely great connect-working events.

Coach Anna has been an inspiration in my life. She helps me realize that I can accomplish my dreams. I now know that they will not happen by my simply wishing for them; rather, they will happen by my knowing that I am capable of doing, that I have within me what is necessary to make them happen, and that I just need to act on them—I must be a doer! This women's organization is an inspiration to me. Watching Anna develop and grow this organization has inspired me to reach out for my dreams, figuring out which ones I want to pursue and walking towards them.

Learn more about

...

Woman Act Now Covenant

This covenant is an agreement between a woman and her word, which holds her accountable for her own success. With the joint effort of others, she will achieve it. Embrace these words, live them, and act on them. Become all that you are meant to be.

I make conscious decisions in my now that positively affect my future—right now.

I value education and sharpen my "saw" monthly by exploring and learning about people, places, or events that expand my view of the world.

I commit my time and my mind to thinking creatively, envisioning my future, and acting on my dreams.

I am an executor of my ideas, and I will master closing the gap between my thoughts and my actions.

I am a God-size dreamer; I search my heart, my soul, and my mind to deliver to the world everything I was created to give it.

I materialize my thoughts, my ideas, and my dreams.

I give more than is required and value relationships with other like-minded individuals.

I demonstrate character, integrity, and leadership in the marketplace.

I am a woman of an excellent spirit—it is my right and my essence—and I seek improvement continuously.

I am a woman of my word, I am intentional with my actions, and I keep my commitments to myself, my family, and my community.

Becoming a Member of Woman Act Now

Visit www.womanactnow.com to join today. The cost is $199 per year for a discounted annual membership, or $19 per month.

The Benefits of Joining Woman Act Now

Online Coaching

You will be encouraged to share your goals and objectives and will receive online coaching to hold you accountable to those goals.

Videos/MP3s

These media files provide content on business and personal development in order to teach you various principles and techniques to help you achieve personal and business success.

Online E-business Seminars

These seminars provide access to entrepreneurship e-business seminars at no additional cost to WAN members.

Information Resources

WAN provides you with information resources relating to more than fifty areas of training in starting, growing, and managing your business.

Focused Business Opportunities

You have the opportunity to create a Web presence in the Woman Act Now community and can list and respond to various opportunities for employment, collaboration, and so forth.

Visibility in the Business Community

You will have the opportunity to connect-work with other like-minded women who can help you start, grow, and manage your business.

15 Minutes to Destiny Weekly Tele-Calls

These powerful fifteen-minute calls will propel your growth in many areas of business and personal development. Calls are scheduled for fifteen minutes each and are available on a first call, first served basis. Each call can accommodate up to one hundred and fifty callers and is designed to charge you up and move you forward.

Create and Send Audio/Video Postcards

You can create audio/video postcards to send to customers to showcase your product or service. There is nothing to download; with a Webcam and microphone, you are off to a running start.

Financial Learning Center

This center is a tremendous resource to help you spend less, save more, and plan for your financial future. The Financial Learning Center provides e-seminars, portfolio management, relevant articles, and newsletters, and it is updated monthly with new information.

Member-to-Member Advertising

Take advantage of special rates that allow you to advertise your business to other members of the WAN community for one dollar per day. Get noticed and get customers! Woman Act Now members also receive discounts on various products, conferences, and chapter member events.

Private Messaging System

The messaging system allows members and coaches to communicate directly with one another via both video and e-mail.

Video Chat and Live Broadcast

Contact other members and coaches via video chats and live broadcasts.

Appendix C

Becoming a Chapter Leader

By joining WAN, you can start a chapter in your own community if none exists there. Woman Act Now is actively seeking like-minded women leaders who are passionate about empowering other women.

Perhaps you have a desire to gather women together to encourage, train, and support one another. Woman Act Now will equip you to help women by bringing them together and promoting an atmosphere that provides an audience of intelligent women with whom to explore and achieve success.

In each leader, we look for:

1. A woman with a passion for seeing dreams become realities.

2. A woman who wants to help others while she helps herself.

3. A woman who believes she can lead others through the valley of execution.

4. A woman who can tap into her circle of influence and encourage other women to act on their dreams.

5. A woman who has a dream to help other women achieve their dreams.

6. A woman who believes in the power of giving.

7. A woman who believes that the Woman Act Now vision mirrors her own vision.

Frequently Asked Questions

Where can chapters be established?

Chapters are established nationally and internationally. Multiple chapters can be formed in a metropolitan area. For example, Dallas/Fort Worth, Texas, may have ten chapters within the metropolitan area, in places like Dallas, Fort Worth, Irving, Frisco, Plano, Arlington, South Dallas, Desoto, North Richland Hills, and Grapevine. There may be many chapters in a given area, and all of them may act independently of each other.

Maybe your community already has a women's organization or ministry but you would like a WAN chapter established there, as well. You do not have to start a completely new chapter; rather, you can use the principles of WAN within your existing structure.

For example, if you have a chapter of the organization called Women on the Move and you also want to join WAN, you can assimilate them both into a joint organization. In the WAN community, your chapter would be known as Women on the Move WAN Chapter, Anywhere, USA. Collaboration, not duplication and separation, is the key. Combining organizations and starting new chapters are both embraced by Woman Act Now.

How many chapters will you start?

We will start as many chapters as we have women leaders. Our objective is to have more than one hundred chapters in the U.S. and abroad by the end of 2009. Within five years, we desire to become the leading women's organization worldwide that empowers women to execute their ideas through the use of technology as they do business and build relationships without geographic or cultural borders.

How can I establish a chapter?

Each chapter applicant is interviewed personally by the founder, Anna McCoy, to ensure that her vision, passion, ethic, and character align with Woman Act Now. After further discussions, steps will be taken to help you establish a chapter in your local area.

How much does it cost to start a chapter?

It will cost an approved applicant a minimum startup fee for a chapter, plus travel to Dallas, Texas, for leadership training. The cost per applicant will differ depending on applicant's location.

What is the benefit to the person who starts a chapter?

Chapter leaders will be provided with specialized training, curriculum, support, and personal encouragement. If you are an individual who meets the seven criteria above, then you will be aligning with an organization that can help you achieve your goal of helping others, which you will have the resources to do both online and in your local area.

How many members should a chapter have?

We like small numbers, which ultimately will lead to larger numbers if women experience real value in coming together. A chapter can start with as few as three women. If you bring three people together and begin to share ideas and think out loud, you can begin something spectacular.

Why three and not two? Well, two can easily get on the same page and move in any direction, but when you have three people, accountability is stronger because you can listen to ideas and get three opinions rather than two. Thus, each chapter should comprise three or more individuals. It's easy to get a table at Starbucks, our official "home away from home."

So, start your chapter: gather two or three of your friends at the nearest Starbucks, grab a latte, and start thinking about how you are going to turn your dream from an idea into a physical reality. Each chapter can grow as large as its leader can handle.

How do I get started?

Call 877-751-5700 or visit www.womanactnow.com to learn more about Woman Act Now and to register as a member. Also, refer to the last page of this book for a special offer for interested and new members!

About the Author

Anna McCoy is a powerful, stimulating, and thought-provoking speaker. Her witty, no-nonsense, stand-on-your-feet, practical approach to getting life done will challenge you and equip you to live your best life every moment!

Anna is a seasoned executive and business and life coach with more than twenty years' experience in sales, marketing, and operations management. She is the Chief Encouragement Officer of Act Now, Inc., a personal development and success training organization, and founder of Woman Act Now, an online, chapter-based membership organization dedicated to empowering women to dream, believe, execute, and connect with other like-minded women to achieve their goals in the now.

Anna and her husband, Richmond McCoy, are founding partners of UrbanAmerica, a multibillion-dollar, private real estate fund in New York. She attended Spelman College and earned her Bachelor of Science in business administration from California State University. She is the recipient of an Honorary Doctorate of Divinity from Saint Thomas Christian College, and she is a certified NLP coach with Coach Academy Texas. Additionally, Anna is a skillful golfer.

She resides in Fort Worth, Texas, and Newark, New Jersey, with her husband, Richmond. She has an exceptional daughter, Daryl, and two outrageously special canines, Ricky Jr. (named after his daddy) and Tommy (named after his uncle).

Special Offer

You've read the book, you've learned about Woman Act Now…now, let it change your life as it has changed the lives of so many other women! This is a special invitation for you to enjoy a free 30-day trial membership to Woman Act Now.

To take advantage of this outstanding offer, visit **www.womanactnow.com** and enter **W1A5N9** as the promotional code.

Explore the online community and its many benefits. Connect with like-minded women who will encourage and empower you. And if one month isn't enough (and I guarantee that it won't be), join Woman Act Now and receive a 20 percent discount on your first year of membership (a $40 value).

Woman, join now!

—*Coach Anna*

Free 30-day trial membership
www.womanactnow.com
promotional code: W1A5N9
Enjoy a 20 percent discount on first year of membership, too!
(A $40 value)